WOMEN AND
PUBLIC POLICIES

WOMEN AND PUBLIC POLICIES

Reassessing Gender Politics

Joyce Gelb

and

Marian Lief Palley

with a new prologue
and epilogue

University Press of Virginia
Charlottesville and London

The University Press of Virginia
© 1996 by the Rector and Visitors of the University of Virginia

First University Press of Virginia printing 1996

∞ The paper used in this publication meets the minimum
requirements of the American National Standard for Information
Sciences—Permanence of Paper for Printed Library Materials, ANSI
Z39.48-1984.

Library of Congress Cataloging-in-Publication Data

Gelb, Joyce, 1940–
    Women and public policies : reassessing gender politics / Joyce
Gelb and Marian Lief Palley.—Rev. and expanded ed.
      p.   cm.
    Originally published: Princeton, N.J. : Princeton University
Press, 1987.
    Includes index.
    ISBN 0-8139-1695-X (pbk. : alk. paper)
    1. Feminism—United States.   2. Women in politics—
United States.   3. Women—Government policy—United
States.   I. Palley, Marian Lief, 1939– . II. Title.
HQ1426.G35   1996
305.42′0973—dc20   96-27069
                                                     CIP

Printed in the United States of America

*To Andrew, Elizabeth, Jonathan, and
Stephen and Katie, who we hope will live
in a more equitable society.*

CONTENTS

LIST OF TABLES

PROLOGUE

In the decade since the publication of the second edition of *Women and Public Policies,* changes have occurred on the American political landscape and in the women's movement itself. The political environment has shifted sharply to the right, with significant consequences for the women's rights agenda and the women's movement. The movement has continued to grow and change, and it retains considerable vitality, particularly when measured against other social movements that became politicized in the 1960s and 1970s. New issues have come to the fore and expanded the agenda of women's activism beyond a focus on individual rights. In 1980, with the election of Ronald Reagan, hostility to organized feminism gained a new legitimacy. Although the election of Bill Clinton in 1992 seemed to promise a more "women-friendly" regime in Washington, its ascendancy was short-lived. The 104th Congress (elected in 1994) vigorously challenged feminist policies, as have state governments dominated by right-wing Republicans.

BACKGROUND

The last decade has seen considerable backlash against the women's rights agenda; women's reproductive rights, affirmative action, and welfare have been particular targets of right-wing groups. There has been a rapid feminization of poverty and a frontal attack on the social programs that support poor women and children. And yet the women's rights movement not only survives in this hostile political environment, it has achieved some victories. These successes are in large measure due to the political adroitness of the movement's leadership. The assumptions we made in the earlier editions of this book regarding appropriate political behavior and playing by the rules of the game continue to explain the success of the women's movement even as the political terrain has become harsher and the opponents of the movement have become better organized. The authors of this volume take issue with the idea that the "'peak period' for groups has passed, that political opportunities have narrowed, consciousness has diminished, and organizations are just concerned with maintaining themselves."[1] There is little evidence that the women's movement has become complacent, is beset by organizational inertia, or is in a state of decline. Organizational change should not be interpreted as the death knell of feminism.

The women's rights movement has changed in the past ten years. Organizations have proliferated and have been forced to compete for scarce resources in an often hostile political and economic environment. Whereas the political agenda during the 1970s and 1980s was generated largely by national women's movement groups, in the past decade some concerns of locally based women's organizations have moved onto center stage. Violence against women and day care, for example, were initially issues of only local concern. The Clarence Thomas–Anita Hill confrontation in 1991 brought the issue of sexual harassment national visibility, although the women's rights community had been concerned about sexual harassment since the passage of the Civil Rights Act of 1964. Of course the more direct economic concerns of the women's right's movement have not been fully resolved, and considerable attention is still given to achieving educational equality, retaining reproductive choice, and removing the "glass ceiling" in upper-level positions and obstacles to employment mobility. These economic issues began and have remained a primary concern of the national women's rights movement.

Published in 1987, the second edition of this book continues to stand on its own as a series of case histories. Furthermore, the theoretical framework developed for the study and the lessons learned from the individual cases remain as valid in the 1990s as they were in the 1980s. In the last decade, however, there have been policy agenda changes, new policy directions, changes in the politics of the organized women's movement, changes in the broader political environment—and more women have become involved in local, state, and national politics. This new prologue assesses the recent politics of the women's movement, the transformation of women's participation in U.S. politics, and changes in the broader political environment. The epilogue for this new edition discusses several new policy directions.

THE POLITICAL ENVIRONMENT

In 1992 Bill Clinton was elected President of the United States. Women's rights groups supported and welcomed his victory because Clinton seemed to share many of their concerns. Though in 1992 the national Democratic ticket focused primarily on the economy and not on cultural issues such as family values, reproductive rights, freedom of choice, sexual harassment and violence against women, the Bush-Quayle campaign, as well as many state and local campaigns, kept these issues alive.[2] The political vitality of these cultural concerns became apparent in the 1994 election, when Republicans captured both the House of Representatives and the Senate as well as a majority of state houses and state legislatures. Some observers contend that for several decades a culture war has been raging in the United States between the egalitarians and the patriarchists, with men and women on both sides.[3]

Many successful Republican candidates in 1994 were supported by right-wing groups and voters who focused more of their attention on cultural agenda items—which are in part a backlash against the women's rights agenda—than on the nation's economy. There can be some natural overlap between cultural and economic agendas, such as the opposition to providing payments to women and girls on welfare if they have another child. In fact, almost immediately after Congress considered the Republican *Contract with America* in 1995, the Christian Coalition came forward with its *Contract with the American Family,* with warnings to the Republican leadership to ignore it at their own risk.

Women's groups opposed to the organized women's rights movement are also active players in the right-wing backlash. Concerned Women of America (CWA), led by Beverly LaHayne, has a "pro-family" agenda that is anti-choice, supports abstinence-only sex education, and opposes comparable worth measures to support women in the workplace. In a word, the Concerned Women of America is antifeminist. Organized in local chapters, the CWA has a national staff in Washington and publishes a monthly newsletter, *The Family Voice.* The Eagle Forum, led by Phyllis Schlafly, was organized in 1972 to oppose the Equal Rights Amendment. It now supports the full agenda of the religious right: it opposes comparable worth legislation and freedom of choice and champions "family values."[4]

No discussion of the right-wing backlash and its impact on women would be complete without mention of the Right to Life Movement, particularly the activities of Operation Rescue and its leader Randall Terry. The harassment of doctors and women and the murders of abortion providers have successfully reduced the availability of abortion despite the legal freedom of choice that women retain.

POLITICS OF THE WOMEN'S MOVEMENT

Despite this frontal attack on women's rights, the women's right's movement has survived and expanded. The organization of the women's movement has not remained static for the past decade. New organizations and groups have formed that are now playing significant roles in national, state, and local politics. In fact, given the diversity of interest and issue concerns that comprise the movement, it is often necessary to speak of many women's submovements, rather than one movement, all united by their concern for discrimination against women. Though the number of women's groups active in Washington leveled off during the early 1990s, by 1993 their number had begun to increase again. From 1982 to 1995 the number of active groups increased from 75 to approximately 140. Mayer Zald, among others, has remarked on the unusual staying power of the women's movement among the new social movement groups.[5] Also, new coalitions have emerged with the rise of "new" issues—such as the Coalition on Women and Job Training, the National Network to End Domestic Violence, and the National Committee on Pay Equity—and new leaders have appeared on the scene.

Though we have focused our attention on organized women's rights groups, it is significant that public awareness among both women and men has been raised during the past ten years. Women's rights marches and rallies draw large crowds, and interest in women's studies courses in colleges and universities has increased. Though many young women do not self-identify as "feminists," many do support the principles advanced by the movement.

The organized women's rights movement has always had a serious "free rider" problem: it is not necessary for women to join a movement group in order for them to derive the benefits (e.g., new legislation and increased opportunities).[6] It is not clear how many young women are joining the groups associated with the women's rights movement. As the leadership of the movement ages, young women may be becoming complacent about the rights they have gained as a result of the activities of the organized women's rights community. Nonetheless, a February 1966 meeting in Washington D.C. organized by the Feminist Majority to discuss new directions in empowerment for women was cosponsored by 299 groups and attracted large numbers of young women. Of the 3,200 people in attendance, 35% were either high school or college students, many of whom were explicitly concerned about the challenges to affirmative action and to other rights that feminists have struggled to gain.[7] New groups that mobilized in the late 1980s with a more radical direct action agenda, including WAC (Women's Action Coalition), WHAM (Women's Health Action Mobilization), and Third Wave, have members who are primarily 20 to 30 years old.[8]

College women in the 1980s were more likely to endorse feminist issues than to accept the label "feminist," much as was the case in the 1970s.[9] According to a Gallup survey, women under the age of 45 were more likely to identify as feminist as they grew older. Attitudes toward the women's movement have become steadily more positive. In 1970 40 percent of women favored efforts to "strengthen and change the status of women"; in 1980 that figure had increased to 64 percent; and in 1990, 77 percent of women said they supported such efforts. In a 1989 survey, 89 percent of women agreed that the women's movement had given women more control over their lives and 82 percent of women thought the movement was "still improving the lives of women." Approximately one third of U.S. women identify themselves as feminists, and 65 percent think that NOW is "in touch with the average American women." About 4.5 million people claim to have made a contribution at one time or another to an organization affiliated with the women's rights movement.[10]

THE STRUCTURE AND RESOURCES OF
TODAY'S WOMEN'S MOVEMENT

The continued existence and even expansion of a Washington-based women's rights policy network defies all predictions of the 1980s. Organizations have survived and flourished regardless of their origins—leadership by board or staff experts, or collective and membership oriented, state-based coalitions with a national presence and strength. Single-issue groups, expert research and policy-related groups, electoral groups, and new coalitions continue to proliferate. It is true that some of the groups discussed in earlier editions of this book have ceased to exist, most notably the Women's Equity Action League (WEAL). WEAL, among the groups studied earlier, seems to have failed in the late 1980s for several reasons. It was a multi-issue organization that lost a clear policy niche. Its emphasis on careers and professional mobility for individual women may have seemed less relevant than issues related to the feminization of poverty, the problems of blue-collar women, women and family issues, and violence against women. Also, it was too dependent on support from one or two key foundations. By contrast, the Center for Women Policy Studies (CWPS), which also faltered in the 1980s, was able to develop a new policy agenda under dynamic new leadership and with diversified funding sources.[11]

It is impressive that most of the women's rights groups, old and new, continue to pressure Congress for changes, recruit supporters, and influence public opinion despite diminished resources and political opposition. Most organizations continue to rely on a liberal feminist language of rights and opportunities and to avoid radical and left-wing approaches.[12] Policy alternatives continue to be presented in narrow, nonconfrontational ways. Thus "comparable worth" has become "pay equity," "wife beating" has evolved into "domestic violence," and "child care" and "working women's rights" are now called "family and medical care leave."[13]

Women's rights groups have broadened their policy agendas beyond issues associated with women's individual rights to address societal concerns such as race, poverty, and sexual preference. In addition, NOW and the Center for Women's Policy Studies, among other groups, encourage increased participation of women who lack other representation.[14] Some groups have added references to homophobia and lesbian rights to their policy statements, agendas, and publications.

Issues related to working women and poor women are often included in new policy agendas, as are concerns about low wages and gendered valuation of work. In the view of some observers, women's rights organizations were not as active as they might have been in defending the rights of children and women welfare recipients. These rights came under attack by the right when Aid to Families with Dependent Children (AFDC) was being debated in 1995 as part of the *Contract with America*. However, NOW and the NOW Legal Defense and Education Fund (NOWLDEF) were more active than other women's rights groups in defending welfare recipients and other low-income workers. Women's rights groups have not given up their "feminist claims" by adding new issues related to diversity and empowerment to their agendas. They have simply broadened the sweep of issues they consider crucial to a feminist agenda.

One consequence of organizational proliferation and defensive adaptation in the 1980s and 1990s has been group specialization, which we discussed in earlier editions of this book. Thus new "submovements" have organized around issues such as women's health, rape, domestic violence, and reproductive rights. Tendencies toward fragmentation are offset by the Council of Presidents, a forty-nine-member, Washington-based women's network that coordinates the activities of women's rights groups. State and local policy-based networks and coalitions augment these national efforts.

Numerous scholars note the longevity of women's rights organizations that emerged in the 1960s. Jack Walker has emphasized the proliferation of women's rights groups from 1966 through the 1980s, while Mayer Zald contends that of "all social movements on the current scene, the feminist movement appears to have the best chance for continued high levels of mobilization and activity."[15] David Knoke's study of women's organizations finds that these groups' leaders have learned to structure and maintain open access political economies that are conducive to high-energy involvement more than groups involved with other social movements.[16] Nancy Whittier decries the "post feminist myth," in part a tribute to the success of the movement. She also recognizes the difficulty of remaining an activist in the 1980s and 1990s in the face of mounting opposition, financial stress, and aging.[17] The movement survived the 1980s and remains vibrant in the 1990s, though it has changed in significant ways.

Many interest groups have relied on government support and other external patronage for survival. Women's movement groups have been especially dependent on these sources. Walker finds that, compared with other contemporary social movement organizations, women's rights groups have been remarkably successful in garnering contracts and grants from public and private sector organizations.[18] Recognizing their dependence on outside patrons, however, and the frequent uncertainty of continuing support due to economic and political change, many women's rights groups have sought to diversify their funding sources. They have tried to depend less on government and foundation support and more on membership-based funding. One of the most successful women's groups in the early 1990s was the campaign-focused group, EMILY'S List. This group, which provides early money to Democratic women candidates who are pro-choice, enjoyed phenomenal growth in the 1990s. By 1994 it had 33,000 members. During the 1992 election year cycle it contributed more money to congressional candidates than any other group. The success that women had raising money from women may be one of the factors leading other women's rights groups to lessen their reliance on outside funding and generating financial resources from women themselves.

Other women's rights groups have increased their budgets and staff size in the 1990s.[19] This partial trend toward increasing membership-based income has helped ensure the continued organizational success and survival of the women's rights community. Restructuring the distribution of power within organizations has helped some groups in their struggles with new issues and changed agendas. The process of self-examination engendered by divisive issues has strengthened the movement.[20] Many groups have developed new mechanisms of accountability and conflict resolution to emphasize process as well as outcomes. The willingness of women's rights groups to incorporate and reassess elements of collectivism and bureaucracy within their structures may offer a new conceptualization of power, one which helps to explain the relative longevity of such groups among social movement groups.

There is clearly no one form of women's rights organization that dominates. In fact, the diversity of organizational forms we identified in the second edition of *Women and Public Policies* still remains. The individual leaders who were instrumental in the formation of many of these organizations continue to play major roles in setting agendas and insuring organizational survival.[21] For example, Leslie Wolfe, the present head of the Center for the Study of Women and Society, had been a leader of the Project on Equal Education Rights (PEER), Pat Reuss has moved from WEAL to NOW-LDEF, where she has continued her advocacy role as the Senior Policy Analyst, and Tish Sommers, who organized the Displaced Homemakers Grassroots Movement, went on to form the Older Women's League (OWL). These women, and many others, represent the "spillover" occurring among women's organizations within the same movement, highlighting an important aspect of their organizational success: strong leaders and activists who carry the movement's work beyond the life of any single group.

William Gamson characterizes two dimensions of social movement success: the ability to gain recognition as a legitimate actor in politics and the ability to reward its beneficiary community.[22] Other scholars have expanded this definition by pointing to other dimensions of social movement success. A movement's success can be measured by evaluating its role in challenging existing ideas, practices, and means of socialization.[23] The creation of resources for further mobilization may also indicate organizational success.[24] Although policy initiatives developed by the women's rights movement contribute to its success (and are assessed in the epilogue), the movement's ability to maintain a constituency for future struggles and its success in helping to restructure thinking about feminist issues may set it apart from other contemporary social movements.

CHANGING PATTERNS OF
WOMEN'S POLITICAL PARTICIPATION

Continued advocacy by women's rights groups is particularly striking given their reliance on outside support from government and foundations.[25] Since the late 1960s, many women's organizations have pressed for changes in both the public and the private sectors. Despite the fact that women hold far fewer than half of all elected offices, women's groups have helped shape the nation's policy agenda. However, increasingly women see the need to be not only group participants and voters but office holders themselves. In 1992 women cast 54 percent of the votes for president. In 1994 there were eight women in the U.S. Senate and forty-seven women in the House of Representatives, and in forty-two states women held at least one statewide elective office. In nine states women held at least half the statewide constitutional (elective) offices. In 1995 women held 21 percent of state legislative seats and 18.3 percent of mayors across the country were women.[26]

Women's groups' financial support of women candidates has greatly increased in the 1990s. These groups, characterized as "campaign sector" groups in our earlier work, include organizations such as the Women's Campaign Fund, the National Women's Political Caucus, and Voters for Choice. These older groups have been joined by EMILY'S List and the Republican WISH list as well as by other PACs that support women's rights. The *Almanac of Federal PACs, 1994–1995* reported that fifteen federally registered PACs supported candidates who were aligned with women's rights' positions.[27]

More women vote than men, and there are more women than men in the electorate. As a consequence of the women's movement, more women have become active in the political fray and more women are winning elections. Carol Mueller has suggested that a major achievement of the American feminist movement of the last thirty years has been to increase women's candidacies for elective office and in turn to insure that elected women "have made women their constituency and women's issues their issues."[28] (However, in 1994, for the first time in twenty years, the number of women running for legislative positions declined. When the Republicans took over the House of Representatives, the Congressional Caucus for Women's Issues, which had been a force for collective action in behalf of women's rights, was eliminated along with all of the other special-interest congressional caucuses.)

Despite the fact that the majority of voters are women, women do not win a majority of elections. This is due in part to the fact that gender is only one factor that influences the way a person votes. Other circumstances such as economic status, place of residence and employment status influence voting decisions, as well. Women and men tend to agree on many issues if education, income, age, profession, ethnicity, etc., are the same. For example, men and women support freedom of choice in equal numbers. It does appear, however, that on women's rights issues, women adhere to their positions with greater intensity than men. This helps explain the gender gap, or differential voting patterns between men and women, evident since the 1980 election.

The gender gap, attributable in part to the success of the women's movement in making women conscious of their gender at the ballot box, suggests differences in party identification and voting behavior between men and women. Women are more likely to identify as Democrats and to support Democratic and politically liberal candidates for public office than are men. Although this trend is evident in presidential elections, it is also true of state and congressional races. Also, women seem to be predisposed to vote for female candidates if they are politically liberal. However, women have supported Democratic men in preference to Republican women when the man has been the more liberal of the candidates.[29]

In 1994 there was a gap of 4 percentage points between the proportion of male and female votes garnered by electoral winners. Women Democratic candidates such as Barbara Boxer and Dianne Feinstein, both senators from California, and Ann Richards, the defeated candidate for Governor of Texas, were disproportionately supported by women voters.[30] Women voters affected the outcome in the February 1966 senatorial election in Oregon. Women supported the Democratic candidate by a 7 percent margin; men preferred the Republican candidate by a 10 percent margin. The Democrat, Ron Wyden, won the election because 57 percent of the voters were women.[31]

Of course the gender gap in these elections can also be attributed in part to the economy. A March 1996 national survey of voters conducted jointly by the *Washington Post,* the Kaiser Family Foundation, and Harvard University found that women are more concerned with the economic circumstances of other Americans than they are with their own economic situations. The survey findings suggested the widening electoral gender gap may be rooted in different attitudes towards economic concerns.[32] The *New York Times/CBS NEWS Poll* in April 1996 also attributed the increase in the gender gap to a sense of economic insecurity among women. According to this poll, in an early presidential preference question men divided their loyalty evenly between the two presidential candidates, while 34 percent of women favored the Republican, Dole, and 52 percent favored the Democrat, Clinton.[33]

When women are elected to public office they often help create a more hospitable environment for political change and reform. Many women legislators are members of women's groups and women's rights organizations. One study found that 40 percent of all elected women belong to a women's rights organization.[34] Women legislators are likely to owe their elections in part to the activities of these groups. Women's groups provide strong support, including money and volunteers, to female candidates, and women candidates are more likely than men to identify such organizational support as crucial to their electoral success. Women legislators, reflecting their support base and their interests, tend to be more liberal and more feminist than their male counterparts. They are more likely to prioritize issues related to women and children.[35] Sue Carroll, for example, points to support for women's issues among women legislators. Other observers suggest that, as the number of female legislators increases, they are even more likely to provide support for women's issues.[36] In the 103rd Congress, women and men voted differently on the Crime Bill, Freedom of Access to Clinic Entrances Bill, the Family and Maternal Leave Bill, the Brady Bill, the Hyde Amendment, and the reauthorization of the National Institutes of Health.[37] Because women also bring to legislative bodies their concern for women's rights, women's issues are more likely to be championed in legislative bodies where there are women members and especially where there are women in leadership positions.

It is on issues of special interest to women that female lawmakers are often identified as opinion leaders in legislative bodies. They raise the questions, focus the debate, and are seen as cue givers. However, they are not always in a position to control debate. When issues are defined in terms of role change rather than role equity, the agenda becomes more difficult for women legislators to control, since opposition to these issues may be fueled by religious and moral justifications. This has been the case with issues of reproductive rights and services for poor women and children. Similarly, those opposed to affirmative action and equal employment opportunity contend that such policies involve the government too heavily in the lives of Americans.

The organized women's rights community has also had considerable success in the administrative arena. In part as a recognition of the support of many women for his candidacy, Clinton appointed seven women to cabinet-level positions and a record number of women to the federal bench. As of 1994, thirty of his ninety-one judicial appointees were women.[38]

CONCLUSIONS

The political environment has changed, new issues have emerged, and the women's movement has redirected its focus in response to the evolving political and social environment. In the past decade, the concerns of the movement have broadened. Grassroots concerns have become national movement concerns, and local and state spokespersons for women's rights are increasing in number. "While local groups reach women where they live, national groups can bring their knowledge and struggles to the national policy arena and to the agendas of national feminist organizations."[39] This is reflected at the polls on Election Day, and its impact is seen in state, local, and national legislative bodies.

The women's rights community tries diligently to define issues in terms of role equity, and its greatest successes continue to be in policy domains that do not raise the specter of role change or any significant redistribution of power. Groups continue to rely on the language of rights and opportunities to access power and gain legitimacy. As Roberta Spalter-Roth and Ronnee Schreiber remind us, feminist policy initiatives have gained political capital and legitimacy. Their approach is generally nonthreatening, and thus acceptable, and their issues have became part of the public-policy discourse. Terms such as "domestic violence," "pro-choice" and "family leave" have gained common currency.[40] Advocacy of women's economic rights, equal educational opportunity, and reproductive choice are still central to the women's rights movement agenda. In addition, their concerns have broadened to include violence against women, sexual harassment, and the broader issue of political empowerment. The women's rights groups continue to be consummate political players—lobbying, testifying, mobilizing constituents, and litigating—as they adhere to the rules of the game that constrain political change in the American political system.

NOTES

1. Anne Costain, *Inviting Women's Rebellion* (Baltimore: Johns Hopkins Univ. Press, 1992), 141.

2. Marian Lief Palley, "Elections 1992 and the Thomas Appointment," *PS* 26 (March 1993), 28.

3. Deidre English, "Through the Glass Ceiling," *Mother Jones* (Nov. 1992), 50.

4. Lori Forman, *The Political Activity of the Religious Right in the 1990's* (New York: American Jewish Committee, 1994), 10.

5. *Washington Representatives, 19th Edition* (Washington DC: Columbia Books, 1995), 964–65. Mayer Zald, "The Trajectory of Social Movements in America," *Research in Social Movements: Conflict and Change* 11 (1988), 10, 19–41; Women's and Racial-Ethnic Voluntarist and Activist Organizations, 1955–1985," *Social Forces* 71 (June 1993), 887–908.

6. For a discussion of the free rider problem see Mancur Olson, *The Logic of Collective Action* (Cambridge: Harvard Univ. Press, 1965).

7. Feminist Expo for Human Empowerment, Washington, DC, 1–4 Feb. 1996.

8. Myra Marx Ferree and Beth Hess, *Controversy and Coalition: The New Feminist Movement across Three Decades of Change* (New York: Twayne, 1994), 190–92.

9. Ibid.

10. Ibid., 190–92, 199.

11. Joyce Gelb and Jennifer Disney, "Success and Survival in Femi-

nist Organizations." Unpublished paper presented at the annual meeting of the American Political Science Association, San Francisco, September 1996. The Aspen Institute funded this study.

12. Roberta Spalter-Roth and Ronnee Schreiber, "Outsider Issues and Insider Tactics: Strategic Tensions in the Women's Policy Network in the 1980's," *Feminist Organizations: Harvest of the New Women's Movement,* Myra Marx Ferree and Patricia Yancey Martin, eds. (Philadelphia: Temple Univ. Press, 1995), 105–28.

13. Ibid.

14. Ferree and Hess, *Controversy and Coalition,* 183.

15. Jack Walker, *Mobilizing Interest Groups in America* (Ann Arbor: Univ. of Michigan Press, 1991), 31. Zald, "The Trajectory," 13.

16. David Knoke, "The Mobilization of Members in Women's Associations," *Women, Politics and Change,* Louise Tilly and Patricia Gurin, eds., (New York: Russell Sage, 1990), 376.

17. Nancy Whittier, *Feminist Generations: The Persistence of the Radical Womens Movement* (Philadelphia: Temple Univ. Press, 1995), 3.

18. Walker, *Mobilizing Interest Groups,* 31.

19. Gelb and Disney, "Success and Survival."

20. Ferree and Hess, *Controversy and Coalition,* 104, 112.

21. Gelb and Disney, "Success and Survival."

22. Cited by David Meyer and Nancy Whittier, "Social Movement Spillover," *Social Problems* 41:2 (1994), 280.

23. Carol Mueller, "The Organizational Basis of Conflict in Contemporary Feminism," *Feminist Organizations,* 263.

24. Suzanne Staggenborg, "Can Feminist Organizations Be Effective?," ibid., 341.

25. Walker, *Mobilizing Interest Groups,* 31.

26. *Fact Sheet on Women's Political Progress* (New Brunswick NJ: Center for American Women and Politics, April 1995).

27. Edward Zuckerman, *The Almanac of Federal PACs, 1994–1995* (Arlington VA: Anward Publications, 1995), 354.

28. Carol Mueller, "Collective Consciousness, Identity Transformation and the Rise of Women in Public Office in the United States," *The Women's Movements of the United States and Western Europe,* Mary Katzenstein and Carol Mueller, eds., (Philadelphia: Temple Univ. Press, 1987), 104.

29. Nancy McGlen and Karen O'Connor, *Women, Politics and American Society* (Englewood Cliffs: Prentice Hall, 1995), 70–72; Center for American Women and Politics, *News and Notes* (winter 1994), 37.

30. Center for American Women and Politics, *News and Notes,* 7–8.

31. William Schneider, "Women Made the Difference in Oregon," *National Journal* (10 February 1996), 342.

32. "The Backlash Begins," *Notes from EMILY* (March 1996), 2.

33. Robin Toner, "With G.O.P. Congress the Issue, 'Gender Gap' Is Growing Wider," *New York Times* (21 April 1996), 1, 26.

34. Robert Darcy, Susan Welch, and Janet Clark, *Women, Elections and Representation* (Lincoln: Univ. of Nebraska Press, 1995), 37.

35. Ibid., 187. Center for American Women and Politics, *News and Notes* (summer 1995), 2.

36. Sue Carroll, *Women as Candidates in American Politics* (Bloomington: Univ. of Indiana Press, 1985), 171. Darcy, Clark, and Welch, *Women, Elections and Representation,* 183.

37. Center for American Women and Politics, *News and Notes* (summer 1995), 2.

38. *Women's Political Times* (winter 1994), 1.

39. Leslie Wolfe and Jennifer Tucker, "Feminism Lives: Building a Multicultural Women's Movement in the United States," in *The Challenge of Local Feminisms,* Amrita Basu, ed. (Boulder: Westview, 1995), 457.

40. Spalter-Roth and Schreiber, "Outside Issues," 113–27.

LIST OF ABBREVIATIONS

AAUP – American Association of University Professors
AAUW – American Association of University Women
ACE – American Council on Education
ACLU – American Civil Liberties Union
ACLU-RFP – Reproductive Freedom Project
ACLU-WRP – Women's Rights Project
AIAW – Association for Intercollegiate Athletics for Women
BPW – Business and Professional Women
CARASA – Committee for Abortion Rights and Against Sterilization Abuse
CLASP-WRP – Center for Law and Social Policy-Women's Rights Project (now National Women's Law Center, NWLC)
CWPS – Center for Women Policy Studies
ECOA – Equal Credit Opportunity Act
EEOC – Equal Employment Opportunities Commission
ERA – Equal Rights Amendment
GFWC – General Federation of Women's Clubs
HEW – Department of Health, Education, and Welfare
IUE – International Union of Electrical, Radio, and Machine Workers
LCCR – Leadership Conference on Civil Rights
LWV – League of Women Voters
NAACP – National Association for the Advancement of Colored People
NARAL – National Abortion Rights Action League
NCAA – National Collegiate Athletic Association
NCJW – National Council of Jewish Women
NOW – National Organization for Women
NOW-LDEF – Legal Defense and Education Fund

NWLC – National Women's Law Center
NWPC – National Women's Political Caucus
OCR – Office of Civil Rights, HEW
OWL – Older Women's League
PAC – Political Action Committee
PEER – Project on Equal Education Rights (of NOW-LDEF)
RCAR – Religious Coalition for Abortion Rights
UAW – United Auto Workers
WEAA – Women's Educational Equity Act
WEAL – Women's Equity Action Alliance
WLDF – Women's Legal Defense Fund

NARAL – National Abortion and Reproductive Action League
NAWE – National Association for Women in Education
NCADV – National Coalition against Domestic Violence
WAC – Women's Action Coalition
WHAM – Women's Health Action Coalition

WOMEN AND
PUBLIC POLICIES

CHAPTER 1

FEMINISM
AND THE AMERICAN
POLITICAL SYSTEM

INTRODUCTION

Students of American politics have long recognized the existence of a "mobilization of bias" that limits access to power for new "out-groups" on the political scene. According to E. E. Schattschneider, political systems and subsystems develop a "mobilization of bias," a set of predominant values, beliefs, rituals, and institutional procedures that operate systematically and consistently to the benefit of certain groups and at the expense of others. Defenders of the status quo occupy key positions of power, from which they promote their vested interests. Schattschneider called attention to the narrow scope and bias of the American system, stressing the difficulties present for groups seeking to expand their participation and increase their impact on policy.[1]

Nonetheless, within the past two decades a plethora of new groups have appeared to press their demands on the policy-making process. Among these are groups representing the interests of racial and ethnic minorities, the poor, the aged, consumers, and environmentalists. In addition, after some fifty years of dormancy, a feminist movement emerged in the late 1960s and 1970s, and in the brief twenty years of its existence this movement, rooted in the middle and upper-middle classes of society, has developed a sophisticated organizational struc-

[1] E. E. Schattschneider, *The Semisovereign People* (New York: Holt, Rinehart and Winston, 1956), 71, quoted in Peter Bachrach and Morton Baratz, *Power and Poverty* (New York: Oxford University Press, 1970), 43.

ture and has established itself as a significant presence in national policy making. The evolution of a strong feminist presence in national politics parallels the expansion of interest-group activity in general in Washington. The decades of the 1970s and 1980s witnessed an increase in the number of organized interests coming to the nation's capital to make demands on the political system. This development seems to have been propelled by an expanding federal role in politics and by an apparent decline in the role of political parties with a concomitant increase in constituency and group influences on members of Congress.

Despite references to *the* feminist movement, it is important to understand at the outset of this analysis that there are numerous components within what is popularly described as the feminist movement, and these multiple groups are referred to as "the movement" merely for the sake of convenience. Feminisin is defined here as a movement seeking to operationalize self-determination for women in political, economic, and social roles. In the succeeding chapters the roles of women in affecting national public policies during the 1970s and 1980s will be considered. Thus the focus of this book is on politics and on the groups active in the political process.

In this study we are concerned more with group leadership behavior than with mass membership behavior. This focus is determined by the predominance of leadership as opposed to mass membership groups in the organized feminist movement. There is, however, broad support for the goals of the feminist movement even though formal membership in most of the primary feminist interest groups is relatively small.

There are five major types of groups that comprise the feminist political community as it is discussed here: mass-based feminist organizations, single-issue groups, specialized litigation and research organizations, electoral groups, and the traditional women's groups such as the League of Women Voters. The group participants will be considered in detail in the second chapter.

It is our contention that feminists in politics have conformed

2

to both the scope and bias of the system and simultaneously, by virtue of their presence and demands, have expanded the range of decision making to include a broader segment of the populace. Feminists are not inclined to rely on public agitation in order to achieve their goals; rather, they support changes in social policy through conventional lobbying efforts. Feminist groups are represented by "movement" women who share a commitment to changing discriminatory social and economic policies albeit through reformist as opposed to radical techniques. Feminist advocates in Washington are thorough-going professionals who maintain a visible presence on a variety of issues. Their reputation for legal and technical expertise coupled with tenacity has gained them access to policy makers at all levels. For example, they are often consulted by federal agencies when regulations are being written, though their clout does not always equal that of their rivals. In contrast, feminists have had an uncertain history in the federal courts, which have pursued ambivalent and often contradictory approaches to issues of sex discrimination. Although some issues raised and advocated by women's groups have prevailed in the courts, the Supreme Court's rejection of the race/sex analogy has meant that feminists have had to develop strategies different from those of civil rights groups that preceded them in several areas under discussion here.

We will demonstrate that feminists can claim primary credit for a series of successes in the adoption and implementation of policies including the Equal Credit Opportunity Act of 1974, the Pregnancy Discrimination Act of 1978, Title IX of the Education Amendments of 1972, and the Retirement Equity Act of 1984. When they are most successful, feminists participate in broad-based coalitions in which often they play pivotal roles. Increasingly, playing the game of coalition politics, with several coalitions organized around specific issues, has been of major importance to feminists' success.

In addition to the policies analyzed in depth here, feminists have either benefited from or influenced other equal rights legislation related to women. Thus the Equal Pay Act of 1963, Title VII of the Civil Rights Act of 1964, which makes sex-based discrimination in employment unlawful, Executive Order 11246 (September 1965), amended by Executive Order 11375 of October 1967, prohibiting discrimination in employment under federal contracts, and a prohibition against sex discrimination in mortgage lending in the Fair Housing Act of 1974 all have aided women. In the area of federally funded child care, since President Nixon's veto of the Comprehensive Child Development Act of 1971, which would have brought day care within reach of all families, efforts to gain congressional passage of even a scaled-down measure have been defeated. However, the Tax Reform Act of 1976 does provide a maximum child-care tax credit of $400 for one child or $800 for two or more children.

Feminists also devoted considerable resources and energy to the struggle for the ratification of the Equal Rights Amendment (ERA). The amendment passed Congress easily in 1972, after a fifty-year period of seeking a constitutional amendment to advocate equal rights for women, but faltered in the state ratification process (after early success in gaining ratification in 35 of the 38 needed states). Nonetheless, feminists did gain a major victory again in Congress when, in 1979, they were able to persuade Congress to extend the deadline for ratification of the ERA for another three years. But the amendment ultimately failed to be adopted by June 1982.

Scope of the Book

The role of women in effecting changes in five separate policy areas—credit, education, pregnancy disability, free choice regarding abortion, and economic equity—will be considered in this study. Other issues could have been selected, but these five were chosen because they provide a particularly good mix of feminist experiences from an organizational and political perspective.

We will discuss each of the five issues in separate chapters, tracing their development through the legislative and administrative process. Thus the case of credit will be presented within the context of the Equal Credit Opportunity Act of 1974; education will be discussed by focusing on Title IX of the Education Amendments of 1972; pregnancy disability will be highlighted by consideration of the Pregnancy Discrimination Act of 1978 (Amendments to Title VII of the Civil Rights Act of 1964); the discussion of free choice regarding abortion will center on the annual Hyde Amendments for the years after 1976 (these are amendments to the annual appropriations for the Department of Health, Education, and Welfare and the Department of Labor); and economic equity will be considered by looking at several titles of the Economic Equity Act—the Retirement Equity Act of 1984 and the yet to be enacted Nondiscrimination in Insurance Act. Each of the issues selected for study is broadly representative of the policy-making process since each deals with legislative and administrative enactments and, when relevant, their interpretation by regulatory and judicial authorities. From the analysis of specific cases, we will determine which issues and strategies are most likely to produce success for feminists in the political process and will specify parameters of such success. Before looking at the actual policies, we will examine the major feminist groups that have been especially central to the public policy efforts put forth by women in the past decade.

For each issue discussed, the analysis will include: the underlying problem the issue addresses; the nature of the goal sought; the organizational structure of the feminist movement; efforts at coalition-building both within and outside the feminist movement; the existence of a countermovement to oppose feminist interests; and the interactions of feminist groups within the policy process. We contend that when an issue is perceived as one affecting *role equity* rather than *role change*,[2] success is most likely.

---

[2] The terms "role change" and "role equity" were suggested by Maren Lockwood Carden, *Feminism in the Mid-1970's* (New York: Ford Foundation, 1977), 40-43.

Role equity issues are those policies which extend rights now enjoyed by other groups (men, other minorities) to women and which appear to be relatively delineated or narrow in their implications, permitting policy makers to seek advantage with feminist groups and voters with little cost or controversy. In contrast, role change issues appear to produce change in the dependent female role of wife, mother, and homemaker, holding out the potential of greater sexual freedom and independence in a variety of contexts. The latter issues are fraught with greater political pitfalls, including perceived threats to existing values, in turn creating visible and often powerful opposition.

The analysis is based largely on interviews with participants in the policy-making process who have affected the enactment of the laws considered. They include members of Congress and their aides and members of executive agencies and their staffs. In addition, lobbyists and advocates for both the "women's movement" and its opponents, including the anti-abortion "right-to-life" movement, the credit and insurance industry, and the professional athletic community have been interviewed. The interviews were not intended to achieve a quantitative portrait of policy inputs and outputs, but rather to aid in understanding the nature of the policy-making process. (See Appendices 1 and 2 for a sample questionnaire and list of persons interviewed.)

THE THEORETICAL APPROACH

In this study the role of women in politics will be examined from the vantage point of the convergence of contemporary interest-group theory and social-movement theory.[3] It is our belief that emergent groups in American politics such as the feminist movement provide a unique example of both political

[3] This convergence was suggested to the authors in remarks made by Terry Moe at the Annual Meeting of the Western Political Science Association, Denver, Colorado, March 26, 1981.

mobilization and interest-group development. To examine the feminist movement without examining this convergence would be to provide an incomplete analysis of this important group.

Those techniques which appear most effective in achieving even limited change for emergent groups like the feminist movement will be analyzed: Does a new group seem to achieve the greatest gains bv adhering to traditional tactics, including interest-group lobbying, or is a more radical threat to the "system" more effective in achieving change? Is it reasonable to anticipate fundamental changes in the status quo, or is incremental change the only likely result of reformist political challenge? In addition, we will assess the importance of a mass constituency for groups seeking to effect social change, as well as the constraints placed upon such groups by limited economic resources. The relevance of increased campaign and electoral activity will be considered as well.

Though we suggest a systematic set of rules indicating the kinds of issues, necessary organizational structures and coalition partners, degree of opposition, and techniques likely to produce even marginal political gains for new political groups, it should be emphasized that we are *not* discussing the development of a systematic causal model for either group formation or group behavior. Rather, we will consider those behavioral patterns which, based on the experiences of the contemporary feminist movement, are most likely to facilitate success for emergent groups trying to positively effect changes in the status quo.

More specifically, there are four rules that an emergent group must follow effectively in order to influence public policy:

1. To be effective in American politics, groups must be perceived as legitimate.[4]

[4] See David Truman, *The Governmental Process* (New York: Knopf, 1951); Robert Dahl, *A Preface to Democratic Theory* (Chicago: University of Chi-

2. In order to appear legitimate, groups will find it necessary to focus on incremental issues.[5] In this regard, role equity issues are less threatening than role change issues.

3. In order to appear legitimate, groups will stress the provision of information[6] and concentrate on mobilizing their allies. They will seek to avoid confrontation that comes from the use of protest tactics. They will form policy networks, and they will be willing to define success in terms of "increments."

4. Like other conventional interest groups, emergent groups will engage in a struggle over the definition of the situation. This struggle will almost always involve the manipulation of symbols favorable to one's cause. At times, these symbols will be employed to socialize conflict. At other times, symbols will be used to privatize conflict (for example, by defining the issue as one involving just role *equity*).[7]

These rules suggest the continuing relevance of E. E. Schattschneider's observation that our policy system is marked by a "mobilization of bias." However (and in this regard we are suggesting a modification of Schattschneider's notion), it is sometimes possible to achieve significant change in the guise of incrementalism if the importance of a seemingly narrow issue is not recognized by key political actors. Continued success

---

cago Press, 1956); David J. O'Brien, *Neighborhood Organization and Interest Group Processes* (Princeton: Princeton University Press, 1975).

[5] Charles E. Lindblom, "Still Muddling, Not Yet Through," *Public Administration Review* 39 (Nov./Dec. 1979), 517-26; Theodore Marmor, *The Politics of Medicare* (Chicago: Aldine, 1970), 14-16.

[6] Raymond Bauer, Lewis A. Dexter and Ithiel de Sola Pool, *Business and Public Policy* (New York: Atherton, 1963) as noted by Michael T. Hayes, "The Semi-Sovereign Pressure Groups," *Journal of Politics* 40 (Feb. 1978), 135.

[7] Murray Edelman, *Politics as Symbolic Action* (Chicago: Markham, 1971), ch. 1.

may be achieved by intensive organizational intervention, with the knowledge that no easy victories are likely.

Several social scientists have called attention to the need for "thinking small." The broader the goals of a social movement, the more central its focus, and the greater its threat to the status quo, the less likely it is to succeed.[8] Single-issue reformist politics that does not threaten displacement of existing power configurations, then, may often provide the easiest route to success for emergent groups. Feminists have been reformist in focus, distinctly nonradical in method, and have tended to deal with each issue as discrete and separable from others, conforming to the above hypotheses. Correspondingly, the broader the goal sought and the more visible the issue, the more prevailing values are likely to be perceived as threatened and countermovements to form in intense opposition to change. Thus narrower *role equity* issues are most likely to produce success while *role change* issues often lead to intense, and not always resolvable, political conflict. As has been the experience for blacks in the political process, it may be that even the feminist thrust for equity is sometimes perceived as broadly redistributive of traditional values and resources. This has the potential for producing conflict with those people who wish to maintain existing power relationships.[9]

Using the distinction between role change and role equity explained above, we may say that the issues of equal credit opportunity and the portions of the Economic Equity Act that address insurance and pensions conformed more closely to the role equity construct than the other three issues. Pregnancy disability was a role equity issue that generated divisiveness on the question of coverage for abortions. Title IX was a role equity issue that became controversial as aspects of the law and its regulations were perceived as affecting role change. Finally, abortion is an issue perceived as having profound implications

[8] Roberta Ash, *Social Movements in America* (Chicago: Markham, 1972), 29.

[9] See Harlan Hahn and Timothy Almy, "Ethnic Politics and Racial issues," *Western Political Quarterly* 33 (Dec. 1971), 728.

for role change. Thus, of the issues examined in this volume, it has engendered the most controversy. In addition to this difference between role equity and role change, other factors sometimes influence opposition to feminist interests.[10] There is, for example, strong moral and religious opposition to abortion. Issues that are perceived as influencing role change have been more likely to produce united opposition than have issues seen to involve role equity. The feminist movement often has been able to effectively neutralize opposition on the equity issues.

On four of the issues examined here—credit, pregnancy discrimination, education, and economic equity—women have been able to provide a relatively united front despite some differences in opinion on specific tactics. However, on the abortion issue, women (although not the feminist movement) have been divided among themselves. Furthermore, when a group is able to manipulate the symbols of politics, it is in a position to help define the limits of debate.[11] In the case of changes in the credit law, women's groups were able to invoke the symbol of equal economic opportunity. On abortion there has been a continuing struggle over which political symbol will prevail— individual freedom or murder.

Contrary to the experience of public interest groups, the sometime allies of feminists for whom expansion of conflict has brought considerable success,[12] feminists have achieved most when they have stressed the technical nature of an issue and have sought to contain conflict within clear bounds. An example may be seen in the politics of the Equal Rights Amendment. In Congress, where the ERA succeeded in 1972 with broad majority support, the amendment was perceived as a legal issue and was discussed in abstract and technical terms.

[10] Hayes has distinguished beween consensual and conflictual demand patterns, stressing the importance of political opposition ("The Semi-Sovereign Pressure Groups," 142).

[11] Edelman, *Politics as Symbolic Action*, ch. 2.

[12] Mark Nadel, *The Politics of Consumer Protection* (Indianapolis: Bobbs-Merrill, 1971), 160-205.

In the ratification process, where the ERA faltered, the issues dealt with became broader and the process came to highlight ideological values regarding society and change. Thus the presence of conflict has represented a bias against the adoption of any new policy: once conflict arises, differing views are presented; decision makers seek to avoid taking action; the politics of expediency can no longer prevail; and potential coalition partners may choose to stay aloof. Put in somewhat different terms, the group that succeeds in defining and limiting the parameters of debate may have a headstart on victory.

PLAN OF THE BOOK

In the next chapter there is a discussion of the mobilization of the contemporary women's movement and its evolution over the past decades. Chapter 3 considers the organization, funding and strategies employed by feminist advocates. In the remainder of the book the five policy issues selected for analysis are examined. Finally, in the last chapter an assessment of the movement in relation to the policies studied is provided.

CHAPTER 2

FEMINIST MOBILIZATION

INTRODUCTION

Feminism lay dormant during the fifty-year period following the passage of the Nineteenth Amendment. The "new wave" of feminist activism is a product of the 1960s and 1970s. The contemporary feminist movement arose in a climate of social reform during a time when gaps between expectations and reality became more apparent. Technological advances and changes in societal values and lifestyles, together with changed consciousness, fostered development of the movement and finally the formation of formal group organizations.

The feminist groups that emerged as a social movement in the late 1960s and early 1970s evolved in the later years of the 1970s into a stage of political development that emphasized interest-group organization and professionalization. It must be remembered that feminist groups, despite their relatively broad support, have small formal memberships and have relied upon traditional women's organizations and a public generally supportive of equal rights for a constituency base. Feminists may benefit from decision makers' knowledge of increasingly widespread support for the basic principles of equal rights feminism. A 1984 *Ms.* magazine poll found that 86 percent of Americans of both sexes considered it important that women's rights be strengthened. In contrast, 1970 poll data indicated that 43 percent of men and women accepted this view. A University of Michigan study found that support exceeded opposition for an equal role for women and for the women's rights movement. Women in voluntary traditional women's groups and local civic associations that are nonfeminist often demonstrate receptivity to women's rights issues, as long as they are related to equal rights and are presented in terms that do not threaten traditional lifestyles.[1] This point will be elaborated in Chapter 3.

In the pages that follow, we will discuss the stages in the development of feminist groups—specifically, the social, political, and economic factors leading to group consciousness, the process of group mobilization, and the structure of groups.

THEORIES OF GROUP ORIGINS

The feminist groups that evolved in the past twenty years have tended to be leadership, not membership, based. Both the National Organization for Women (NOW) and the National Abortion Rights Action League (NARAL) are exceptions, however. Thus, the theoretical frameworks used in this volume for understanding the contemporary feminist movement provide only partial explanations for their development because they emphasize mass membership groups.

David Truman, in *The Governmental Process*, provides some general insight into the development of groups in American politics when he calls attention to the "phenomenon of organization in waves," suggesting that the formation of some groups may give rise to other groups.[2] Hence it can be suggested that the increased activities of the black civil rights movement influenced the mobilization of feminists.

William Chafe illuminates the emergence of the feminist movement in particular by attributing it to a point of view

[1] Debrah Bokowski and Aage Clausen, "Federalism, Representation and the Amendment Process: The Case of ERA" (paper presented at the Midwest Political Science Association convention, Chicago, Ill., April 1979), 5; Susan Gluck Mezey and Trudy Haffron Bers, "Support for Women's Issues Among Local Civic Leaders" (paper presented at the American Political Science Association convention, Washington, D.C., Sept. 1, 1979), 6-14; Mary Thom, "The All-Time Definitive Map of the Gender Gap," *Ms.* (July 1984), 55.

[2] David Truman, *The Governmental Process* (New York: Knopf, 1951), 60. For a more complete discussion of Truman's "disturbance" theory, see Jeffrey M. Berry, *Lobbying for the People* (Princeton: Princeton University Press, 1977), 19.

around which to organize, a positive response by a portion of the aggrieved group, and a conducive social atmosphere.[3] Charles Tilly has similarly contended that collective action involves recognition of a common interest, mobilization or control of resources (which provide the capacity to act on interests), and opportunity. A movement's formation and growth require an experience of events common to many people, strong emotional feelings of dissatisfaction, focus upon an outside object, and leadership.[4] The contemporary women's movement did in fact evolve in such a manner. No one event precipitated its mobilization. Rather, a convergence of conditions over time created an environment that was amenable to the reemergence of feminism.

Students of feminist politics like Jo Freeman have argued that when a movement emerges, it must rest on a preexisting communications network or infrastructure—like-minded people whose background, experience, or location will make them receptive to a new movement.[5] Once a social movement has appeared, it may develop components of interest-group action. Interest-group organization reinforces leadership, communications, and incentives to participation.

The importance of leadership in the mobilization of previously unorganized interests is highlighted by Robert Salisbury, whose analysis of interest-group origins identifies entrepreneurial dominance as the major precondition for group development.[6] In the early years of the feminist movement, such figures as Betty Friedan provided a focus for both communication and development of leadership. Salisbury, in his article on

[3] William Chafe, *The American Woman: Her Changing Social, Economic and Political Roles, 1920-1970* (New York: Oxford University Press, 1972), 227.

[4] Charles Tilly, *From Mobilization to Revolution* (New York: Addison Wesley, 1978), 7.

[5] Jo Freeman, "Origins of the Women's Liberation Movement," in Joan Huber, ed., *Changing Women in a Changing Society* (Chicago: University of Chicago Press, 1973), 32.

[6] Robert Salisbury, "An Exchange Theory of Interest Groups," *Midwest Journal of Political Science* 13 (Feb. 1969), 1-32.

"An Exchange Theory of Interest Groups," suggests that "interest group origins, growth, death and associated lobbying activity may all be better explained if we regard them as exchange relationships between entrepreneur/organizers, who invest capital in a set of benefits, which they offer to prospective members at a price—membership."[7] Accordingly, his theory posits that individuals join groups because they derive benefits from participation.

The nature of incentives for individuals' involvement in groups has been the subject of much analysis. Peter Clark and James Q. Wilson identify three kinds—purposive, solidary, and material. Purposive incentives are ideologically based, solidary are socially rooted, and material are related to tangible rewards.[8] Mancur Olson further refines the notion of incentives for group membership by arguing that it is possible to organize latent support for groups only through the provision of selective incentives—nonpolitical positive inducements available only to group members.[9] Terry Moe has modified Olson's framework by suggesting that "purposive benefits can operate as selective incentives. . . . The support and pursuit of worthwhile collective goods" may provide sufficient rewards to some participants.[10] This notion of "in-process" benefits helps explain the nature of participation in feminist interest groups. "The individual will gain certain benefits from the process of participation itself, regardless of the outcome of the process, . . . [and] these in-process benefits will outweigh [the] costs of contribution."[11] In the period during which the women's movement reemerged and developed an intricate network

[7] *Ibid.*, 2.

[8] Peter B. Clark and James Q. Wilson, "Incentive Systems: A Theory of Organizations," *Administrative Science Quarterly* 6 (Sept. 1961), 129-66.

[9] Mancur Olson, *The Logic of Collective Action* (Cambridge, Mass.: Harvard University Press, 1971), 132-33.

[10] Terry Moe, "A Broader View of Interest Groups," *Journal of Politics* 43 (May 1981), 536.

[11] Allen Buchanan, "Revolutionary Motivation and Rationality," *Philosophy & Public Affairs* 9 (Fall 1979), 68.

of policy-related interest groups, it is clear that incentives for participation were primarily of the "in-process" kind, and the societal conditions outlined by social movement theorists help account for group development and mobilization.

GENESIS OF THE MOVEMENT

As suggested above, the women's movement appears to have originated in changed social conditions. Without giving equal weight to all the factors cited below, we can say that there were several causes for the reemergence of feminism. Among these causes were socio-political conditions and technological innovations that served to transform the role of women as mothers and homemakers, albeit gradually over time. The latter included advances in medical science, especially contraception, which lowered the birthrate and consequently the time devoted to childrearing, and laborsaving devices that freed women from housework so that they had more time to perform other tasks. In the two decades from 1950 to 1970, moreover, female labor force participation almost doubled, reaching 40 percent by the end of the sixties. By the end of 1982, 57.3 percent of American women over the age of 16 were employed either part-time or full-time.[12] These trends and others helped reinforce an environment of changing lifestyles, later marriage, more frequent divorce, greater sexual freedom, and the changed (if not diminished) role of the family, providing a favorable context for the resurgence of feminism.

In the 1960s a prevalent atmosphere of social reform contributed to the conditions that fostered feminist mobilization. One avenue into the feminist moverment was participation in the civil rights and new left moverments where, despite their rhetoric of equality, women were relegated to subordinate roles and feminist interests were both neglected and scorned.

[12] Marcia Lee, "The Equal Rights Amendment," in David Caputo, ed., *The Politics of Policy Making in America* (San Francisco: W. H. Freeman, 1977), 16-17; "The Changing Face of the Workforce," *National Journal* 16 (July 7, 1984), 1327.

This experience "radicalized" some women and led them to organize a variety of newer groups—*women's liberation groups*—that stressed, along with other concerns, "consciousness-raising," reflecting the shared experiences and discrimination suffered by women, and "alternative structures" such as self-help clinics and day-care centers. Many of these feminist activists began to question the validity of existing societal modes. From such women there emerged the more radical segment of the women's movement, which emphasized nonhierarchical, democratic, virtually leaderless (anti-) structures.

There were stark discrepancies between expectation and reality for educated middle-class women in the 1950s and 1960s. These women grew up encountering numerous contradictions in their lives; in particular, achievement-oriented values were incompatible with the traditional feminine role. In 1963 Betty Friedan wrote *The Feminine Mystique* describing the plight of overeducated women who were consigned to the role of homemakers and mothers. Her work was followed by that of Kate Millett, Germaine Greer, and others. The awareness aroused by these books, along with the model of tactical action and concern with oppression provoked by the civil rights and new left movements, was reinforced by the experiences of many women activists with the state commissions on the status of women, which brought together older middle-class women. The commissions produced considerable evidence that legal inequality existed for women, creating the expectation that change would occur. At the Third National Conference of State Commissions held in 1966 feminists were rebuffed by conference organizers who prevented them from submitting a formal motion that would have had the effect of urging government implementation of legislation forbidding sex discrimination.[13] This disappointment provided a major catalyst for the development of the *women's rights movement.* This movement was reformist, and its adherents were con-

[13] This account is presented in Maren Lockwood Carden, *The New Feminist Movement* (New York: Russell Sage, 1974), 103-104.

cerned with altering the status quo by using the traditional tools of American politics. After the meeting, in protest against the limitations on action or dissent, feminists came together to create the National Organization for Women. Other organizational mobilization of rights groups soon followed: the Women's Equity Action League (WEAL) was founded in 1968 and the National Women's Political Caucus (NWPC) in 1971.[14]

By the early 1970s the women's rights groups that emerged in the 1960s, as well as older and more traditional women's groups such as the League of Women Voters (LWV), American Association of University Women (AAUW), Business and Professional Women (BPW), and the General Federation of Women's Clubs (GFWC), were involved in a sophisticated endeavor, dividing responsibility for political activities and gaining congressional passage of the Equal Rights Amendment. The movement for the enactment of the ERA created policy networks—friendships, overlapping group memberships, and the like—which comprised the basis for renewed efforts in other policy areas. Mutual problem-solving, sharing of information, division of labor, efforts at creating coalition and unity, mobilization and recruitment of activists, and the gaining of positive access to media and government—all of which were to be built upon in future political efforts—emerged.

In addition, the relationship between women's liberation and women's rights groups began to change. By the late 1970s there was no longer a sharp distinction that could be drawn between women's rights and women's liberation groups.[15] Many of the ideas once held only by "liberation" advocates were now espoused by most feminists.

The liberation groups had adhered to strong priniciples based on anti-authoritarianism, participatory democracy, and

[14] Lee, "The Equal Rights Amendment," 16.

[15] Maren Lockwood Carden, *Feminism in the Mid-1970's* (New York: Ford Foundation, 1977), 6.

utopian communalism.[16] Sara Evans and Jo Freeman observed that the anti-leadership consensus adhered to by these groups proved inadequate as a basis for organization. "A preoccupation with internal processes . . . took precedence over program or effectiveness. As a result, women's liberation groups tended to oscillate between total formlessness at one extreme or a kind of collective authoritarianism on the other."[17] Among women's liberation groups, those women who developed an ability for public leadership received harsh criticism for being "stars." However, despite difficulties, a considerable portion of the more militant branch of feminism survived by joining with the mainstream of the movement. Other liberation groups began to organize numerous activities in communities throughout the nation. Liberation groups continue to exist in many local areas. These organizations publish myriad newspapers, magazines, and newsletters. They organize "Take Back the Night" marches to protest violence against women, speakouts on rape, consulting and support services for women (including bookstores), and such direct action efforts as shelters for battered women and child-care centers. Local feminists have organized collectives and have also developed caucuses and discussion groups within trade unions and professional organizations.

Much of the participatory ideology of early liberationists has remained an integral part of mainstream professional feminist politics. The relationship between liberation- and rights-oriented variants of feminism may be seen in the largest women's rights group, the National Organization for Women.[18] Although NOW remains a pragmatic and reformist group, it has

[16] See Wini Breines, "A Review Essay," *Feminist Studies*, Fall 1979, 502; also Joan Cassell, *A Group Called Women* (New York: McKay, 1977), 168.

[17] Sara Evans *Personal Politics* (New York: Viking, 1980), 223. See also Jo Freeman, "The Tyranny of Structurelessness," in Jane Jaquette, ed., *Women in Politics* (New York: Wiley, 1974).

[18] Sheila Rothman, *Women's Proper Place* (New York: Basic Books, 1978), 245.

altered some of its more moderate mainstream positions.[19] For example, NOW and several other feminist groups have come to view the oppression of lesbians as an integral part of mainstream professional feminist politics, recognizing the right of individuals to determine their own sexuality and lifestyle. (Prior to 1970 lesbian rights were not part of NOW's program.) NOW has also increased its involvement in such broadly humanist areas of policy as prison reform and racial discrimination. In its earlier years it took no position on these issues.[20]

The current leaders of feminist groups might be termed "executive" rather than "charismatic"; their stress is not on concentrating their own power but on countering bureaucratic tendencies that place more and more people under control of a few. What Rosabeth Kanter has defined as "flattening hierarchy"—spreading authority and gaining greater participation—seems to be the prevalent mode in feminist groups, although it is difficult to generalize for all those groups discussed here.[21] As Maren Lockwood Carden wrote with reference to NOW: "Although NOW has moved steadily in the direction of greater institutionalization, . . . its members remain self-consciously determined to avoid becoming an impersonal bureaucratic organization and intend to combine the goal of organizational effectiveness with the goal of concern for the individual participant."[22]

Although feminist leaders (such as Betty Friedan and Gloria Steinem) were instrumental in the mobilization of a feminist movement that had remained dormant from the early 1920s to the mid-1960s, the ideology of the movement itself seems to have led over time to a modification of leadership roles for the contemporary movement. Most feminist leaders are well known within the moverment but have little media visibility or public recognition. While individual leaders who had great de-

[19] *Ibid.*

[20] Carden, *The New Feminist Movement*, 117.

[21] Rosabeth Moss Kanter, *Men and Women of the Corporation* (New York: Basic Books, 1977), 276.

[22] Carden, *The New Feminist Movement*, 131.

termination and skill were largely responsible for the formation and early development of these groups, no feminist organization could echo these words used to describe Common Cause: "[John] Gardner's influence permeates the entire structure of Common Cause. It is hard for the staff of Common Cause to imagine their organization without Gardner, and thus when he hinted publicly that he might retire . . . many were genuinely shocked." Nor is there a feminist counterpart to Ralph Nader, of whom it has been written: "the ascetic, dedicated prophet of the public interest is the object of widespread admiration. Thousands of young people seek to emulate him."[23] The absence of personalized leadership among feminists may be attributable in part to movement ideology, which inspires women to be autonomous, take responsibility, make decisions, and develop their own positions. Group staffs are committed less to a specific leader than to the "movement" and its goals. Another factor mitigating against personalized leadership may be the early ideology that stressed "sisterhood," implying decentralization, internal democracy, nonhierarchical control, and the like. Although no longer dominant among such groups as NOW, whose "sisterhood" does not extend to total intraorganizational equality, there is still a prevailing belief in maximizing participation by the rank and file.[24] NOW builds in leadership change by holding biennial elections for new national leaders, a reflection of the desire to prevent domination by a single person or small elite. It seems evident that this commitment to avoidance of domineering leadership, and decision making through compromise and participation, is directly attributable to the ties of the movement to earlier liberation politics.

Organized feminism, though professionalized, has not lost its spontaneity and commitment—new elements continually

[23] Andrew McFarland, *Public Interest Lobbies* (Washington, D.C.: American Enterprise Institute, 1976), 20-21.

[24] Jo Freeman, "Resource Mobilization and Strategy: A Model for Analyzing Social Movement Organization Action" in Meyer Zald and John D. McCarthy, eds., *The Dynamics of Social Movements* (Cambridge, Mass.: Winthrop, 1979), 178.

join and renew organizational vigor, although groups themselves (including NOW) have become more hierarchical in structure and traditional in established procedures. The experience of NOW and other feminist groups seems thus to refute the view of Weber and Michels that bureaucratization and accommodation replace a movement's initial momentum. That model suggests that as an organization gains societal acceptance, it becomes bureaucratized and accommodates to society. Bureaucrats develop a vested interest in maintaining their organizational position and, in order to maintain their primacy, lead their organization toward conservatism and oligarchy. The desire for organizational maintenance, even at the expense of achievement of movement goals, becomes paramount, and the wish to avoid conflict becomes overriding.[25] Yet, as Zald and Ash have pointed out, this need not be the only fate of groups oriented to change.[26] The organizations in the contemporary women's movement have not fallen prey to the perils of bureaucratization. They have remained agents for change in the status of women in society even as they have worked to broaden understanding for the goals of the movement.

The Structure and Types of Contemporary Feminist Groups

Virtually all the women's groups discussed in this study have a traditional bureaucratic organizational structure. In addition, some have chapters or branches and a dues-paying membership. All of the groups have operating rules or by-laws and a prescribed governing system. Usually governance consists of a board (comprised of professionals, business persons, and often leading group activists) that plays a role in raising money and in determining priorities and strategies. There is substantial overlap among board members within the feminist commu-

[25] Max Weber, *The Theory of Social and Economic Organization* (New York: Oxford University Press, 1947) 363-86; Robert Michels, *Political Parties* (New York: Dover, 1959), 370-73.

[26] Mayer Zald and Roberta Ash, "Social Movement Organizations: Growth, Decay, and Change," *Social Forces* 421 (1966), 327-40.

nity. Most boards set broad policy but do not interfere in day-to-day staff activities. An exception is the Reproductive Freedom Project of the American Civil Liberties Union where board and staff functions are blurred among the eight attorneys who share joint concerns and consult frequently. Several feminist groups (WEAL and NOW-LDEF) have developed professionally from once largely voluntary organizations, have built stronger staffs in recent years, and have emerged from an era of board dominance. Most of the groups began as leadership or cadre organizations lacking a mass base. Some, such as NARAL and NOW, have developed constituencies while still others (WLDF, for one) would like to. Some, such as WEAL, prefer to exist with a small membership.

Although groups have become bureaucratized, they have not tended to rigidify or become more conservative. Rather, they have reinforced and even expanded their initial range and activities while sustaining or deepening their commitment to social change, albeit incremental in scope.

The growth and development of feminist groups were aided by the existence of traditional women's voluntary groups such as the American Association of University Women, National Council of Jewish Women, and League of Women Voters. Feminist political consciousness and mobilization were heightened by the struggle for congressional ratification of the ERA, which helped create a network of contacts, communication, mutual problem-solving, and information-sharing. Feminist groups proliferated in the 1970s so that the initial movement spearheaded by NOW diversified with groups specializing in litigation, research, policy formulation and analysis, and constituency development—though some groups participate in more than one activity.

Like their earlier black civil rights counterparts, feminist groups are frequently based in Washington or New York. By 1973 many of the groups including the (now defunct) Women's Lobby, WEAL, NOW, and NWPC had opened Washington offices in order specifically to influence the national policy process.

The groups whose roles will be considered in this chapter include the Women's Rights Project (WRP) and Reproductive Freedom Project (RFP) of the American Civil Liberties Union (ACLU), Women's Rights Project of the Center for Law and Social Policy (CLASP), now called the National Women's Law Center, the National Organization for Women (NOW) and its affiliates, the NOW Legal Defense and Education Fund (NOW-LDEF) and the NOW Project on Equal Education Rights (PEER), Women's Equity Action League (WEAL), Women's Legal Defense Fund (WLDF), National Women's Political Caucus (NWPC), Center for Women Policy Studies (CWPS), and National Abortion Rights Action League (NARAL).

It should be noted that several groups maintain different arms, each with a different tax status and different purpose. For example, NOW with 501(c)(4) status—which means that while the organization is tax-exempt, contributions to it are not tax-deductible—has established a Legal Defense and Education Fund that has a 501(c)(3) tax status; contributions are tax-deductible, but the organization is limited as to the time it can expend in lobbying activity. NOW has also established a Political Action Committee (PAC) to engage in campaign-related activities.

There are five types of groups that comprise the national feminist political community. Together they have created a network of complementary alliances in national politics, despite the existence of potential strains that exist owing to the presence of their often disparate constituencies. Four types of groups have been on the scene for a decade or longer: *mass-based* or *membership* feminist organizations such as NOW and NWPC; *specialized* feminist groups, including litigation and research groups, which often provide the technical expertise and legal acumen that have led to feminist successes in the administrative, legislative, and judicial arenas; *single-issue* groups such as NARAL, AIAW (Association for Intercollegiate Athletics for Women), PEER (which monitors Title IX in education), and SPRINT (a WEAL Fund affiliate concerned with equal athletic opportunity); and *traditional* women's groups, which support many but not all feminist goals (for example, some are avowedly "pro-choice" and some are not) and whose support of these goals is not the major objective or function of the group. Political efforts by feminists have been facilitated on numerous occasions because of the mass constituency base and contacts maintained by these more established women's groups (see Tables 1 and 2).

The newest type of group in feminist politics is an *electoral campaign sector*, which developed in the late 1970s and gained additional momentum in the election campaigns of 1980, 1982, and 1984. In addition to the political action committees (PACs) established by the NWPC, NOW, and NARAL in accordance with new campaign finance regulations, autonomous groups such as Voters for Choice now seek to "target" legislators opposed to abortion. They have borrowed this technique from the efforts portrayed as successful by the media in which anti-feminist groups have used the electoral system to pursue their goals. The campaign-oriented groups rely extensively on direct mail in order to raise money. These efforts mark a new stage in feminist political development. In addition, the Women's Campaign Fund provides resources for fe-

TABLE 1

Membership of
Traditional Women's Groups (1980)

American Association of University Women	190,000
B'nai Brith Women	120,000
League of Women Voters	115,000
General Federation of Women's Clubs	600,000
National Federation of Business and Professional Women's Clubs	154,000
National Council of Jewish Women	100,000
United Methodist Women	1,244,000
Total	2,523,000

SOURCE: Telephone survey, July 15, 1981.

TABLE 2
Feminist Groups' Membership (1985)

Group	Membership
ACLU-WRP/RFP	none
CLASP-WRP (NWLC)	none
CWPS	none
NARAL	100,000
NOW	156,000
NOW-LDEF	none
NWPC	77,000
WEAL	7,000
WLDF	1,500

SOURCE: Annual reports of the groups, telephone interviews, and the *Washington Post*, July 14, 1985.

male candidates seeking electoral office who have a commitment to women's rights. Support for ERA and "pro-choice" views has qualified prospective recipients for backing by the group.[27]

Feminist Membership Groups

Among the earliest feminist groups to develop were the National Organization for Women and the National Women's Political Caucus. Although these organizations are membership organizations, they lack the mass constituency of such traditional women's groups as the General Federation of Women's Clubs (cf. Tables 1 and 2). NOW is patterned (though

[27] In addition to the groups we examine in the text we also interviewed attorneys from the League of Women Voters (Maureen Thornton) and the Women's Law Fund (Jane Picker) as well as directors of Voters for Choice and Women's Campaign Fund. Because of space constraints, their comments are not analyzed in depth, but some of their insights are included. One other group, the Women's Lobby, under the direction (and considerable financial support) of Carole Burris, has been the feminist movement's first casualty.

perhaps not consciously) after the National Association for the Advancement of Colored People (NAACP). Following the NAACP model, NOW has developed different components in order to maximize fund-raising and flexibility. In addition to the mass-membership-based NOW organization, a NOW Legal Defense and Education Fund was established, as well as PEER to emphasize monitoring of Title IX enforcement and a PAC to stress ballot-box reprisals against recalcitrant legislators.

NOW increased its membership from 1,122 and 14 chapters in 1967 to 125,000 members and 700 chapters in each of the fifty states in 1978, largely owing to its campaign for ERA ratification. After Ronald Reagan's election in 1980 and the defeat of the ERA in 1982, NOW's membership increased to 181,000. By 1985 NOW's membership had decreased to 156,000. Other reform groups have experienced similar membership fluctuations as their issue concerns ebb and flow in the public consciousness.[28] Members receive the group's publication, *National NOW Times*. Local chapters are autonomous. In contrast to the NAACP and Urban League, which derive significant revenue from local affiliates and branches, NOW rebates 4 percent of its revenue to state chapters.

NOW is the largest feminist constituency group. It has an unusually strong board, which is elected by regional representatives on a biennial basis, and five national officers, who are selected at a national convention. The two-year-term national officers, who manage the Washington offices, are salaried by the organization. Utilizing a somewhat unusual structure, these officers are involved in the daily operations of the organization as well as in decision making. A thirty-person staff includes ten field operatives, researchers, organizers, lobbyists, and specialists in specific areas such as reproductive freedom, lesbian rights, and economic rights. They all operate under the direction of national officers. (NOW's Legal Defense and Ed-

[28] *Washington Post*, July 14, 1985; Andrew McFarland, *Common Cause* (Chatham, N.J.: Chatham House, 1984), 203-204.

ucation Fund and the Project for Equal Education Rights will be discussed below in the section on research and litigation groups.)

During its history NOW has been beset by attacks internally from both the right and the left: members who have opposed its current and past advocacy of abortion rights and sexual self-determination, and members who oppose NOW's reformist, pragmatic approach to changing the existing political system, respectively. Nonetheless, it has weathered internal conflicts such as these as well as those engendered by creation of and communication with local chapters.[29]

NOW and other feminist groups have experienced major changes in leadership and organization since their formation but have sustained and strengthened their political role. NOW's 1967 Bill of Rights still remains a guide to the general demands of the feminist movement:

1. an equal rights constitutional amendment;
2. enforcement of laws banning sex-biased employment discrimination;
3. maternity leave rights in employment and social security benefits;
4. tax deductions for child and home care expenses for working parents;
5. child-care centers;
6. equal and unsegregated education;
7. equal job training opportunities and allowances for women in poverty;
8. the right of women to control their reproductive lives.[30]

Another constituency organization in the women's movement is the National Women's Political Caucus, which expanded its membership from 271 members in 1971 to 77,000

[29] Carden, *The New Feminist Movement*, 103-18.
[30] Barbara Deckard, *The Women's Movement* (New York: Harper and Row, 1979), 348.

in 1985. Most "members," however, are merely "associates" or contributors rather than active group participants; "governing" members number 11,000 and play a more participatory role in the organization. The NWPC publishes a newsletter, *Women's Political Times*. It is governed by a steering committee comprised of state and local caucus representatives. The staff includes eight professionals and several seasonal consultants. The NWPC focuses on electing women as national convention delegates and on electing women to public office. Hence, while the caucus does lobby and is active in Washington-based coalitions, its primary orientation is the electoral process and, in recent years, the ratification of the ERA as well.

Like NWPC, the Women's Equity Action League has a membership base but is not primarily a membership organization. WEAL was founded in Ohio in 1968 as a reaction to what was then perceived as NOW's radical stand on abortion and in an effort to provide "respectability" to the feminist movement. In 1972 its tax-exempt arm, the WEAL Fund, was established largely to support lawsuits and to monitor implementation and enforcement; it has focused on Title IX and academic discrimination and in recent years on economic equity. In 1981 WEAL and the WEAL Fund merged. At the present time WEAL operates SPRINT (a clearinghouse on women and athletics) and a legal defense fund. It issues a monthly *WEAL Washington Report*. The membership of WEAL doubled from 3,500 in 1978 to 7,000 in 1982. WEAL's primary constituency of professional and executive women has sought to mobilize expertise rather than numbers.[31]

Specialized Groups

The growth of WEAL from a small office operation to an organization with a staff of twenty-one employees in 1978 is paralleled by the growth of the Center for Women Policy Studies, a small nonmembership organization founded in 1972 to provide technical expertise on various women's issues. In 1985 it

[31] Freeman, "Resource Mobilization and Strategy," 185.

had a staff of five professionals, four full-time and one part-time. The scope of the organization's issue concerns ranges from equal credit to battered women. The board of three (consisting of the director, former co-director, and academician Jessie Bernard) plays a strong role. The Center has published numerous scholarly works documenting economic discrimination as well as other systematic discrimination against women.

In addition, there are several groups with litigational focuses, though not necessarily extensive litigational capacity,[32] whose strategy is to become involved in precedent-setting cases, much like their civil rights predecessors. However, there is no one dominant feminist legal group comparable to the NAACP Legal Defense and Educational Fund for civil rights groups. This is the result of several factors, including foundations' funding practices that have encouraged a multiplicity of groups, the role of several strong personalities who have fostered the growth of multiple organizations, and specialization by issue-specific organizations.

Thus several groups, each with three or four attorneys plus support staff, coexist. In this respect, they resemble the small-scale operations of the NAACP and ACLU in their formative stages from 1940 to 1960.[33] Many litigation groups do far more than just case law, and they increasingly devote their time to other tasks. The executive director of one such group operates as a "linkage" person among feminist interests and among civil rights groups coordinating, bringing them together, sharing information, and "politicking." She spends relatively little time actually litigating.

The Center for Law and Social Policy, now called the National Women's Law Center, began in 1969 as a public interest law firm, initiated its women's rights project in 1974, and now

[32] Several feminist law firms exist outside the Washington/New York axis; they include the Women's Law Fund in Cleveland and Equal Rights Advocates in California. They are not being considered here.

[33] Robert Rabin, "Lawyers for Social Change: Perspectives on Public Interest Law," *Stanford Law Review* 28 (Jan. 1976), 213.

employs three attorneys on this project. Its advisory board is predominantly local (Washington-based), and its Litigation Committee serves to advise on the broad nature of cases to be dealt with. The Center's lawyers have been particularly active on Title IX and on health issues as they relate to women. One observer has remarked that the Center functions as a law firm for women's organizations that do not yet have the skills or resources necessary to support litigation. It has developed expertise in analyzing government regulations and securing their enforcement.

The American Civil Liberties Union has given rise to two feminist-oriented litigation groups. The first was the Women's Rights Project, an outgrowth of the 1971 Supreme Court case *Reed* v. *Reed*,[34] which provided the ACLU with the idea that the equal protection clause might have potential as a vehicle to increase rights for women. With the aid of Ford Foundation funding and matching grants from other foundations, the project began in New York City. Three attorneys now work on the Women's Rights Project.

The ACLU office in Washington employs a full-time lobbyist on women's and other rights issues, funded by the ACLU itself. In 1974, prompted in part by the reluctance of contributors (primarily the Ford Foundation) to support abortion-related cases and in part by the concentration of the Women's Rights Project leadership on other areas, the Reproductive-Freedom Project was founded by the ACLU with the aid of funding from John D. Rockefeller III. Monthly meetings between the staff and a four-person advisory committee (all feminist attorneys) have come, by all accounts, closest of all groups examined to blurring distinctions between board and staff in function and expertise. The meetings are strategy sessions, which are supplemented by more frequent intraoffice consultations. Today the feminist legal staff of seven at the ACLU is the largest "group" in the organization, leading one

[34] 404 U.S. 71.

writer to suggest that feminists have "coopted" the ACLU.[35] The RFP both litigates on abortion rights and functions as an informational resource center.

The growth and development of the Women's Legal Defense Fund, as well as NOW's Legal Defense and Education Fund, may be attributed to their directors. WLDF was founded in 1971 by a small group of well-known feminist lawyers in Washington, D.C., with the aid of a start-up grant from the Junior League. Originally a volunteer organization that borrowed from the model of the ACLU and the Lawyers Committee for Civil Rights under Law in obtaining *pro bono* private counsel, the Fund now employs fifteen people, including five attorneys. It still does no in-house litigation. Under the direction of Judith Lichtman, the Fund has grown from an organization with a $30,000 budget and 85 members to one that in 1984 had 1,500 members and a budget of over $400,000.[36] The organization has a board of elected members and chairpersons of standing committees, most of whom are attorneys. A nine-person screening committee determines what cases the Fund should accept. Volunteers continue to play a key role in the organization's work, which alone among feminist groups discussed here operates a local service facility—a shelter for battered women.

NOW's Legal Defense and Education Fund is linked to its parent organization NOW through an intricate corporate relationship. NOW-LDEF is governed by its own board (and by-laws) consisting of NOW officers, ten elected directors, and eight directors appointed by the board. At least five members of the board must be attorneys. A Defense Committee reviews participation in litigation. The Fund's headquarters are in New York while both national NOW and NOW-LDEF's offshoot PEER are located in Washington, D.C. Similar to the board of the WEAL Fund, NOW-LDEF's board is active and involved although no longer dominant, owing to the new role

[35] Freeman, "Resource Mobilization and Strategy," 175.
[36] WLDF, *1984 Annual Report*, 23.

of the enlarged and strengthened staff. Like the NAACP Legal Defense and Educational Fund, whose model it has emulated, NOW-LDEF is seeking to develop a group of cooperating attorneys. Director Phyllis Segal inherited a litigation budget of $4,000 when she came to the Fund as its first full-time staff attorney in 1976, and it grew to over $625,000 in 1984. By 1984 the staff had been enlarged to include four attorneys, and the total budget was estimated to be over $2 million. The major focus of NOW-LDEF is education and public information, not litigation.[37]

Single-Issue Groups

The National Abortion Rights Action League, a single-issue "pro-(abortion) choice" group, is an outgrowth of an earlier feminist organization that sought to repeal restrictive abortion laws at the state level. At that time it was known as the National Association to Repeal Abortion Laws. In 1973, in response to the Supreme Court decisions on abortion, and fearing a countermovement from the right, the group's name was changed and its headquarters moved from New York to Washington, D.C. NARAL is not only a feminist organization; it also has numerous ties to population and health groups. It has always counted among its members public health activists and medical professionals as well as feminists. Like NOW, WEAL, and several other civil rights groups, NARAL has several arms—one that lobbies, having 501(c)(4) status, a 501(c)(3) Foundation, and a PAC to engage in electoral campaign activity. NARAL, like NWPC and CWPS, has no litigation capacity, although it can contract legal work to be done. With a staff of twenty-eight and an active Executive Committee of fifteen (which meets every six weeks), NARAL, under pressure from right-to-life opposition, seems to be expanding its focus from being primarily a Washington-based group to developing grassroots organization as well. By 1985 it had grown from an organization of 20,000 to 100,000 members as a result of a di-

[37] NOW-LDEF, *1979 Annual Report*, 15.

rect-mail recruiting effort. The emergence of single-issue groups like NARAL has freed organizations like NOW to participate in more diverse causes.

NOW's Project on Equal Education Rights (PEER) was founded in 1974 to monitor enforcement of Title IX in Washington, D.C. Its nine-person staff was supplemented by a project in Michigan to initiate grassroots activity on Title IX through organizing, monitoring, and bringing complaints from the local level. PEER has its own (albeit inactive) advisory council.

CONCLUSION

Feminist organizations evolved as energetic interest-group actors in the 1960s and 1970s. Their development was based in large measure on changed societal relationships that fostered the generation of new demands on public policy makers. The women's movement has been able to integrate many divergent interests, by virtue of group proliferation and concern for inclusivity.

CHAPTER 3

THE GROUP ACTORS:
RESOURCES AND
STRATEGIES

INTRODUCTION

As Chapter 2 makes clear, the organized feminist movement
has grown remarkably, in both the number of constituency
groups and its political influence, since its relatively recent be-
ginnings in the 1960s. Today it is poorer than its counterparts
in the civil rights movement, having entered politics together
with a large number of other competing "rights" groups.
Group resources including staff, funding, and membership
both dictate and constrain possibilities for political influence.
Nonetheless, feminist groups have proliferated, and new and
old groups alike have grown and become increasingly professionalized in the last several years. These groups come together
regularly in numerous coalitions and exchanges, linked by intersecting sets of personal relationships and contacts. Feminists have been particularly effective in developing autonomous, specialized organizations while preserving the
cohesiveness of the movement. Bound to the movement and its
abstract ideology rather than to a specific leader or set of leaders, feminists have avoided rivalries based on personal loyal-
ties.

Feminist groups examined here are reformist or "norm-ori-
ented" in setting their goals.[1] Though their very existence represents a commitment to changing the social structure and the
distribution of rewards within society, they reflect the scope

[1] Neil Smelser, *Theory of Collective Behavior* (New York: Free Press, 1963),
270-312.

and bias of the system. They are committed to gaining equal rights within existing society rather than creating a new society based on new values. In other words, they seek change in institutions instead of new institutions. Policy makers within the movement are trained professionals who are pragmatic, compromise-oriented individuals willing to settle for incremental change. They largely eschew expressive for more instrumental politics and deemphasize long-range planning and program development.

However, though there is an absence of overall "strategizing" and planning within the movement, it seems that the ad hoc nature of policy development is particularly well suited to constraints determined by the structure of the political system, a system characterized itself by incrementalism and shifting policy concerns. In the absence of ideological rigidity, flexibility may be maximized. It is possible, nevertheless, that some groups may find that they will need to define their own role and mission more precisely should they wish to maintain or augment membership and funding as well as gain greater rationality in resource allocation in the future.

Finally, the women's movement, like other reform movements, has had a problem recruiting and mobilizing latent constituencies, in whose name they gain credibility, owing to the "free rider" problem. Mancur Olson has pointed out that a group's ability to mobilize constituents may be severely limited when collective benefits or goods obtainable by group efforts accrue to group members whether or not they are active participants in the organization.[2] There is no material incentive for mass participation unless selective benefits or services are obtainable only by virtue of group membership. That feminist groups have been unable to develop such selective incentives (in contrast to the aged, for example, who may receive insurance and medical benefits with formal group membership) may provide a partial explanation for their failure to recruit more than a fraction of potential members. They are thus *re-*

[2] Mancur Olson, *A Theory of Collective Action* (Cambridge, Mass.: Harvard University Press, 1971), 48.

sponsive but not *responsible* to a broad constituency base. Nonetheless, feminists may be in a stronger political position than membership figures only would indicate owing to their relationship with traditional women's groups on whose support and numbers they rely. In addition, as suggested above, these groups have the sympathy of countless men and women who adhere to many movement principles but do not hold formal membership in any organization.

GROUP RESOURCES

For feminist groups, organizational resources such as staff, finances, and membership tend to structure patterns of advocacy and impact. We will examine the resources available to feminist groups and then examine tactics and strategies for utilizing these resources in the political arena.

Staff

A major resource for all of the feminist groups examined in this study is their dedicated staff. Mancur Olson has hypothesized that individuals tend to join and maintain interest-group membership if they gain "separate and selective" incentives, normally of a nonpolitical nature, and when all access to those incentives is monopolized by the group. In the case of ideologically oriented interests, such as the women's movement, material incentives are not applicable. Terry Moe and Allen Buchanan have pointed out that the satisfaction of participating in a worthy cause may provide its own "selective incentives" for members of noneconomic groups.[3] In addition, incentives for staff and activist leaders may differ from those attractive to members—an issue not discussed by Olson and other incentive theorists.

On the basis of the interviews conducted for this study, it is clear that most feminist group staff and leaders have made a

[3] Allen Buchanan, "Revolutionary Motivation and Rationality," *Philosophy & Public Affairs* 9 (Fall 1979), 68; Terry Moe, "A Broader View of Interest Groups," *Journal of Politics* 43 (May 1981), 536-37.

conscious decision to place strictly economic rewards in a secondary position because of their basic concern for achieving social reform. Substantial numbers of female recruits join feminist organizations (often directly from law school or graduate school) because of a commitment to the particular cause, work with the feminist organizations for several years, and, when they do leave the groups, often remain in the public interest arena or join government agencies in areas where their training and movement identification are crucial.

Recruits to feminist activism tend to be well educated and middle class. Most of those interviewed were relatively young (under 50, many under 40), and many had law degrees or graduate degrees, primarily from good Eastern colleges or large public universities. They are predominantly attorneys. Salaries paid by feminist groups are clearly lower than those paid by the private sector and lower than those paid by government. In 1985 most of the salaries were in the range of $15,000 to $55,000. Nonetheless, even accounting for inflation, they compare favorably to salaries paid public interest lobbyists.[4]

The incentives that motivate initial recruitment and willingness to remain are purposive (ideological) and solidary (social).[5] Individuals are drawn into the movement's network by ideology and often personal relationships, and they remain part of the complex organizational structure described below through extensive contacts, networks, and social ties.

One compensation for lack of economic rewards may be the access to power and even media publicity that participation in the movement can bring. Young women, even those with lim-

[4] Telephone interviews with Jane Chapman (WCPS), Eleanor Braun (NWPC), Elaine Loiello (NARAL), and Noel Salinger (ACLU), Sept. 18-20, 1985; Joel Handler, Ellen Hollingsworth, and Howard Erlanger, *Lawyers and the Pursuit of Legal Rights* (New York: Academic Press, 1978), 85; and Jeffrey M. Berry, *Lobbying for the People* (Princeton: Princeton University Press, 1977), 102, Table IX-7.

[5] See Robert Salisbury, "An Exchange Theory of Interest Groups," *Midwest Journal of Political Science* 13 (Feb. 1969), 16. James Q. Wilson, in *Political Organizations* (New York: Basic Books, 1973), discusses incentive structures in a similar manner.

ited experience, may find themselves involved with exciting issues, talking with well-known politicians, and coming before the public in leadership roles. These rewards may provide a rationale for continued hard work, long hours. and low salaries.

Interviewees did complain of frustration in their work and spoke of a "burn-out" period—loosely estimated to be seven years—caused by delays, red tape, and other governmental foot-dragging as well as the never-ending nature of monitoring, necessary even after favorable legal decisions or acts of legislation have been achieved. Nonetheless, despite financial and psychological pressures and the inevitable turnover that results, a substantial number of leaders have remained with their groups.[6] It should be noted that, in addition to student interns, many groups (including WEAL and WLDF) supplement their regular work force through the use of volunteers, although feminists are sensitive to the issue of "exploitation" without "compensation."

Although the focus of this study is not on internal decision-making processes within feminist groups, the importance of staff dominance in most groups should be noted. Increasingly, as feminist groups have emerged from an era of board dominance and reliance on volunteers, staffs have assumed leadership roles in selecting issues and employing tactics and strategies for political influence. In addition, as Jeffrey Berry suggests, a group's concentration on particular issues is also restricted by previous commitments and focus and by financial resources as well.[7] We now turn to the crucial matter of funding for feminist interest groups.

Funding

Sources of funding for women's movement groups are diverse, with membership and nonmembership contributions (especially from foundations), assistance from other groups, and

---

[6] Among those who have endured for a lengthy period are Marcia Greenberger and Margaret Kohn of CLASP-WRP, Jane Roberts Chapman of the CWPS, Holly Knox of PEER, and Char Mollison of WEAL.

[7] Berry, *Lobbying for the People*, 203-205.

government aid all providing some of the revenue. (See Table 3.) However, a 1976 study of public interest groups (which included many of the groups considered here) found that law centers serving racial and ethnic minorities were better funded than feminist groups. The latter had the smallest percentage of contributions as a proportion of their available revenues.[8] All the groups considered here have financial constraints, and almost all are dependent on contributions from outside funding sources whose impact may be to distort organizational goals and resource allocation. Many groups have received grants or contracts from such diverse government agencies as the Equal Employment Opportunity Commission, U.S. Civil Rights Commission, Department of Labor, and the Department of State. However, during the years of the Reagan presidency, the extent of this federal government funding has declined substantially. Women's groups have been forced to seek replacement resources elsewhere in a climate hostile to funding groups seen as (pejoratively) "feminist." WEAL, like other groups, has lost all of its federal support, which had comprised half of its 1980 budget. From 1980 to 1982 WEAL's budget decreased somewhat, but it was able to survive through increasing membership and contributions by one third and tripling publication, sales, and foundation support. The loss of federal support has been offset in part by the increase in foundation grants to women's groups from 1.7 percent (or $20 million) in 1980 to almost 2.8 percent ($50 million) in 1983 and 3.69 percent ($60 million) in 1984.[9] No feminist groups have been forced out of existence as a result of fiscal difficulties, although several have had to curtail their activities, share space with other groups, and eliminate some programs in order to survive.

One source of funding for groups that have a public "image" is direct-mail soliciting of contributions from individuals.

[8] The Council for Public Interest Law, *Balancing the Scales of Justice* (1975), 95 and 107.
[9] *National Journal* 15 (Aug. 6, 1983), 1630 and 1632; *Foundation Grants Index*, 14th ed. (New York: Foundation Center, 1985).

NOW-LDEF received $591,769 in individual contributions in 1984, more than double its 1978 revenue from individuals.[10] Direct mail also has helped NOW and NARAL increase their memberships. WLDF now utilizes this method as well. Direct mail thus seems to be a growing source of revenue for both membership and contributions, although it is costly in staff time and mailing expenses. Several groups have indicated that they tap individual contributors—men as well as women— several times annually. Increasingly, feminists may seek funds from women themselves as female work-force participation and income grow. A problem with reliance on individual funding may be its ephemeral nature; as economic conditions and popular issues change, such contributions may decrease.

Other sources of income include membership dues. For NOW and NARAL, for example, this comprises the major source of revenue. Many groups have several categories of paying members. One drawback is that membership often requires organizations to provide some sort of service, however limited, in the form of newsletters, periodicals, or the like, which may cost almost as much as the revenue that can be raised from dues.

Some litigation groups derive a portion of their funds (shifting as different cases are settled each year) from recoveries for attorney's fees. It should be noted that the Supreme Court's 1975 decision in *Alyeska Pipeline Service Co.* v. *Wilderness Society*[11] curtailed the award of attorneys' fees unless there is a specific statutory authorization for such an award. This has limited fee awards in many feminist cases that do not entail such authorization, except those relating to Title VII, which does authorize fee awards. However, groups that obtain *pro bono* legal services derive the equivalent of thousands of dollars annually in "free" legal time from cooperating attorneys.

A growing source of revenue for some groups, including NOW and NWPC, comes from charges for dinners and recep-

[10] NOW-LDEF, *Report 2000.*
[11] 421 U.S. 240.

TABLE 3
Change in Annual Budgets (1978-1984) and
Major Sources of Revenue (1984)

Group	1978 Annual Budget	1984 Annual Budget	Funding Sources	Amount
ACLU-WRP	$ 300,000	$ 280,000	foundations	$ 280,000
ACLU-RFP	156,000	547,000	grants	357,000
			attorney fees	116,000
			other	74,000
CWPS	209,476	171,810	federal government	51,543
			foundations/corporations	32,644
			subscriptions/publications	79,032
			other	8,591
NARAL	1,800,000	2,600,000	membership dues and fees	2,600,000
NOW	2,654,000†	5,637,000	membership dues	3,600,000
			contributions	1,715,000
			sales	232,000
			other	90,000
NOW-LDEF	602,828	2,143,449	corporations/foundations and individual contributions	1,827,291
			other	316,158

CLASP-WRP (NWLC)	156,000	700,000	corporations/foundations and individual contributions	700,000
NWPC	750,000‡	1,000,000	dues	250,000
			direct-mail contributions	350,000
			foundations and individual contributions	400,000
WEAL	379,674	n.a.		
WLDF	243,076	583,326	government grants	12,733
			foundation and other grants	427,852
			contributions/membership dues	69,223

SOURCE: All data derive from available annual reports and telephone interviews: 1984 annual reports for NARAL, NOW-LDEF, and NWLC telephone interviews with Neal Salinger (ACLU); Jane Chapman (CWPS); Elaine Loiello (NARAL); Eleanor Braun (NWPC). *National NOW Times,* Aug.–Sept. 1985, 11.
† Only 1979 figures were available.
‡ Includes NWPC/ERA.

tions. Selling pins, t-shirts, and posters, as well as magazine subscriptions and the use of advertising space in publications, is another new way of building revenue.

It should be noted that groups that are part of a larger organization (the WRP of the ACLU) receive in varying degrees valuable "in kind" services from their sponsoring organization. These services include access to telephones, administrative help and the like, which would require raising further revenue if they were not made available gratis.

Perhaps most significant, finally, is the role of foundations. In 1967 the Ford Foundation "made a major commitment to civil rights and disadvantaged minorities," listing four areas of action: community development, civil rights litigation, civil rights advocacy, and public interest law[12] (see Table 4). Only in a few instances have foundations other than Ford contributed more to any one feminist group's revenues, though the PEER project to monitor Title IX received $275,000 from Carnegie as part of its joint support arrangement with Ford. Major foundation contributors to feminist groups other than Ford include the Rockefeller Foundation, the Carnegie Corporation, Rockefeller Brothers Fund, the Field Foundation, and the Edna

TABLE 4
Ford Foundation Grants (1983-1984)

ACLU-RPF	$ 50,000
ACLU-WRP	300,000
CWPS	24,650
NOW-LDEF	150,000
NWLC	440,000
WEAL	200,000
WLDF	155,000

Source: *Grants for Women and Girls* (New York: Foundation Center, 1984), 131-39.

[12] Robert McKay, *Nine for Equality under Law: Civil Rights Litigation* (New York: Ford Foundation, 1977). 9.

McConnell Clark Foundation. Kellogg, the New York Foundation, and others contribute in varying amounts to different groups. Several feminist groups have received small grants from the Playboy and Ms. Foundations. A grant from John D. Rockefeller III was instrumental in getting the Reproductive Freedom Project of the ACLU started; the Rockefeller gift helped generate other contributions as well. Its funding pattern is unusual because the Project draws small grants, generally under $50,000 and often under $20,000, from a number of different foundations.[13]

As a rule, established black civil rights groups receive far more substantial funding than feminist groups. According to figures provided by Susan Berresford of the Ford Foundation, Ford funding for all feminist groups (including educational institutions and programs as well as advocacy groups) from 1972 to 1979 averaged 2.1 percent of the total grants that were made (compared with 40 percent for black civil rights groups in 1970). By 1983 funding priorities had been altered and women's groups were receiving 11 percent of all Ford Foundation grants. In this same year black and Hispanic groups received 10 percent and 6 percent of Ford grants, respectively.[14]

Numerous studies have documented the relatively impoverished state of feminist groups. In 1976 feminist litigation groups received only 3 percent of all foundation grants, and all of these women's groups had incomes of less than $300,000. Further evidence indicates that, from 1972 to 1974, $12 million of $2 billion in grants provided by foundations went to improve the status of women—less than one-fifth of 1 percent.[15] A 1979 study of funding of women's groups by the Ford Foundation included *none* of the groups examined here among

[13] Telephone interviews with Aryeh Neier and Ira Glasser of the ACLU, Feb. 22, 1980.

[14] Telephone interviews with Susan Berresford, Vice President, Ford Foundation, Jan. 1980 and Sept. 1985.

[15] Mary Jean Tully, "Funding the Feminists," *Foundation News* (March/April 1975), 26.

the "top ten" women's group recipients noted. This study also reported that most feminist groups that are grant recipients receive only one grant from each foundation (whereas many black civil rights groups receive more than one grant).[16] Of six foundations that derived their assets primarily from sales of cosmetics to women, only 4.7 percent (of $26 million) of their grant awards went to women's programs in 1975-76.[17] The only cosmetics-based foundation that provided significant support for women's groups was the Helena Rubenstein Foundation.

Why have feminist groups been disadvantaged in their ability to raise funds from foundations? Several explanations seem plausible. Feminist groups are the most recent entrants into the political process, and they appeared in a period of economic downturn.[18] In addition, most foundations are dominated by men at both board and staff levels, and they have not given priority to women's issues.[19] Groups such as NOW and others may be perceived as having a "radical" image or may be caught in a "Catch 22" situation without an established "track record" and, lacking funds, inability to get one.[20]

Despite limited foundation support, feminist groups have grown substantially since the 1976 study cited above. While still grossly underfinanced, feminists have gained some access to foundation as well as government funding, and several feminist groups more than doubled their incomes in the late 1970s. Although financial problems remain, many groups have experienced growth over the past decade, as measured

[16] *Financial Support of Women's Programs in the 1970's* (New York: Ford Foundation, July 1979), 7.

[17] *Survey of Six Foundations that Derive their Assets Primarily from Sales of Cosmetics to Women* (New York: Women and Foundations/Corporate Philanthropy, April 1978).

[18] See *Financial Support of Women's Programs in the 1970's*, 23, and Tully, "Funding the Feminists," 28-30.

[19] *Balancing the Scales of Justice*, 95.

[20] Karen O'Connor, *Women's Organizations: Use of the Courts* (Lexington, Mass.: D. C. Heath, 1980), 119.

both by expanding staff and by increasing funding. [21] Groups such as WEAL and NOW-LDEF have grown from office operations with one professional staff person and volunteer aides a decade ago to operations with several paid professionals and support staff.

Foundation support comprises at least half the annual budget for several groups and a significant portion for the others. This dependency creates problems for feminist groups, while at the same time this funding has permitted the groups' very existence and expansion in the past decade. As suggested above, foundations tend to favor funding established groups, significantly limiting possibilities for aiding feminist groups. Second, foundations tend to donate money on a project basis or for issue areas for a specified period of time. Few groups analyzed here are able to gain substantial general unrestricted funding. This pattern of funding tends to limit both the scope and the flexibility of groups, which are then locked into those projects deemed fundable. Several groups examined have become involved in projects they would not have undertaken had special funds not been made available for specific studies or conferences. Many group leaders feel that foundations prefer to fund educational programs and are loath to fund litigation. Leaders of other groups indicated that foundations were fond of funding programs for interns, which were sometimes of limited value in contributing to fulfillment of organizational goals. Some groups have accepted money for "earmarked" projects and have sought to utilize them "loosely" in order to gain flexibility. In general, funding may shape a group's entire focus and distort its initial priorities.[22] Project-by-project funding fragments an organization and hinders a holistic approach to policy development. Finally, it is unclear what methods are used by foundations to determine the success of their ventures. The "follow-up" and evaluation techniques used in

[21] Interview with Jane Chapman, CWPS, Oct. 10, 1979.
[22] *Balancing the Scales of Justice*, 107.

many instances seem haphazard at best and call into question the rationality of allocation processes.

Because foundations are such a major source of support, a decrease in their funding of an organization may have adverse consequences. In 1979 the Ford Foundation cut its appropriations to some groups and warned of further cutbacks.[23] All groups must compete with one another and with newer groups for the same (increasingly) scarce resources. Put in somewhat different terms, funding continues to be a serious problem for all groups.

Although most groups have been creative in their efforts to augment traditional sources of funding, this is not an easy task. One feminist group that relies heavily on one government agency and one foundation (Ford) for its funding was rebuffed in 1979 by virtually every other new source approached.[24]

Membership

Membership too may be a valuable resource. For the feminist community, the issue of constituency remains a controversial one. In 1984 NARAL, NWPC, WEAL, and NOW had a combined dues-paying membership of about 341,500—a substantial increase from 75,000-80,000 in 1971.[25] NOW and NARAL, in particular, increased their paid membership dramatically. Nonetheless, members of these groups still comprise but a small segment of women in the United States. Several leaders and policy makers interviewed for this study emphasized the importance of constituency-based groups, arguing that the absence of such mass organizations significantly weakens efforts to influence policy at every level of the politi-

[23] *Foundation Grants Index, Bi-Monthly* (March/April 1979), G87. In December 1980 the Ford Foundation announced that it was doubling its grants for women's activities, from $4 million to $9 million a year. It is not clear what percentage of these funds were directed to the groups considered in this study. *Women in the World* (New York: Ford Foundation, Nov. 1980).

[24] WEAL Fund, 1979 *Development Highlights*, Nov. 1979.

[25] Maren Lockwood Carden, *The New Feminist Movement* (New York: Russell Sage, 1974), 140.

cal process. Even (and perhaps especially) at the administrative level, the image of organizational strength may aid in changing an agency's perspective and priorities through the development of a new constituency. For example, analysis of Title VI of the Civil Rights Act of 1964 enforcement suggests that civil rights groups greatly increased their political effectiveness when they belatedly began to mobilize and represent their mass constituency.[26]

The concern for a mass base has been expressed by scholars and activists alike. One student of feminist politics worried about the gap she discerned between active feminists and constituents' observing that isolation from the grassroots often produces policy commitments out of touch with actual mass needs.[27] The leadership of at least one group examined (WLDF) determined that it had to develop a membership base because such a course would increase accountability, credibility, and funding capacity. It is undeniable that as laws and their regulations reach the stage of implementation in issue areas such as education, grassroots efforts provide the information on compliance or noncompliance as well as the general feedback necessary to determine to what extent the laws are effective. In another context, "pro-choice" forces, routed continually in legislative efforts in recent years (although not always in the courts), have turned increasingly to constituency-building, partially to replicate the success of "right-to-life" groups that so effectively have organized at the community level and have brought pressure to bear in state and national legislative politics and at the ballot box.

But building membership also requires servicing it in some fashion; frequently groups barely break even as a result of mailing newsletters and other materials. In addition, member-

[26] See Gary Orfield, *Reconstruction of Southern Education* (New York: Wiley, 1969), 122; Beryl Radin, *Implementation, Change and the Federal Bureaucracy* (New York: Columbia University Teachers College Press. 1977).

[27] Margaret Berger, "Litigation on Behalf of Women: An Assessment," (New York: Ford Foundation, May 1980), 87, and personal discussions, Dec. 1979 and Jan. 1980.

ship expressing its wishes via annual conventions or other mechanisms may limit organizational flexibility and maneuverability in the political process. It is difficult to engage in compromise—as most groups in the feminist group matrix customarily do—when an emotional issue is at stake and when leadership must be accountable to members. Mass issues often tend to create opposing constituencies, and as more emotions are inflamed and media attention focused on an issue, change-oriented groups such as feminists may well lose out. Moreover, feminist groups face major obstacles to organizational recruitment; they face the "free rider" problem. Under such circumstances, organization-building is especially difficult.

It seems that the benefits of membership organizations are significant but that highly specialized lobbying, research, and litigation groups also perform key functions in our highly fragmented political system. At this juncture, feminists may have the best of both worlds in that they may call upon membership without necessarily incurring the cost of maintaining it through their relationships with traditional women's groups and a public generally supportive of equal rights.

TECHNIQUES FOR EXERTING POLITICAL INFLUENCE

Techniques used by feminist groups are reformist and involve traditional approaches to advocacy, lobbying, litigation, and monitoring. The flexibility with which groups approach political activity is notable; they will use any technique that has promise, and they will change tactics if necessary. There are, of course, several favored techniques for influencing the political process.

Protest

In contrast to the civil rights movement in the late fifties and early sixties, protest has never been the dominant means of political expression for feminists. NOW activists disrupted a 1970 Senate Judiciary Subcommittee meeting in order to dramatize the demand for the ERA, and at the state level some demonstrations in support of state ERA ratification have been held. In 1970 a mass rally, "Women's Strike for Equality," was held around the nation, bringing together disparate elements in the movement to advocate day care, abortion on demand, and equal education and employment opportunity.

More recent demonstrations of militancy have been limited, though they have occurred. Thus in March 1986, over 85,000 people joined a march in Washington, D.C. coordinated by NOW in support of reproductive freedom. In general, equity-oriented feminists have seen protests as unnecessary in part because other channels of access to the political system were opened without much difficulty in the 1970s and 1980s. Perhaps one reason for this *relative* openness in the political system is that women comprise a majority of the population in the nation and many politicians perceive that potentially they comprise a formidable bloc that *may* vote on women's issues. Also, sympathetic and articulate women in Congress, legislative aides to members of Congress, and administrative staff members in the bureaucracy have continued to provide access to women's groups.

Litigation

While litigation has been employed by feminist groups, it too has never occupied the central role it did for civil rights groups. There is no feminist group comparable to the NAACP Legal Defense and Educational Fund in funding and status, although the combined legal resources of the two ACLU women's related programs make the ACLU a major force for litigation. The use of *pro bono* attorneys has been less well developed by feminists, despite the fact that general resources or resources earmarked for litigation have been hard to come by. Funds for "special projects" have been more readily available from foundations and other contributors. One reason for feminist restraint regarding the use of litigation may be that the Supreme Court has never declared sex to be a suspect classification in the same manner as race, thus making judicial victory uncertain.

Groups that specialize in law-related activities spend a good deal of time on actual litigation, although increasingly even their work has come to include other activities, such as educating the public, gathering and disseminating information, analyzing and drafting legislation, commenting and testifying on proposed regulations, and monitoring enforcement. For example, the director of one litigation group interviewed for this study estimated that she devotes only 20 percent of her time to actual litigation; another feminist attorney gave 40 percent as her estimate.

Litigation is seen as a mechanism for developing case law and precedents for an entire class and as a "consciousness raiser" for the public and the political system even if a case is lost. Cases also are seen as having a "spillover effect" on the private and public sector beyond the confines of a particular suit. Thus *General Electric v. Gilbert*,[28] which dealt with pregnancy discrimination, was lost by feminists in the Supreme Court in 1976 but provided a catalyst for coalition-building in the Congress, leading ultimately to the enactment of the Pregnancy Discrimination Act, which amended Title VII of the Civil Rights Act of 1964. The ACLU Reproductive Freedom Project (together with other groups) pressed unsuccessfully for a judicial ruling against the Hyde amendment in *Harris v. McRae*[29], but won a judicial victory in 1983 in *City of Akron v. Akron Center for Reproductive Health*.[30] After success in *Reed v. Reed*[31] and *Frontiero v. Richardson*,[32] in 1975 the ACLU Women's Rights Project successfully fought gender-based discrimination in the awarding of social security benefits in *Weinberger v. Weisenfeld*[33] and gained increased court rec-

[28] 429 U.S. 129 (1976).
[29] 491 F. Supp. 630 (1980).
[30] 456 U.S. 988 (1983).
[31] 404 U.S. 71 (1971).
[32] 411 U.S. 677 (1973).
[33] 420 U.S. 636 (1975).

ognition of the need for a "higher standard of review" in subsequent cases on sex-discrimination issues relating to social security and welfare.

In addition to setting precedents, litigation is also used as a tool to prod the political process into action regarding enforcement, by establishing seriousness of purpose and credibility. Thus in *WEAL* v. *Califano*[34] attorneys from the CLASP Women's Rights Project sought compliance with Title IX of the Education Amendments of 1972 regarding sex equity in education (settled in 1977). Some observers attribute the final release of Title IX athletic guidelines in 1979, which were favorable to feminists, to their efforts to obtain a contempt citation against HEW for continued nonenforcement. Although the contempt citation was dismissed by the presiding judge, its existence may have served as a form of pressure to hasten the release of the long-overdue new guidelines. (Feminists were opposed on this issue by the National Collegiate Athletic Association and a coalition of college and university presidents.)[35]

Some litigation groups do little actual litigation because of their limited funds. They must often rely on outside counsel—preferably *pro bono*—to do their actual case work. These groups tend to become involved in suits primarily through the filing of *amicus* briefs. NOW-LDEF, WLDF, and WEAL are among those whose litigation efforts have been limited by inadequate resources.

As litigation costs have risen and funding for litigation has become more limited and more dispersed among nonprofit groups (for example, CLASP and others were severely cut back by the Ford Foundation), and as effort expended on cases and appeals appears to become more and more protracted and burdensome, it is not surprising that groups have sought other techniques to achieve their goals.

[34] U.S. Dist. Ct. for D. of C., Civ. Act no. 70-3095 (1977).
[35] Interview with Cindy Brown, former Deputy Director, Office of Civil Rights, HEW, Nov. 13, 1979.

Lobbying and Monitoring

Virtually all of the groups analyzed here now do some legislative (and administrative) lobbying since the relaxation of Internal Revenue Service rules that now permit even 501(c)(3) groups to lobby up to 20 percent of their time. Hence legislative drafting, expert testimony, negotiations with members of Congress, and dissemination of research have become part of the daily activity for nearly all feminist groups. Feminist groups have been active in the legislative arena ever since their successful efforts to secure passage of the Equal Credit Opportunity Act and the Pregnancy Discrimination Act and their success in having prevented weakening amendments and riders from emasculating Title IX of the Education Amendments of 1972. With regard to the Hyde amendments and other "pro-life" legislation that have in successive years systematically limited federal payments for abortions, they have been less successful, but nonetheless persistent. More recently they were successful in having the Retirement Equity Act of 1984 passed into law.

Advocacy and monitoring at the agency level have increased for all groups with the recognition of the importance of the administrative process in sustaining and consolidating legislative and judicial gains. Supplying information, commenting on proposed regulations, and the monitoring of enforcement policy is now common for all groups. Because federal agencies—some newly created, others now pursuing missions different from their original assignments—have been operating in a variety of new issue areas, groups with constituency or informational resources have often been able to play a key role. In fact, several groups devote themselves primarily to research, recognizing the impact that informational resources may have on policy development. Thus CWPS was founded to provide a scholarly research focus for the feminist movement and has published several books documenting economic and other kinds of discrimination against women. Most groups publish newsletters or informational flyers. Among them are *In the*

Running, a quarterly publication of WEAL Fund's SPRINT, and the ACLU-WRP's *Women's Rights Report.* Many groups issue frequent reviews of federal policy affecting their particular area of interest, disseminated to members (if any) and interested citizens. Special publications issued by groups serve to prod the policy process into action by calling attention to failures of enforcement and commitment of resources. Particularly notable was PEER's *Stalled at the Start,* a critique of HEW's enforcement of Title IX. This document received considerable publicity and dissemination when it was issued in 1978. An ACLU-RFP Report on the *Impact of the Hyde Amendment on Federally funded Abortions* (1978) documented the virtual elimination of such abortions (almost 100 percent) since passage of the initial congressional amendment.

Many of the groups discussed here are recognized as being expert in their field, and they are asked by policy makers to prepare analyses of existing or proposed legislation or regulations or to assess the impact of existing rules and laws. Many serve as informational clearinghouses to which elected and appointed officials, other interest groups, and the general public turn for specific information and data. SPRINT responds to numerous requests by phone or mail regarding sex equity in education and sports. WLDF responded to over 6,000 requests for information in 1984, up from 2,000 in 1976. Other groups providing such services include the CWPS, NARAL (which answers over one hundred letters per week), and ACLU-WRP.[36]

Constituency Organizing and Leadership Training

Several groups including NWLC, WEAL, NARAL, and NOW-LDEF have internship programs that have the dual function of training new practitioners for the feminist movement and obtaining additional workers at reduced cost. The

[36] WLDF, *Annual Report, June 1978-July 1979,* Appendix 2; WLDF, *1984 Annual Report,* 2; WCLU-WRP, quarterly reports; interview with Karen Mulhauser, NARAL, Oct. 10, 1979. The WRP reports almost 1,000 annual requests.

ACLU-WRP originated with a clinic at Columbia University Law School. NWLC had ten student interns in 1984 and relations with several law schools. Individuals who have received training within feminist groups often remain as staff members in these groups or are employed in related government or advocacy organizations where their skills and expertise prove invaluable. Virtually all groups hold seminars and conduct lectures for lawyers, students, and others on a wide range of feminist issues. These functions sensitize large groups of people to feminist approaches and issue concerns.

Organizations like NOW that have mass memberships are, of course, involved with constituency organizing and relations. In addition, several other organizations maintain community-organizing components. NARAL has sought to build a grassroots constituency through direct mail because of a belief that the best way to combat the "right-to-life" opposition is to emulate its strategy of developing constituency strength. WLDF is eager to build a membership organization, partially to develop financial independence but also "to provide accountability—to assure that the Fund takes positions which have support in a national feminist community"—and to "provide a base" for referring women throughout the country to feminist-oriented attorneys and counsellors.[37] Many groups use grassroots activity to aid the enforcement process. PEER has sought to develop monitoring strength at the grassroots for Title IX through the dissemination of a local action kit called *Cracking the Glass Slipper*, emulating a technique pioneered by NOW in its issuance of equal credit kits, which provides instruction on how to assess discrimination and file complaints. Finally, all groups discussed devote considerable time and effort to internal administration and fund-raising.

Leadership and Coalition-Building

As suggested earlier, feminists have been able to rely on a preexisting structure of traditional women's groups (such as

[37] Women's Legal Defense Board, "Report on Long-Range Planning of the WLDF Board of Directors (Washington D.C.)," unpublished report, 8-9.

the League of Women Voters and General Federation of Women's Clubs) whose shared interest in many feminist issues has produced numbers and assistance that would otherwise have been costly and probably unattainable. The civil rights movement served as a model of structure and tactics and provided considerable assistance to the incipient feminist movement as it developed. Indeed, some legislative gains by feminist groups have involved use of civil rights legislation; for example, Title VII of the Civil Rights Act of 1964 (provisions against race and sex discrimination) was amended to include pregnancy discrimination insurance protection. Feminist successes, in turn, have helped other groups: the Equal Credit Opportunity Act served as a model for minorities and the aged, who lobbied to amend the law to cover their groups as well.

Despite the existence of numerous autonomous subgroupings that compete for funding and influence, there is, as noted previously, extensive coalition-building and remarkable unity among feminists. Individuals and groups join together in a variety of contexts linked by loose commitment to feminist ideology, shared symbols of group identity, and the friendships and contacts they have developed.

There is no one central point of contact, but there are intersecting sets of personal relationships and other intergroup exchanges that provide a network for common activity. Friendships among group activists as well as multiple group memberships provide linkages and facilitate the sharing of information, the mobilization of activity on specific projects, and the planning of joint strategy. Groups also come together at meetings, rallies, and conferences.[38] The movement for the ERA and more recent state and national meetings for the International Women's Year (1977) served this function, too. Communications media within the movement provide links regarding issues, projects, and activities, while issue specialists form their own subunits for sharing information.

Feminist coalitions with varying degrees of institutionalization and permanency exist for a number of issue areas: for ex-

---

[38] Joan Cassell, *A Group Called Women* (New York: McKay, 1977), ch. 8.

ample, regarding educational equality, there is the National Coalition for Women and Girls in Education; for abortion rights, there is the "pro-choice" caucus; and there are coalitions on women and health, women and poverty, and women in the military. Ad hoc coalitions are created as necessary both within the movement and with allied groups. An example of this phenomenon was the Coalition to End Discrimination Against Pregnant Workers, in which representatives of over 300 groups comprised largely of feminists and labor unionists successfully persuaded Congress to amend Title VII of the Civil Rights Act of 1964 to include pregnancy as an insured health-care benefit. A newer group, the Coalition for Reproductive Rights of Women, seeks to prevent employers from using classifications of "hazardous employment" to bar only women from holding specific jobs. The Coalition to End Discrimination Against Pregnant Workers may be characterized, in Berry's terms, as "participatory," with no one dominant group, resource commitment from many groups, and temporary existence. Others, such as the National Coalition for Women and Girls in Education, are "independent"; the Education coalition has permanence and a letterhead, although several groups (AIAW, NWLC, WEAL, and ACE) have tended to play major roles within it.[39] In addition, feminists have also joined together in the Washington Women's Network, Coalition on Women Appointments, and the Judicial Selection Panel. Thus they have consciously engaged in network-building and have created an effective mechanism for both specialization and cohesion. Also, in their efforts to legislatively overrule the Supreme Court's decision in *Grove City* v. *Bell*,[40] the women's groups have joined with the broader civil rights community under the aegis of the Leadership Conference on Civil Rights.

Effectiveness of the movement is enhanced by division of labor; differing goals and approaches have not caused perma-

[39] See Berry, *Lobbying for the People*, 257-60.
[40] 104 S.Ct. 1211 (1984).

nent splits or paralysis. There are particular people whose personalities are well suited to coordination and providing informational feedback and resources. Thus such women as Judith Lichtman, WLDF's executive director, help bring groups together as well. Networking—consciously facilitated by feminists—has both positive and negative features. While it may retard efforts at seeking immediate tangible goals when concerted action is necessary, ultimate success may be more likely because flexibility and experimentation are encouraged. In fact, the movement is capable of energetic action through intergroup mobilization when necessary, as the Pregnancy Discrimination Act case demonstrates.

Finally, another example of coalition behavior among feminist groups is to be found in what may be termed "interlocking directorates." A striking feature of many of the groups considered is the overlapping memberships of their boards (people who hold formal staff or board positions in one or more groups). These persons serve as links between organizations because of their dual (and sometimes multiple) memberships in feminist groups. Table 5 illustrates these overlapping memberships. In addition, organizations are also found as each other's clients; for example, CLASP attorneys represented WEAL in its suit *WEAL* v. *Califano*.

CONCLUSION

In this chapter we have suggested that despite the existence of significant deficiencies in their resources, among them limited funding and membership from potential constituents, feminists have been creative in the utilization of those resources they do possess. Among the latter are dedicated and committed staff personnel and creative and pragmatic use of existing funds. Feminists have exercised flexibility in choosing strategies and approaches and have employed traditional pressure-group tactics with considerable skill, as the five case studies that follow demonstrate to varying degrees. Finally, the simultaneous reliance on groups' specialization and coalition activity has maximized the effective use of existing resources.

TABLE 5
Interlocking Directorates among Feminist Groups (1978)

	WLDF	NOW-LDEF	NWPC	ACLU	CWPS	WEAL	CLASP	NARAL
Barbara Bergmann						•	•	
Jessie Bernard					•	•		
Margaret Gates	•			•	•	•		
Ruth B. Ginsburg		*	•					•
Krysten Horbal	•						•	
Margaret Kohn			•					•
Odessa Komer	•						•	
Brooksley Landau		•		•				
Sylvia Law						•		
Judith Lichtman				•				
Margaret Moses				•		•		•
Harriet Pilpel				•		•		
Bernice "Bunny" Sandler†								
Diana Steele								
Gloria Steinem			•	•		•		•

SOURCE: Annual report and personal interviews.

* Once director.

† Director, Project on the Status and Education of Women of the American Association of Colleges.

CHAPTER 4
WOMEN AND
CREDIT DISCRIMINATION

INTRODUCTION

In 1974 Congress passed, and the President signed into law, the Equal Credit Opportunity Act (ECOA), which banned credit discrimination on the basis of sex. One year later, in October 1975, regulations promulgated by the Federal Reserve Board were completed, and the provisions of the 1974 law were implemented. The history of the Act's passage and implementation provides us with a good example of specialization on issues and formation of coalitions among women's groups as they worked to achieve very specific equity goals in both the congressional and administrative arenas.

It can be argued that activist women were able to place the issue of credit reform to eliminate sex discrimination on the political agenda because they adhered effectively to the prerequisites of the "mobilization of bias" or existing configuration of influence and access to power. Seen in this light, women succeeded in winning significant credit reforms not because they violated the "rules of the game," but because they conformed to them so well. From this perspective, the ability of women activists to achieve their goals is not necessarily proof of the openness of the system, but rather an indication of its elitist nature. In a political universe in which the critics of pluralist theory have argued that participants speak with a decidedly upper-middle-class accent, the women seeking credit reform were of high social status[1]; and in a political system in which

[1] Maren Lockwood Carden, *The New Feminist Movement* (New York: Russell Sage, 1974), 19-20.

access and representation of one's interests at key points in the decision-making process are crucial, an ongoing "policy system" served the cause of women's rights well.[2] Women activists understood the need for effective use of the media, organizational skill, and expert testimony. In addition, they possessed respectability and a high degree of technical competence, as well as a spirit of group efficiency and unity.[3] Women activists also understood the need to keep the issue under control by limiting its scope—in order to maximize rather than dissipate their resources. Although equal credit opportunity is an issue with profound long-term implications, it was perceived as a role equity issue, and as such it threatened no fundamental values.

There would probably not be an Equal Credit Opportunity Act were it not for the actions of some women's groups. Thus the legislative and later the administrative efforts of these women clearly indicate success. There was not, however, a total victory inasmuch as women's groups had to accept a compromise both in Congress and later at the Federal Reserve Board. Janette Hart, of the Federal Reserve Board's Office of Saver and Consumer Affairs, the body responsible for the administrative regulations for the ECOA, made the above distinction. Throughout the process leading to the enactment of the credit law, representatives of women's groups recognized the nature of incremental politics in the United States and understood the need to compromise. Thus they did not place themselves in support of extreme positions from which they could not deviate with relative ease.

It should be noted that the women's community was united on the ECOA; traditional women's groups were highly supportive of activist groups in their pressure for the enactment and writing of favorable regulations for the Act. While not involved as active lobbyists, they were (as it will be discussed

[2] David Truman, *The Governmental Process* (New York: Knopf, 1951), 322-32.

[3] Darryl Baskin, *American Pluralist Democracy: A Critique* (New York: Van Nostrand-Reinhold, 1971), 92.

later in this analysis) supporters of credit legislation favorable to women and helped create a coalition that gave the appearance of considerable support for the ECOA.

BACKGROUND

Students of the legislative process have argued in recent years that new policies are adopted after a change in opinion, not as a result of group pressures.[4] In fact, several studies have raised doubts about the effectiveness of pressure groups in the legislative process. Viewed from this perspective, women's groups might be expected to play only a negligible role in legislative politics. This section will attempt to demonstrate, however, that despite significant limitations on staff and financial resources, women activists were able to initiate and sustain momentum for legislative action on equal credit opportunity. As one member of Congress put it: "Without the input of women activists pushing for credit reform, there would be no Equal Credit Opportunity Act."

Perhaps because interest in this issue had been heightened by a National Commission on Consumer Finance and subsequent media coverage, making many members of Congress more responsive to the issue, women activists were able to keep it alive for two congressional terms. Women's organizations supplied information, technical expertise, and explicit suggestions on policy to members of Congress. Unlike the campaign to adopt the Equal Rights Amendment, which had a broad scope and vast constituency as well as organized opposition, the efforts made for the passage of legislation on equal credit opportunity were primarily at a leadership level with only a limited amount of grassroots involvement.[5] But, as Jo Freeman suggests, the movement for equal credit opportunity was able to build upon the contacts created during the long fight for the ERA. That

[4] James Q. Wilson, *Political Organizations* (New York: Basic Books, 1973), 330.

[5] Jo Freeman, *The Politics of Women's Liberation* (New York: David McKay, 1975), 217.

battle had, in her words, created a new "policy system," involving lobbyists, volunteers, members of Congress and their staffs, and policy makers in the administrative sector.[6]

The success of advocates of credit reform may also be attributed in part to the existence of a "policy vacuum" in an area of few established political precedents as well as to a lack of clear political opposition. Representatives of industry were aware of the extent of credit afforded women by way of male co-signers and were cognizant of the potential credit worthiness of women. Thus there was apparently some concern by the representatives of industry not to antagonize groups of women on what was perceived as an *equity* issue.

In addition, members of Congress were sensitive to reactions of the potentially active women's groups in their local constituencies.[7] The majority of women vote; many women work in political campaigns. Some local NWPC groups made credit a (local) campaign issue. It is important to recognize that women activists acted as a vanguard, causing legislators to operate in anticipation of voters' reactions and thus to act somewhat in advance of mass consciousness on the issue. However, by 1974, it was apparent that the majority of women had become aware of the credit discrimination they suffered. The 1974 *Virginia Slims American Women's Opinion Poll* indicated that 57 percent of American women believed that women suffered credit discrimination.[8]

THE PROBLEM OF CREDIT DISCRIMINATION

"Hormones, birth control and wedding rings are not matters of credit." When Betty Furness spoke these words before the Subcommittee on Consumer Affairs of the Committee on Banking and Currency of the House of Representatives in No-

[6] *Ibid.*, 220.

[7] Gary Orfield, *Congressional Power: Congress and Social Change* (New York: Harcourt-Brace-Jovanovich, 1975), 305.

[8] *Virginia Slims American Women's Opinion Poll*, Vol. III (New York: Roper Organization, 1975), 5.

vember 1973, she expressed the concerns of the thousands of American women who had been denied credit in their own names as a result of being female.

Discrimination against women because of their sex and marital status had been institutionalized over the years by the credit industry. This discrimination was rooted in a "long standing tradition, outmoded customs, beliefs and attitudes fraught with myth."[9] Whereas in the eighteenth and nineteenth centuries it was not customary for married women with sufficient means to qualify for credit to work, this was no longer the rule in modern society. In 1973 over 40 percent of the nation's labor force was female, and many women worked to provide the sole or major source of income for themselves and their families. Assumptions upon which the credit industry rested its unequal treatment of women were simply no longer true: that all women stop working when they have children; that working mothers are delinquent on payment of bills; that divorced women rely exclusively on unstable support from former husbands; and the like.

In March 1973 42 percent of married women worked (up from 26 percent in 1953).[10] A third of mothers with children under 6 were in the labor force, as were half of the women whose children were between 6 and 17 years of age.[11] In the 22 million families in which husbands and wives both worked, family income had been substantially raised. Women were the heads of 6 million families and, in 1971, 54 percent of them were in the labor force.[12] As of March 1971, 70 percent of all divorced and 50 percent of all separated women were in the labor force (and these women, if working at age 35, had a work

[9] Statement of the National Organization for Women before the Subcommittee on Consumer Affairs of the Committee on Banking and Currency, House of Representatives, mimeo., Nov. 13, 1973, 1.

[10] Howard Hayghe, "Marital and Family Characteristics of the Labor Force in March 1973," *Monthly Labor Review* 97 (April 1974), 21.

[11] *Ibid.*, 23.

[12] Elizabeth Waldman and Kathryn R. Gover, "Marital and Family Characteristics of the Labor Force," *Monthly Labor Review* 95 (April 1972), 6.

expectancy of 27-29 years!).[13] A 1969 study by the Women's Bureau of the Department of Labor found that labor turnover is influenced more by job level, age, record of stability, and length of service than by sex; also, differences in job turnover between men and women are small.[14] In addition, although there is scant research on the subject, available studies indicate that women are good credit risks.[15]

However, despite the changing social and economic role of women, they continued to be treated as "second-class citizens" by the credit industry. Surveys of the lending policies of banks and of savings and loan associations found that few of them would grant full credit to a working wife's income.[16] Single women also had difficulty qualifying for credit. In one classic example, a 40-year-old woman was required to have her father co-sign a bank loan.[17] Married women lacked a credit history since all records were kept in their husbands' names. In order to obtain credit, they often were forced to respond to humiliating questions regarding birth-control techniques and intent to bear children. Divorced and widowed women were subject to particular discrimination. Alimony and child support as

---

[13] *Ibid.,* 7.

[14] U.S. Department of Labor (Women's Bureau), *Facts about Women's Absenteeism and Labor Turnover* (Washington, D.C.: Government Printing Office, 1969), 2-3, 15.

[15] For both married and single women, bad account probability is less than for men with similar marital status. Paul Smith, "Measuring Risk on Installment Credit," *Management Science* 2 (Nov. 1964). 324-40. And, as the percentage of the family income earned by the husband decreases, delinquency in mortgage payments decreases. Leon Kendall, *Anatomy of the Residential Mortgage Market* (Washington, D.C.: U.S. Savings and Loan League, 1964), 59. According to J. Harzog and J. Earley, working wives are no more prone to delinquency and foreclosure than other borrowers. *Home Mortgage Delinquency and Foreclosure* (New York: National Bureau of Economic Research, 1970). In a communication to Jane Roberts Chapman and Margaret Gates of CWPS, Thomas Jones, executive director of Neighborhood Housing Services, Inc., found the mortgage delinquency rate among female-headed families to be 2 percent as opposed to 4 percent for the total group.

[16] *New York Times,* March 25, 1973, 1.

[17] Margaret Smith, "Where Credit is Due," *Ms,* Oct. 1972, 36.

well as other monetary resources were ignored as income when these women applied for credit. The need to alter the discriminatory treatment of women in the credit-granting process first received national attention in May 1972 at the hearings of the National Commission on Consumer Finance.

When the National Commission on Consumer Finance held these hearings to determine the extent of the problems relating to the entire area of consumer credit, among the issues they sought to examine was credit discrimination based upon sex and marital status. Extensive testimony pointed up the conditions relegating women to an inferior legal status as far as the availability and receipt of credit were concerned. The hearings underlined five specific areas of difficulty for women seeking credit. It was determined that single women had more trouble obtaining credit than single men; creditors generally required a woman upon marriage to reapply for credit, usually in her husband's name (whereas similar reapplication was not demanded of men when they married); creditors were often unwilling to extend credit to a married woman in her own name, or to count the wife's income when a married couple applied for credit; and women who were divorced or widowed had trouble reestablishing personal credit.[18]

The Commission's hearings created a rippling effect that has never stopped. Once the situation was accepted as a problem, and the extent of legal inferiority was clearly articulated, the movement for the passage of corrective legislation began.

The reality of credit discrimination attracted great attention from several national women's groups and a number of congressional leaders. Media coverage was extensive—both in the press and in women's magazines—throughout the nation and accentuated the growing interest in the problem. Women's groups, public interest organizations, and human rights commissions undertook credit surveys, which reinforced the fact of

[18] National Commission on Consumer Finance, *Consumer Credit in the United States* (Washington, D.C.: Government Printing Office, 1972), 498-99.

pervasive credit discrimination everywhere. "Credit kits" were prepared by NOW chapters and local women's organizations to educate women on the problem and to stimulate action. Many women became aware of the fact that the discrimination they had faced was not simply a personal experience but, rather, represented part of a pattern of discrimination against over half of the American population. As a shared problem, it became an issue around which women's interests and energies could be mobilized.

The woman most instrumental during the initial period in facilitating cooperation among women's groups and fostering interest in the issue in Congress was Sharyn Campbell, an attorney who, at this time, was the chair of the NOW Task Force on Consumer Credit. During the legislative and administrative process, various other members of NOW emerged as leaders in the quest for equal credit opportunity. (It should be noted that although NOW does have a legislative lobbying office in Washington, this office never participated in the struggle for equal credit. That it did not was due to intragroup factionalism within the organization, pitting a faction loyal to then President Karen DeCrow against the press and legislative offices. Hence the extensive resources of NOW were not available to those members who took a strong stand on equal credit opportunity.) In addition to NOW members, a second group, the Center for Women Policy Studies, played a major role in providing the technical expertise utilized by women's groups. A nonprofit research group, the Center had received a $40,000 grant from the Ford Foundation in order to develop information on the relative role of women as credit risks. When the demands of the legislative and administrative process made it clear that the original issue was no longer as relevant as it had been, Ford permitted the (primarily) two-woman operation to turn its attention to aiding in the formulation of a credit law. The input of the Center was invaluable to the women's cause because the quality of their work came to be highly respected by both legislators and later by the staff attorneys at the Federal Reserve Board (the administrative agency charged with writing the credit regulations); the Center's lawyers were viewed as responsible and reasonable professionals at all levels of the political process. The Center provided most of the background expertise, while women lobbyists determined the strategy to be followed throughout.

Not only was support for the elimination of credit discrimation forthcoming from women's rights groups, but also the credit industry itself was not belligerent, and many members of Congress were supportive. There was, in fact, no strong opposition to the concept of passage of *some* legislation that would eliminate sex discrimination in credit, although the exact form of such a law was controversial.

In part, the tacit agreement among members of the industry and Congress that some corrective legislation was in the offing was a testament to the perceived strength of the women's rights movement. This movement had been legitimized politically by the battle for the ERA, which convinced many members of Congress that support for women's rights could engender significant electoral support in campaigns.[19] Because discrimination in credit-granting was an issue of potential importance to all women, members of Congress were aware of its widespread appeal. In addition, because the issue was not one involving any outlay of public funds, it was easy for legislators to support, particularly in a preelection period. As for the credit industry, it had been made aware of the problems in extension of credit to women and feared a poor public image. This is not intended to suggest that industry welcomed credit regulations with open arms. At the outset of the movement for the passage of legislation, many industry spokesmen were a bit defensive. However, most members of the credit industry recognized that some legislation would be enacted. It was clear that support for legislation was, if not totally positive on the Hill, at least not negative. Hence the industry would not publicly argue the merits of enacting legislation, although it would

[19] Freeman, *Politics of Women's Liberation*, 171; see also Theodore J. Lowi, *The End of Liberalism* (New York: Norton, 1969), 69.

work behind the scenes for desired provisions and testify at legislative hearings to clarify its position. In the long run, the industry must have felt that the extension of credit to more credit-worthy female recipients would be beneficial to business.

LEGISLATIVE INTERACTIONS

At the same time that the National Commission on Consumer Finance was holding its hearings, Representative Bella Abzug (D-N.Y.) introduced legislation—co-sponsored by over one hundred members of the House of Representatives—dealing with several aspects of credit discrimination. Her bills served as the initial thrust within Congress for the gathering momentum of women's groups pressuring for legislation to end credit discrimination.

Early Congressional Considerations

In January 1973 several bills amending the Truth in Lending Act, to prohibit discrimination on the basis of sex and marital status, were introduced in the Senate. The bills, one of which was introduced by Senator William Brock (R-Tenn.), differed with respect to maximum levels of recovery in class actions. Senator Brock's bill had a lower level of maximum liability in class-action suits than other bills that were introduced. He hoped to gain support from liberals who could accept the lower class-action levels and thus back his bill, which broadly defined credit and abandoned attempts to define discrimination.[20] Many of the activist women who were involved in these legislative efforts from the outset accepted his limitations on recovery in class actions.

Senator Brock was a relatively conservative Republican from Tennessee with a rating in 1974 (on a scale where 100 means perfect liberal ideological conformity) of 20 from

[20] Nancy Polikoff, "Legislative Solutions to Sex Discrimination in Credit," *Women's Rights Law Reporter* 2 (July 1974), 31.

Americans for Democratic Action and of 86 from Americans for Conservative Action.[21] His role in introducing equal credit legislation, and subsequently acting as floor leader on it for the Republicans, can be explained by reference to his own experiences and influences on him. As a member of the National Commission on Consumer Finance, he became sensitive to the need to legislate an end to the discriminatory practices suffered by women. Furthermore, on his staff was a feminist political scientist, Emily Card, who apparently was able to transfer her support and enthusiasm for equal credit legislation to Senator Brock. She drafted the initial legislation and acted as a gadfly in promoting the cause of credit reform. When the Senator's preliminary efforts met with resistance from industry, according to Ms. Card, he became even more convinced of the need for such credit reform legislation.

Senator Brock proved to be an excellent sponsor for the equal credit opportunity legislation in 1973 (included in the Truth in Lending Act amendments of that year). In part because he was a conservative member of the Senate, he was able to gain the crucial support of many of his fellow Republicans who might not ordinarily have agreed to such a measure. When the legislation came to the Senate floor in July 1973 (without hearings), it passed 90 to 0. This bill simply stated:

> It shall be unlawful for any credit or card issuer to discriminate on account of sex or marital status against any individual with respect to the approval or denial of any extension of consumer credit or with respect to the approval, denial, renewal, continuation, or revocation of any open end consumer credit account or with respect to the terms thereof.[22]

It also awarded punitive damages of $10,000 or 10 percent of net worth, whichever is less, in class-action suits.

Representative Margaret Heckler (R–Mass.) introduced the

[21] *Congressional Quarterly Weekly Report* 32 (March 30, 1974), 815.
[22] *Congressional Record*, July 23, 1973, S. 14431.

companion bill to the Brock amendment in the House. However, hearings were not held on the bill that Representative Heckler had introduced. Such hearings would have had to be convened by the Subcommittee on Consumer Affairs, whose Chairman was Leonor Sullivan (D–Mo.). Representative Sullivan opposed holding hearings at that time, and many leaders of women's groups felt that her resistance was due to her own lack of interest in feminist issues. (Sullivan, the only female member of Congress to vote against the ERA, however, claimed that she preferred to wait and draft more perfect legislation dealing with problems of credit discrimination against all groups.) In general, feminists distrusted Sullivan, who was viewed both as an anti-feminist and as a poor manager of bills.

The Second Round in Congress

The second session of the Ninety-Third Congress was convened in 1974. Senator Brock reintroduced his legislation as an amendment to the Federal Depositories Insurance Bill. The legislation that he chose to introduce in 1974 was stronger and more detailed than that passed in 1973, and was drafted in consultation with women's rights groups. By this time, business groups sought a more active role in the drafting of the bill, to make it one with which they could comply without great cost and constant danger of nuisance suits. Both industry and women's groups were represented at numerous consultations with legislators. Sharyn Campbell, by then an attorney for National Bank Americard, Inc., sought to wear "two hats" to help resolve conflicts between the credit industry and women. Like its predecessor, the 1974 bill that finally emerged, known as the Equal Credit Opportunity Act, had almost no opposition in the Senate. This time it passed the Senate 89 to 0. Both unanimous Senate votes in favor of equal credit opportunity indicate the perceived importance of this issue to congressmen's constituents, such that all senators wished to be recorded as having voted affirmatively.

Throughout the time that the legislation was being consid-

ered by the Senate, women's rights groups were active in encouraging support for its passage. (There was little doubt that
the bill would pass the Senate, but there was concern that the
House version of the bill might not even pass the hurdle of
being considered in subcommittee—the subcommittee chaired
by Representative Sullivan who had refused to hold hearings
the previous year.) The groups that were most involved both in
devising strategy and in lobbying for equal credit legislation
during this phase of the legislative process included the NOW
Task Force on Consumer Credit, WEAL, NWPC, and the
Women's Lobby. Operating in the background as a source of
technical expertise (as opposed to lobbying activity) was the
Center for Women Policy Studies. Grassroots support in the
form of letters and telephone calls, recruited in part from the
membership lists of NOW, WEAL, and other groups, was also
brought to bear on key subcommittee members. For example,
the Washington office of the National Council of Jewish
Women alerted all of its local offices so that women associated
with the group would be advised to write letters and send tel-
egrams to their senators and representatives in Congress. At
this stage in the legislative process, many of the older and more
traditional women's groups lent their support to the campaign
for the ECOA by encouraging their members to get in touch
with their representatives in Congress.

During the period immediately after the Senate passed S.
3492, the Equal Credit Opportunity Act of 1974, there was
fear among many of its proponents that Representative Sullivan would not hold hearings on a credit bill. She claimed that
if hearings were to be held on any bill, it would have to be an
omnibus bill dealing with more than just sex and marital status—one including age, color, race, and national origin. Most
women's groups felt that legislation of this type would take
several years to be enacted, and that their immediate goal of
ending credit discrimination on the basis of sex and marital
status would thus be postponed. There was concern by wom-
en's groups, and by supportive members in the House of Representatives including Ed Koch (D–N.Y.) and Margaret Heck-

73

ler (R–Mass.), that if hearings were not held prior to the end of the Ninety-Third Congress, a new Congress might not look as favorably upon anti-discrimination legislation, in part because of worsening economic conditions.

Under pressure from Koch, Heckler, and feminist groups, hearings were held by the Subcommittee on Consumer Affairs on two proposed bills dealing with credit discrimination: H. R. 14856, the bill introduced by Representative Sullivan (an omnibus anti-discrimination credit bill) and H.R. 14908, a bill introduced by Representative William Widnall (R–N.J.), which was directed to credit discrimination based on sex and marital status. Koch worked with feminist groups, the Republican minority staff of the Committee on Banking and Currency, and industry representatives to get consensus on a bill.

Prior to the House hearings and during the hearings themselves, women activists were involved in providing information to members of the House Subcommittee, and in trying to influence the outcome of the vote. Again representatives of the credit industry did not try to block legislation; they sought only to influence the substantive details of the final act. Many women's groups—the women's rights groups as well as some of the more traditional women's groups—testified at the subcommittee hearings. Most of these groups used the research and arguments provided by CWPS, and many of the groups that presented testimony at the House hearings took essentially similar positions. Thus, in addition to testimony provided by Ann Scott of NOW, Patricia Massey of WEAL, Carole Burris of the Women's Lobby, and Margaret Gates and Nancy Polikoff of CWPS, testimony in support of legislation to end credit discrimination on the basis of sex and marital status came from groups as diverse as the American Association of University Women, the National Council of Jewish Women, and the National Federation of Business and Professional Women's Clubs, and from outside consumer groups that had been mobilized, most notably the Consumers Union.

This is not to suggest that women's groups were completely unified throughout the entire legislative process. Although

74

they all agreed on the need for immediate legislation, NOW took what some viewed as a pro-industry position whereas other groups sought a more sweeping solution to problems of credit discrimination and enforcement. Among the latter were the Women's Lobby and NWPC, while Margaret Gates of CWPS, who also sought stronger provisions, was characterized by one observer as "taking a more radical view of a not-too-radical issue."

Points of contention included the strength of the class-action provision, the awarding of attorney's fees and court costs of successful plaintiffs, and the right of the plaintiff to recover under both state and federal law for the same violation. Additional differences existed regarding the mandatory disclosure by industry of reasons for denial of credit. The differences, however, did not weaken ultimate support for the passage of the ECOA.

Women's groups accepted an amendment to the bill (sponsored by Koch) that limited the amount of class-action recovery. Ultimately, the concession on the class-action issue was viewed by women involved as a *quid pro quo* for a broad definition of discrimination.

When the bill emerged from the House Subcommittee hearings and mark-up session, it was almost identical to the Senate-passed Brock bill supported by most of the leaders of the women's groups. This bill then went to the Committee on Banking and Currency for a vote. A legislative quirk occurred at about this time in the passage of the ECOA. The Senate passed the Equal Credit Opportunity Act (S. 3492) as well as a House-passed Omnibus Banking Bill (H.R. 11221), Senator Brock attached S. 3492 as Title 5 to H.R. 11221. The Senate was ready to go to conference committee on H.R. 11221. If a conference report were not issued, there could be no final vote in Congress and the bill would die with the end of the Ninety-Third Congress. Thus the House Committee on Banking and Currency assigned members of the Financial Institutions Subcommittee (that had originally considered H.R. 11221) to the conference. As a result, the credit discrimination amendment never reached the floor of the House for a vote, and the conference adopted a version of the bill similar to that passed in the Senate. The conference report (H. Rept. 93-1429) was filed on October 4, 1974, and approved by both Houses of Congress. The Senate approved the conference report by voice vote; the House of Representatives approved it by a vote of 355 to 1. The bill was signed into law by President Ford in October 1974, as the Equal Credit Opportunity Act of 1974. The main provisions of the law were to:

1. prohibit discrimination on the basis of sex or marital status, with respect to any aspect of a credit transaction (although inquiry of marital status is permissible if not used for discriminatory purposes);
2. provide for enforcement by thirteen relevant agencies of the federal government;
3. prohibit dual recovery at the state and federal levels; and
4. award punitive damages in individual suits of up to $10,000 and $100,000 or 10 percent of net worth—whichever is less—in class-action suits.

Credit was construed broadly to cover all aspects of credit extension by the retail industry, credit card companies, banking, home finance, and home mortgage lenders. The Federal Reserve Board was asked to prescribe regulations implementing the legislation before the effective date of the Act (October 1975), thus leaving some key issues to be resolved at the administrative level.

The efforts of women activists to direct congressional attention to the area of credit discrimination, act as informational consultants for congressmen, and play active roles both in presenting testimony and in sustaining legislative momentum resulted in a significant legislative victory for women. The passage of the ECOA suggests that although changes in popular views may be a necessary cause for changes in policy, pressure-group activities often must supply the sufficient cause. Far from being marginal to the legislative process (albeit inadequately financed), women's groups provided crucial informational resources and remained in close contact with Congress throughout. Their success may be contrasted with an account presented by Bauer, Pool, and Dexter, in which legislators characterized women lobbyists as "noble but impractical" and indicated that "the slightest questions on economic issues can embarrass them."[23]

Members of Congress were apparently sensitized to the credit issue and supported it overwhelmingly because they thought it had support of active women's groups in their constituencies. Women activists acted here as a vanguard, somewhat in anticipation of mass consciousness, prompting legislators to think in terms of "anticipated reactions" of female voters on this issue.[24]

The legislation as it emerged seems to fall into that category which James Q. Wilson calls policy with distributive costs and distributive effects that confers benefits on and spreads costs over a large number of persons.[25] While ultimately involving redistributive policy (for example, shifting social and economic resources to women in the long run and indirectly), this issue required no outlay of public funds and conformed to general standards of equity and fair play for women.

WOMEN AND THE FEDERAL RESERVE BOARD

The Administrative Process

The administrative system has been seen by numerous analysts as even more biased in favor of interests with money, technical expertise, and organization than the legislative system. According to Gary Orfield, disorganized groups lacking resources that wish fundamentally to alter the status quo face

[23] Raymond Bauer, Louis A. Dexter, and Ithiel de Sola Pool, *Business and Public Policy* (New York: Atherton, 1963), 394-95.

[24] See 1974 *Virginia Slims American Women's Opinion Poll*, Vol. III (New York: Roper, 1975).

[25] Wilson, *Political Organizations*, ch. 16.

major difficulties in the administrative process. The civil rights forces he studied lacked professional and bureaucratic staff, established access, and centralized organization necessary to work out a consensus on questions of policy.[26] Women's groups shared these characteristics with civil rights organizations. However, the women's groups were conscious of the importance of the administrative process and, however intermittently, did intervene with impact in it. In contrast, according to Orfield[27] and Nadel,[28] for civil rights forces and consumer groups, legislation became an end in itself, and little attention was paid to the administrative process. Also, as suggested earlier, women had the advantage of technical expertise. Several capable women attorneys, who were expert in the credit area, were involved throughout the political process. In addition, and in contrast to the experience of civil rights forces in the Department of Health, Education, and Welfare and other administrative agencies, the staff of the Federal Reserve Board was uniquely sympathetic to women's aims. The feedback and encouragement of the Board's staff were often crucial to women's planning and strategy. Unlike the civil rights groups, the women's groups involved in the process of credit legislation and then administrative regulation were based in Washington and had numerous contacts with government due to their experiences with the passage of the ERA and other legislation. And although several active participants such as CWPS were prevented by 501(c)(3) status from playing an actively political role in Congress, they nonetheless were able to serve a catalytic function at the administrative level for other women's groups (administrative lobbying is not subject to IRS restrictions). Because, in Orfield's words, "administrative technicians are far more responsive to detailed, specific comments couched in the appropriate professional jargon," women who were able to

[26] Gary Orfield, "The Politics of Civil Rights Enforcement," in Michael P. Smith, ed., *Politics in America* (New York: Random House, 1974), 64-65.

[27] *Ibid.*, 65.

[28] Mark Nadel, *The Politics of Consumer Protection* (Indianapolis: Bobbs-Merrill, 1971), 170-72.

supply this type of advice and criticism were in a relatively advantageous position.[29]

The Federal Reserve Board was given responsibility for establishing guidelines to implement the Equal Credit Opportunity Act. The Board has been viewed by some as a group of mandarins, isolated from public pressures but nonetheless subject to domination by monied interests—largely bankers and business groupings.[30] In recent years, the dominance by bankers on the Board has been lessened only by the inclusion of several economists. It was thus not surprising that, once the ECOA was signed into law by the President, business groups sought to use their influence at the Federal Reserve Board to obtain administrative regulations more favorable to their interests. What was more surprising was that they did not ultimately prevail, given what James Q. Wilson refers to as "bureaucratic clientelism"—"sets of established political relations that are extremely difficult to alter and tend to be self-perpetuating."[31]

Politics at the Federal Reserve Board

As noted previously, the Federal Reserve Board was charged with writing the regulations for the ECOA. A task force was appointed for this purpose, and it was headed by Lewis Goldfarb. According to a leading staff member, the staff was selected by the Board's most consumer-oriented member, Governor Jeffrey Bucher, who sought to change the Board's image with regard to emerging issues, such as consumer rights. Because the policy area was a new one for the Board, he sought to select a staff with a substantive background in consumer, civil, and women's rights who could help Board members to understand the complex issues involved in writing the new regulations (Reg. B). The task force took the unusual step of holding public hearings on the proposed regulations, which were

[29] Orfield, *Congressional Power*, 19.

[30] *New York Times*, April 19, 1969, 59; Oct. 23, 1973, 70.

[31] Wilson, *Political Organizations*, 89.

scheduled to appear twice in draft form for public comments and then in a completed form. This was the first time public hearings were held by the Board in the consumer area. The initial draft of the guidelines was issued on April 22, 1975. Public hearings on these regulations were held on May 28-29, 1975. Women's groups played a prominent role in testifying on the regulations; they also contributed extensive written comments. In addition, the task force contracted with CWPS for consulting purposes during the period of time that the guidelines were being developed. Hence women's groups—and especially CWPS—that lacked the extensive research facilities and trained lobbyists of business, but did have technical expertise, were able to provide significant input into the administrative process. The action of institutionalizing the inclusion of a newcomer to the political arena (and even compensating it!) was, to say the least, unusual and demonstrated the pro-feminist leanings of most task force members.

As the April regulations appeared, they were clearly sympathetic to women's groups. Among the provisions irksome to industry—and advocated by women—were the requirements that credit grantors preserve records for two years after a final action had been taken on a request for credit, that they maintain records of accounts in the names of both spouses retroactively, and that they furnish applicants whose credit was denied or terminated a written statement specifying why, if the applicant so requested.

Business opposition to the ECOA "regs" was reflected in an editorial from *Consumer Trends*, a business-oriented publication. The editorial referred to the proposed Reg. B as a "maze of legal booby traps" and called ECOA a "simplistic law" passed by "dishonest" sponsors and proponents. "The National Organization for Women and other elements of the women's lib" movement have forced into Reg. B nearly every type of requirement or prohibition that they protested vigorously they were not seeking, the editorial contended.[32]

At the public hearings and in public testimony, a conflict in

[32] *Consumer Trends*, May 16, 1975, 1.

approach between NOW and the other women's groups became apparent, specifically over how far the guidelines should go in requiring mandatory disclosure of reasons for denial of credit, retroactive recordkeeping in husband's and wife's names, and the like. Susan Onaitis, at this time heading NOW's National Credit Task Force, appeared to agree with industry spokesmen in decrying the probable costs for credit companies of reviewing all their files retroactively. Endorsing a compromise proposed providing for the listing of (old) accounts in both names only upon the borrowers' request, she indicated that women sought only equal, and not unfair, advantages from credit grantors. Under pressure from the other groups, NOW retracted what were viewed as conservative, pro-industry positions and submitted new testimony (on July 14) to the Board more in accord with "pro-feminist views."[33] This incident indicates the degree of communication and, ultimately, unity present in the women's coalition on these complex issues. Nonetheless, Onaitis's initial comments may have weakened the feminist cause in the drafting of the second set of regulations by giving an impression to the Reserve Board of Governors of divided feminist ranks.

At the Federal Reserve Board's public hearings, held on May 28-29, representatives of the banking, consumer finance, and retailing industries told the Federal Reserve Board Governors that some parts of the draft regulations would be an "operational nightmare" and would require more paperwork and expense than the incidence of sex discrimination warranted. Spokesmen from Sears and the American Bankers Association decried the cost of millions of dollars necessary to provide written notice to unsuccessful applicants and carry accounts in names of both spouses, and they contended that the new rules would force small merchants to abandon credit plans, in favor of "impersonal" business by mail that would deny credit to many.[34]

Business groups made a concerted effort to rectify what they

[33] See the *Washington Post*, May 29, 1975, D7.
[34] *Wall Street Journal*, May 30, 1975, 2.

viewed as an imbalance in the Board's first draft regulations; and the second set of proposals, issued in September, emerged as far more favorable to the credit industry and its concerns. Women's groups were less vigilant with regard to the drafting procedure at this stage, and they were caught somewhat by surprise. A good index of the relative concerns of the credit industry and women's groups can be seen in noting the mail responses after each set of draft regulations was issued. After the April draft (viewed as pro-women), of the 467 letters received by the Board, 310 were from business-related groupings and only 91 were from consumer interests. After the September draft (viewed as pro-business), of 420 comments, 191 were from consumer groups or individuals and another 64 were from government sources—many of the latter sympathetic to the feminist point of view.[35]

Immediately upon the issuance of the second set of regulations, women activists swung into action, seeking to mobilize the press, other media, and congressional sympathizers. Television newscasters were approached (primarily by Linda Cohen, Chairperson of the NOW Credit Task Force in Washington, D.C.) and stories were written on the need for affirmative action against credit discrimination. Eileen Shanahan of the *New York Times* and Sara Fritz of UPI wrote several stories sympathetic to the women's point of view. An outraged telegram from Karen DeCrow (President of NOW) to Chairman Arthur Burns of the Federal Reserve Board of Governors, and letters sent to all congresswomen and other members of Congress on relevant banking committees, denounced a "sellout to the banking hierarchy" and betrayal both of women and congressional intent.[36] The letter to representatives and senators urged prompt comment to the Board of Governors. DeCrow demanded a meeting with the Board of Governors in order to present her views to them personally.

[35] Data made available to the authors by the Federal Reserve Board.

[36] These letters made available to the authors by the NOW Task Force on Credit.

At the same time, Representative Bella Abzug requested a meeting with Chairman Burns. She led a delegation of a dozen women congressional representatives to a meeting with Chairman Burns, Governor Jeffrey Bucher (the Federal Reserve Board member most responsible for the regulations and also the most sympathetic to the feminist view), and Janette Hart and Fred Solomon (Deputy Director and Director, respectively) of the Office of Saver and Consumer Affairs of the Board—the office responsible for the preparation of the credit regulations. At the meeting held on September 17, Federal Reserve officials pledged to rewrite provisions of the regulations (1) regarding income from part-time employment (to be allowed in considering credit worthiness), (2) clarifying a ban on all questions about childbearing intentions of credit applicants, and (3) regarding business loans (to prevent creditors from requiring a co-signature on such applications).[37] Women also protested the new regulations' postponement of the effective date of many aspects of the law and the absence from the proposals of a mandatory statement from creditors providing reasons for the denial of credit.

Pressure was kept up on other fronts. Linda Cohen of NOW established contact with Senator William Proxmire, Chairman of the Senate Banking Committee, and gained his limited support. The National Committee on International Women's Year was mobilized, including Senator Birch Bayh, its Enforcement Subcommittee chair. They, as well as Emily Taylor of the Interstate Association of Commissions on the Status of Women, Barbara Bergmann, Director of the Economics of Discrimination Project at the University of Maryland, and Dorothy Haener of United Auto Workers supplied written or oral comments to the Board of Governors, which may have had some impact. Under the aegis of Representative Abzug, a letter from nine women representatives to the Board of Governors made detailed and thoughtful comments on the defects of the

[37] *New York Times*, Sept. 19, 1975, 1.

September draft.[38] The Washington Council of Women Businessowners was especially forceful in pressing arguments advocating the extension of the regulations to many aspects of business loans.

The Board of Governors, clearly astounded at the furor from groups they had thought dormant, was forced to enlarge its domain to include new groups customarily not part of its constituency. The Governors found themselves ill at ease in an issue area far removed from macroeconomics and monetary policy—one in which time was short, the mandate broad, the statute often vague, and the field without precedent. The Board, therefore, sought to play a balancing role, remaining sympathetic to its normal constituencies' anxieties about costs and language, while trying to meet some of the demands of feminist groups. Although the Board operates independently of the staff (whole provisions were rewritten by the Governors), the liberal, consumer-oriented, and pro-feminist character of the staff did serve to provide women's groups with feedback and information that aided in formulation of an effective strategy.

The Outcome

The final regulations, issued by the Federal Reserve Board on October 16, 1975, represented a compromise between the demands of women and creditors. Women activists did achieve a major political success in sustaining their original goal of meaningful credit reform, but the final draft did not constitute a total return to the strongly pro-feminist language of the original April draft—even though there were fewer concessions made to the credit industry in it. Feminist groups won a provision stating that creditors must explain (not necessarily in writing) their reasons for denying or terminating credit to any applicant if the applicant so requests. Although the inclusion of this provision "represented a victory for feminist groups, particularly the National Organization for Women which had

[38] This letter was sent on September 25, 1975; Representative Elizabeth Holtzman also supplied an independent and informed set of comments.

protested the absence of such a requirement in an earlier draft of the regulations," the victory was only partial.[39] Feminist groups felt that, without written statements from creditors, the law could not be enforced, and they were particularly concerned because creditors were not required to inform applicants about the right to such a statement.[40] Although the Board dropped the written notice provision as too heavy a burden on creditors, the regulations do specify a standard form on which creditors can check off reasons for denial. Several other important provisions, which had been fought over by women's groups and creditors, are summarized below. Women activists "won" on several key points:

1. Beginning November 1, 1976, new credit accounts used by husband and wife were to be carried in both names and reported to credit bureaus in both names. This provision permits women to establish a credit history.
2. By February 1, 1977, married couples who had previous accounts were to be informed by creditors that they may have the accounts carried in both names. In addition, as of June 30, 1976, notice of the Equal Credit Opportunity Act's ban on credit discrimination was to be sent to each credit applicant, together with the name of the relevant agency enforcing compliance.
3. Lenders are prohibited from inquiring as to birth control practices or childbearing intentions. This provision represents a stronger pro-feminist view than the September draft.
4. A lender cannot refuse to open a married woman's account in a hyphenated form or form including maiden and married name.

[39] *New York Times*, Oct. 17, 1975, 1.

[40] Amendments to the Equal Credit Opportunity Act, passed by Congress on March 12, 1976, require all creditors to provide unsuccessful credit applicants with written reasons for credit denial and strengthen other provisions as well (including punitive damages in class-action suits) initially sought by feminists in the legislative process.

5. A lender will not be permitted to discount income from part-time jobs, although such income may be evaluated to determine its "probable continuity."
6. Inquiries regarding the income and credit history of a spouse or former spouse are banned if such income is not to be relied upon as establishing credit worthiness.
7. Credit may not be terminated after a change in the applicant's marital status unless there is evidence of a new unwillingness or inability to pay. And, although a creditor may inquire and consider information on alimony, child support, or maintenance payments, if a credit applicant does not choose to rely on such payments to obtain credit, support income from them need not be disclosed. These provisions were eagerly sought by feminist groups.
8. Separate credit may be extended to spouses if each so requests and each qualifies for credit.

But female applicants for business loans would have more limited protection than borrowers of personal goods and services. Business credit would be exempt from the prohibition against inquiry into marital status, the mandatory record-keeping provisions, and the requirement on informational notice. Also, women had wanted unmarried people to be able to open joint accounts, but they lost on this issue. Another key point represented a compromise: creditors were required under the revised regulations to keep credit application records for fifteen months after final action. The credit industry had wanted a one-year retention period; the feminist groups, two years.

However, as a result of amendments to Reg. B (12 CFR 202) passed in Congress in 1976, effective March 23, 1977, several of the original compromises that were accepted by women were modified to comply with the original demands of the feminist lobbyists. Amended Reg. B specifies that notice of an adverse credit decision must be given to the applicant with the written reasons or a notice of the applicant's right to written

reasons within thirty days. Reg. B also establishes a higher
level of liability for punitive damages at the lesser of $500,000
or 1 percent of the creditor's net worth in class actions. In addition, records are to be retained by creditors for twenty-five
months after action is taken. All of these modifications were
consistent with the earlier preferences of most of the women
lobbyists.

ASSESSMENT

Potentially sweeping change was launched by the contribution
of women activists to the Equal Credit Opportunity Act,
which operating in a vacuum created new policy in an area potentially affecting millions of women. While women thus succeeded in broadening the political agenda, they did so only by
conforming to the system's mobilization of bias. The issue was
relatively noncontroversial, involving distributed costs and
distributed benefits; although business may incur greater
costs, they will be passed on indirectly to the consumer, and
large groups of both women and men may profit from the extension, for example, of mortgage credit to a two-income family. Issue demands were specific, and they challenged no fundamental societal values. Though ultimately a role change
issue in the sense that economic power may be transferred to
women, this policy was perceived as one of *equity* or equal
rights and as such had no formal opposition. The issue did not
involve mass publics and was resolved at the leadership level
of politics. There was no national precedent to rely upon,
hence a "policy vacuum" developed that facilitated possibilities for innovation.

In contrast to some other feminist issues (such as abortion
reform and the Equal Rights Amendment), women presented
a united front with regard to equal credit opportunity. Their
broad-based coalition was bolstered by the presence of an ongoing "policy system," created in part by the battle for an
Equal Rights Amendment, which included sympathetic members of Congress, their legislative aides, Federal Reserve Board

87

staff and members, and the press. In addition, women were perceived as a significant "potential" interest group that might be mobilized to defeat recalcitrant legislators at the polls. Thus a multilevel and multifaceted coalition, whose strength rested upon the "anticipated reaction" of women voters, was crucial to success.

Women activists showed themselves ready to accept less than total feminist victory; women compromised in both their legislative demands and, later, in their regulatory demands.

POLICY IMPACT

The ultimate test of a policy's success is its impact on the public and the degree with which the spirit and letter of the new law are accepted. It should be noted that virtually all monitoring by feminist groups of equal credit ceased with the enactment of Reg. B and the amendments to it that were passed in 1976 (largely at the initiation of other disadvantaged groups). For example, the Center for Women Policy Studies, which played such a crucial role in providing background expertise for the issue's acceptance, has moved on to study other issues such as battered women and has been rebuffed in its efforts to obtain further funding to assess compliance with the ECOA. The League of Women Voters was alone in pursuing a case in the courts in a class-action suit against Central-Charge and Riggs National Bank. In the end, private counsel took over and the suit was ultimately dismissed for lack of statistical evidence determining a pattern of discrimination, although the individual plaintiff did gain relief.[41]

Public awareness of the ECOA is difficult to measure; the available evidence is somewhat contradictory, but appears to suggest that the Act has produced considerable change in credit practices due to both public interest and creditors' compliance. A 1977 Consumer Credit Survey came too early after the Act's passage to measure public awareness and impact

[41] Interview with Maureen Thornton of LWV, Oct. 25, 1979.

meaningfully; nonetheless, it did indicate limited awareness by respondents of credit discrimination based on sex and marital status (in contrast to the data reported by the Virginia Slims Poll cited earlier). The Federal Reserve Board has made the suggestion, based on previous experience with other credit laws, that public awareness of these laws tends to develop very slowly.[42] Nevertheless, a Federal Reserve Board survey in November 1977 of eight large creditors found that, of 48.5 million notices of rights to separate credit history for married customers mailed by the *seven* respondents, 5 million replies were received: 11 percent of the customers requested separate credit histories.[43] The survey also showed that the revised Reg. B, requiring creditors to inform rejected applicants of reasons for credit denial either initially or upon request, produced considerable change as well. According to the survey, "many of the rejected credit applicants who were initially given reasons for credit denial supplied additional information and a high proportion of these were then granted credit."[44] A 1978 survey by the Commercial Credit Corporation found that more than 80 percent of women surveyed had applied for credit in their own name in the past two years, and a majority of these indicated that they had "experienced problems"; 56 percent of those surveyed said that the ECOA had made it easier for women to obtain credit.[45] Most women who were turned down in their request for credit asked for a written explanation or reapplied and were later approved. The survey found that more women with family incomes of below $10,000 applied for credit than did women with incomes of over $15,000. The survey sug-

[42] Board of Governors of the Federal Reserve System, *Annual Report to Congress on the Equal Credit Opportunity Act for the Year 1978*, Feb. 1, 1979, 13

[43] "Exercise of Consumer Rights under the Equal Credit Opportunity and Fair Credit Billing Acts," *Federal Reserve Bulletin*, May 1978, 363-64.

[44] *Ibid.*, 365-66.

[45] Commercial Credit Corporation Public Relations and Corporate Marketing Research Departments, *A Survey of Women and Credit: How They Use It and What They Think*, Aug./Sept. 1978. Of 2,080 women surveyed, the response rate was 33.3 percent.

gests, then, that the ECOA may have had a considerable impact on credit awareness and credit worthiness among women, even among lower-class women. A study of equal credit accessibility to mortgage funds by women conducted under the auspices of HUD from 1976 to 1978 found limited discrimination on the basis of sex or marital status of the applicant. This may be the result of compliance with the ECOA, although we lack complete information on cause/effect relationships.[46] More recently, a *New York Times* report on female home ownership found single women as purchasers of one-third of all condominiums and one-tenth of all homes sold in the United States in 1980, a transformation surely due in large measure to equal credit legislation.[47]

With regard to federal enforcement of the ECOA, reports reveal a relatively small number of complaints specifically dealing with discrimination based on sex or marital status. The 1978 Report of the Federal Reserve Board does indicate, however, that noncompliance with the Act rose substantially during 1978, but attributes the apparent rise to better staff training and enforcement techniques. One difficulty in the process of enforcement involves the absence of an "effects" test; that is, there is only a limited effort to take into account practices that may not be motivated by the intent of the creditor to discriminate but do have a discriminatory effect. The Federal Trade Commission, which responds to the largest number of consumer complaints under ECOA, did settle a $50,000 agreement in civil penalties against Bloomingdale's Department Store in an attempt viewed by the FTC as a warning to other companies that might be in violation of the ECOA. Under the direction of Lewis Goldfarb, who headed the Bureau of Consumer Protection at the FTC (and who was one of the ECOA's most fervent supporters in his position at the Federal Reserve

[46] U.S. Department of Housing and Urban Development, Office of Policy Development and Research, "Equal Credit Opportunity: Accessibility to Mortgage Funds by Women and Minorities" (Summary of Results), May 1980.

[47] *New York Times*, April 23, 1981, 1.

Board during the writing of Reg. B), there is an attempt to enforce the law with vigor. The Department of Housing and Urban Development has a special program to educate consumers on equal access to mortgage credit and to study the ECOA's impact, while the Federal Reserve Board and other agencies have sought to educate the public as to their credit rights through the issuance of brochures and a film strip called "To Your Credit." In its 1978 Report, the Department of Justice suggested that firms with questionable credit policies change them quickly after complaints are filed or after enforcement agencies bring them to their attention. Another factor contributing to what appears to be low ECOA activity is the tendency of creditors to accept those applicants who complain—although this process may not necessarily result in abandonment of all illegal practices by creditors.[48]

Proposed revisions of Reg. B on March 18, 1985, addressed possibilities for simplification of creditor burdens and more effective implementation despite the finding that the regulation was found to have substantially achieved its goals. Consequently, only modest procedural changes are being recommended. Comments from creditors, enforcement agencies, and consumer and civil rights representatives concluded that the regulation should be maintained in its present form.[49] Enforcement agencies reported that there were no major compliance problems; creditors considered the requirements as manageable; and civil rights and women's groups felt the regulation provided important protections. Consumers appeared to be satisfied with the treatment they were receiving with regard to credit. A 1982 survey showed fewer than 10 percent of respondents believing that personal characteristics such as race and sex were crucial in obtaining credit. Although the respondents thought that members of ECOA-protected groups still had more difficulty obtaining credit, they felt that less dis-

[48] The Attorney General's Report to Congress Pursuant to the ECOA Amendment of 1975, submitted Feb. 1, 1976, 6.

[49] *Federal Register*, v. 50, no. 52 (March 18, 1985), 12 CFR, part 202, 10691.

crimination occurred in 1981 than in 1977 and indicated that they found the written disclosure statement regarding negative credit decisions useful.[50]

CONCLUSION

The current status of the ECOA is fraught with several paradoxes. The number of complaints under the Act has fallen off, and there have been relatively few law suits and no successful class-action claims since the enactment of the law. Is this relative dearth of activity due to compliance or to lack of public awareness? An attorney for the Office of Saver and Consumer Affairs of the Federal Reserve Board commented on the difficulty of proving discrimination under the law; in the absence of comparative data on the treatment of other consumers, it is difficult to establish discrimination.[51] Is the limited monitoring effort by feminist groups due to limited feedback, feminist preoccupation with other issues, or to the Act's success? To what degree does the multiple enforcement structure of the Act reflect disparate policies between agencies that are often unresolved? While the ultimate impact of the ECOA remains to be seen, we can at least point to preliminary data suggesting both creditor and consumer awareness of the Act's importance.

[50] *Ibid.*, 10898-9.
[51] Telephone interview with Delores Smith, Federal Reserve Board, April 28, 1980.

CHAPTER 5

TITLE IX:
THE POLITICS OF
SEX DISCRIMINATION

INTRODUCTION

To change the society in which one lives it is first necessary to modify the belief system of the people living in that society. One institution for transforming belief systems is the school. Thus, to alter beliefs regarding equal opportunities for women, one available route is education. In the past decade two legislative forays into the schools by feminist groups interested in improving opportunities for women were reasonably successful. More recently their efforts to press for the passage of civil rights legislation in the wake of the Supreme Court's decision in *Grove City* v. *Bell*[1] have met with some strong opposition. In 1972 Title IX of the Education Amendments outlawed sex discrimination in elementary and secondary schools as well as in post-secondary institutions; and in 1974 the Women's Educational Equity Act (WEEA) was enacted, providing funds for research and development to undergird women's efforts toward gaining equality in education. No real conflict arose in regard to WEEA in either the legislative or the administrative arena. But controversy began to rage in response to Title IX as soon as the implications surfaced. In this chapter we consider the politics of Title IX. It will be shown that issue-specialization and coalition-development can balance a strong countermovement on an emotionally charged issue.

[1] 104 S.Ct. 1211 (1984).

In 1984 the women's movement joined with representatives of the larger civil rights community to work for the enactment of legislation that would override the Court's narrow interpretation of federal anti-bias laws. We will be discussing the role of the women's movement in both the pre- and post-1984 period. Our generalizations about the feminist groups when they were addressing sex-specific education issues must be modified as a result of their participation in a broader-based civil rights community. Because of the nature of this coalition, the opposition has broadened and changed as well. No longer is it limited to the sports and educational communities; it comes, too, from representatives of the Administration, key members of Congress, and other elected officials, who have effectively blocked enactment of the proposed civil rights law.

In July 1972 Congress passed and the President signed into law the Education Amendments of 1972. Included among these amendments was Title IX, a provision outlawing sex discrimination in education. Emulating the equal protection aspects of Title VI of the Civil Rights Act of 1964, Title IX states that "No person in the United States shall, on the basis of sex, be excluded from participation in, be denied the benefits of, or be subjected to discrimination under any education program or activity receiving federal financial assistance. . . ." The primary responsibility for drafting the regulations for the implementation of Title IX was assigned to the Department of Health, Education, and Welfare, where the staff of the Office of Civil Rights (OCR) was given the job of enforcing this new anti-sex-discrimination clause of the Education Act.

The passage of Title IX did not come about because of pressure from feminist groups; rather, this legislation may be largely attributed to the efforts of Congresswoman Edith Green and Senator Birch Bayh. Controversy and debate over the bill were centered on issues other than Title IX, and no organized constituency opposed its passage. However, when the full extent of the law was understood and the effect of specific implementing regulations comprehended, hard lines were drawn, especially by the male sports establishment and by its

94

defenders in Congress, in efforts to diminish the impact of the 1972 Amendments. A coalition of women's groups—traditional and feminist—has to date been effective as a counterpoise to the forces opposed to Title IX by beating back challenges to the existing legislation in Congress and continuously seeking more vigorous regulations and implementation at the executive level. In fact, when new athletic guidelines were issued in December 1979, it was clear that the women's movement had been successful in holding the line on the intent of Title IX.

Major conflicts regarding Title IX prior to 1984 involved levels of enforcement by HEW and often centered on the issue of sex equality in intercollegiate sports. To the extent that the feminists were successful, they were able to redefine the issues of equal educational opportunity—both in sports and in other educational activities—as issues of role equity as opposed to role change. Title IX falls somewhere between the poles, because while it involves equity, it deals with questions of privacy and potentially radical change in traditionally male-dominated areas of society. Ultimately, as Doris Burton has suggested, "The athletics issue may well mask a growing concern over changing sex roles and not a concern about the impact of Title IX on revenue-producing sports."[2]

Although Title IX was approved by Congress in 1972, it was not until 1975 that regulations for implementing the law were issued. Implementation has lagged and feminists have pressed their efforts at the legislative, judicial, and administrative levels of politics in order to prevent the demise of Title IX. It took until late 1979 to gain release from HEW of a "policy interpretation" largely dealing with intercollegiate athletics. Because the new rules were known as a "policy interpretation" rather than "regulations," they did not have to go to Congress for approval. A congressional debate might have proved

[2] Doris Jean Burton, "Sexual Equality Through Title IX: Potential vs. Performance" (paper presented at the Midwest Political Science Association convention, Chicago, April 19, 1979), 37.

lengthy and would have involved continued efforts to weaken Title IX, possibly resulting in the law's reconsideration and furthet delay of implementation. The "threat of females to participate in activities sacred to male machismo" has produced almost a decade of unrelenting pressure by feminists to end sex discrimination in athletics.[3]

In the pages that follow we will discuss first the conditions that women's groups have been trying to redress and then the legislative and administrative forces that affected the drafting and implementation of Title IX. We will also attend to the interplay of group activities throughout these processes. The specific role of women's groups in influencing policy will be assessed in an effort to show that they used the tools of the status quo to incrementally change that same status quo. Finally, the efforts of a broad-based coalition to override the Supreme Court's 1984 decision will be addressed.

Much of the success of the women's movement has been in keeping the spirit of the law intact against the rather formidable male sports establishment and lackadaisical enforcement by the OCR. Feminists were successful in holding the line because they organized a coalition focused exclusively on sex discrimination in education, were relentless in maintaining pressure on this relatively narrow issue, were vigilant in fending off challenges to Title IX, and were willing to use a variety of strategies to realize their objectives. When in 1984 the scope of the issue and the range of group participants broadened, the task of maintaining gains already achieved became more difficult.

It was of course never an easy task for the feminist community. The values of members of Congress and administrators do not support vigorous enforcement of Title IX while opposition groups—especially the National Collegiate Athletic Association (NCAA)—with financial backing and legitimacy have mobilized to counter feminist efforts through intensive lobbying. The OCR record of enforcement in civil rights gen-

---

[3] Harold Howe, "Sex, Sports and Discrimination," *Chronicle of Higher Education*, June 18, 1979, 72.

erally was best a mixed one—complicated here by what Doris Burton describes as the numerous decision points through which Title IX and other federal programs must pass. Policy initiated by Congress goes to the OCR (which often must clarify and amplify), is then sent to regional offices, and finally to 16,000 school districts and 2,500 colleges.[4]

BACKGROUND

Education for women in American schools has been deemed by critics within the women's movement to be unequal to that provided men. In particular, educational opportunities for women have been seen as limited by educationally reinforced sex-role expectations regarding the proper role for women versus the proper role for men. Thus women have been steered away from pursuing careers involving mathematics and science. Girls have been rewarded for academic and social docility whereas boys have been encouraged to be aggressive and inquisitive. Female students have been discouraged from seeking advanced professional training and, until the last decade, qualified women were often denied admission to law schools, medical schools, and other professional programs. Thus in 1960 women represented only 6 percent of the total medical school enrollment. (By 1974 women made up 22 percent of first-year medical school enrollment.)[5] Similarly, women were often kept by lack of financial support from following their studies toward the Ph.D. Until the 1970s most prestigious business programs did not admit many women applicants to their MBA programs. The number of women in traditionally male-dominated vocational areas of trade, agriculture, technology, and industry remained low (5 percent in 1972). Career opportunities having been limited in these ways, women in 1980 had yearly earnings that on the average were 59 percent of men's.

[4] Burton, "Sexual Equality," 34.

[5] John B. Parrish, "Women in Professional Training—An Update," *Monthly Labor Review* 98 (Nov. 1975), 49-50.

In educational institutions, women are confined to lower-level positions. A 1979 survey found that women held only one of every ten administrative jobs in public elementary and high schools, while women continue to receive fewer tenured faculty positions at all educational institutions. A 1978 study by the American Association of University Women found that, in institutions of higher education, women had made no statistical gains on faculties and only slight gains in administrative positions even since the passage of Title IX.[6]

Equal athletic opportunity similarly has been denied female students. Sports have traditionally been an area where the stereotype of men as participants and women as cheerleaders or observers has been reinforced.[7] Women's athletics are always secondary to men's. In most schools, boys' teams are better funded and equipped, and boys have better practice facilities and more practice time. Coaches for male sports are better paid than their female counterparts, and in college and university communities, athletic recruitment and scholarship opportunities have been dominated by men. Athletic expectations have reflected a general societal view of women as passive, unskilled, and submissive. This, then, is the backdrop against which the politics of Title IX must be considered.

The Passage of the Law

Title IX, as adopted by both houses of Congress and signed into law by the President, bans sex discrimination in education. Several interacting forces seem to have been responsible for the introduction of Title IX into the Education Amendments of 1972. By the late 1960s women on American college and university campuses had begun to recognize the discrimination that they were suffering. Perhaps this awareness was

[6] *On Campus with Women* 24 (Washington, D.C.: Association of American Colleges, Fall 1979), 4-5; PEER *Perspective* 5 (Sept. 1979), 3; *New York Times*, April 8, 1978, 24.

[7] U.S. Commission on Civil Rights, Hearing, July 9, 1978, testimony of Carole Mushier, President, AIAW, 96.

wrought in part by the ripple effects of the civil rights movement on potential women activists, by the emergence of an organized, albeit small, women's rights movement, by the wave
of unmet rising expectations that had been fed by President
Johnson's executive orders of 1965 and 1967, and by the various state meetings of commissions on the status of women.
Also, in 1969, WEAL initiated its first sex-discrimination case
against universities that made a clearly articulated statement
about the status of women in educational institutions. Then, in
1970, Representative Edith Green (D–Ore.) held congressional hearings that addressed questions of discrimination
against women in education. Two volumes of hearings were
published, and she had 6,000 copies printed so as to provide
the widest possible distribution of the testimony. It is interesting to note that apparently *no* post-secondary institutions sent
representatives to testify at these hearings. Two years later
Representative Green introduced Title IX to the 1972 Education Amendments. She requested the women's groups *not* to
testify in behalf of Title IX because she believed that if members of Congress were not aware of what was included in Title
IX, they would simply vote for it without paying too much attention to its content or its ultimate implications. Women's organizations complied with Representative Green's request and
they stayed away from the hearings.

Feminist goals were met in the early legislative encounters
on Title IX. In part this was so because most attention was directed to the other titles of the Omnibus Education Amendments. Title IX was not a central issue for many members of
Congress. It was only in the process of implementation, when
the potential impact was more fully understood, that opposition to Title IX began to take shape.

LOBBYISTS FOR AND AGAINST THE REGULATIONS

The implementation of Title IX was complicated by the passage of the 1974 Education Amendments, which included a
provision giving Congress forty-five days to disapprove by

concurrent resolution any administrative regulations regarding education if they were deemed to be inconsistent with congressional intent. It was especially in this context that conflict arose and strong counterpressures were mounted to the anti-sex-discrimination goals of the women's groups. The male sports establishment (most notably, the NCAA and other groups of coaches) lobbied to prevent what they saw as a potential erosion in their power if equal educational opportunity in athletics and organized sports in particular were provided to all students regardless of their sex.

Though feminist lobbying for equal credit opportunity met some opposition from business groups during the time when regulations were being written for the Equal Credit Opportunity Act, this countermovement was mild in contrast to what women activists encountered at the same stage with Title IX. In the latter case, social values intervened, as well as a strong and well-organized counterlobby, the NCAA. Feminists had to contend with the internalized values of university presidents, Congressmen, and administrators. Nonetheless, Gary Orfield has written that the Office of Civil Rights was "confronted by an active, informed and insistent constituency of women's organizations, a constituency with organizational resources and political power far greater than those of minority groups, as evidenced by the way it transformed the usually invisible process of administrative rule making and then successfully beat down a challenge to the regulations on the floor of Congress." Despite efforts to weaken the athletic regulations from local officials and influential House members, mobilized women's groups quashed the rebellion.[8]

Some sixty groups were initial participants in the Title IX forays. In addition to WEAL, NOW, NWPC, CLASP-WRP, and other feminist groups, more traditional organizations such as the LWV, the Association of American Colleges' Project on the Status and Education of Women, the AAUW, the ACE, the AAUP, and the Girl Scouts, to name but a few, have

[8] Gary Orfield, *Must We Bus?* (Washington, D.C.: Brookings Institution, 1978), 347.

been involved. In 1974 these groups joined together to form the Education Task Force, which later changed its name to the National Coalition for Women and Girls in Education. This organization started as an informal lunch group of seven or eight people and then expanded into a larger coalition. The participants were concerned with a single issue—sex discrimination in education—and they always attempted to iron out their own differences on issues as well as tactics prior to taking public positions so as to minimize public divisiveness. Participation has been flexible: members need join only on those matters with which they agree. Perhaps most responsible for the National Coalition's inception was Bernice (Bunny) Sandler, who is with the Association of American Colleges' Project on the Status and Education of Women, which supplied both early moral and financial support for the coalition.

The National Coalition generally worked in conjunction with the AIAW, a member of the group. The AIAW, founded in 1971, was the leadership organization for women's intercollegiate programs, governing scholarships, athletic recruitment, and other regulations for women in sports for 916 member shcools. With the aid of its legal counsel, Margot Polivy, a Washington attorney and feminist activist, it played a crucial role in the struggle for Title IX. In addition to the AIAW, SPRINT (a branch of the WEAL Fund that acted as a clearinghouse for sports-related information and case histories) and PEER (a branch of the NOW Legal Defense Fund that exclusively monitors Title IX) occupied major roles in the National Coalition. Other active participants have included Marcia Greenberger and Margaret Kohn (the latter for a long time the chair of the National Coalition's Task Force on Enforcement) of NWLC. They have been highly involved in the area of sex discrimination in education since they brought the *WEAL* v. *Califano*[9] suit in the mid-1970s.

Observers attributed the National Coalition's success to its definable issue area, sharing of power by constituent groups, and narrow range of influence. Resources are limited, and the

[9] U.S. Dist. Ct. for D. of C., Civ. Act. no. 70-3095 (1977).

organization's role is essentially to meet biweekly, discuss issues related to Title IX, and delineate positions on policy. Under these conditions, there is little usurpation of any individual
group's power and influence.

As noted previously, the major opposition to feminist
groups regarding Title IX was mounted by the male athletic establishment. In particular, the NCAA and the leadership of
some universities with major commitments to men's intercollegiate sports were in the forefront of organized opposition.
The major counterforce to feminist efforts was not directed toward the end of funding for Title IX. Rather, the focus was the
exclusion of athletics from Title IX enforcement. The NCAA,
like the AIAW, an organization of institutions, was initially
slow to mobilize opposition through college presidents and
coaches, but became more active.

The countermovement sought to operate in a manner comparable to that of the feminist groups, although a spokesman
for the NCAA claimed that his group was neither as organized
nor as aggressive as the feminists in Washington. However, in
that the countermovement represented the status quo by simply not responding too quickly to demands for change, it was
able to thwart full implementation. Also, many members of
Congress as well as OCR officials, if not active supporters of
the NCAA, are "closet supporters" and have not made vigorous efforts to bring about change. As recently as 1978 the
AIAW issued data that showed wide discrepancies in per capita spending for athletics between men and women at comparable institutions. In NCAA Division I schools, the mean per
capita expenditure for men was $5,257; the figure for women
was $2,156 (see Table 6).

The NCAA is an organization of 726 member institutions.
It has the capacity to raise the political and financial resources
necessary for lengthy litigation. For example, in 1978 its revenues totalled $13.9 million, with self-generated revenues de-
riving from championship games, televised football, and the
production of other television sports programs. The leaders of
major universities can be mobilized. Finally, and not to be
overlooked, although societal values regarding the female role

TABLE 6
Athletes, Budgets, and Per Capita Expenditures (PCE)
at AIAW and NCAA Colleges (1978)
(figures given are means)

•mbership	*Number of Athletes* *Men/Women*	*Men*		*Women*		*Difference between Total Budgets*
		Total Budget	*PCE*	*Total Budget*	*PCE*	
AIAW Colleges W and NCAA	238/102	$ 717,000	$3,013	$141,000	$1,382	− 80.3%
'CAA Div. I	315/138	1,650,000	5,257	276,000	2,156	− 83.3
CAA Div. II	222/105	418,000	1,883	120,000	1,143	− 71.3
CAA Div. III	251/110	79,000	315	24,000	218	− 69.6
NCAA	276/118	1,042,000	3,755	199,000	1,686	− 80.9

ɔURCE: *AIAW Competitive Division Structure Implementation Study: Final Data Summary* ɔciation for Intercollegiate Athletics for Women, Fall 1978, Table XIV.

may be changing, changes in perception among men and women occur slowly. When women do not make demands for athletic participation, then opportunities are not provided. However, if opportunities are not provided, women will often not request them. Thus the men's athletic establishment and academic officials may maintain the status quo while insisting that there is no need to provide equity. As of 1978-79 the OCR reported that a total of 1,179 coeducational institutions provided an average of 5.0 sports for women and 7.4 for men (for two-year schools, the comparable figures were 2.9 for women and 5.0 for men).[10]

WRITING THE REGULATIONS

The Office of Civil Rights of the Department of Health, Education, and Welfare was, as noted previously, responsible for drafting the regulations for Title IX. In July 1972, when the

[10] U.S. Commission on Civil Rights, *Comments on a Proposed Policy Interpretation of Title IX of the Education Amendments of 1972 (Revised)*, Sept. 10, 1979, 2.

OCR staff began to consider this task, they had had only limited experience in enforcing anti-sex-discrimination regulations with regard to faculty and no experience with regard to students. In November of the same year the first draft of the regulations was published. It was a "cut-and-paste version of the existing regulation covering race discrimination under Title VI of the 1964 Civil Rights Act, after which Title IX was modeled."[11] The draft was very general and vague, and after it was reviewed by other officers in HEW and by the White House staff, strong pressure was brought to bear urging much greater specificity. The redrafting procedure was not given a very high priority within HEW—as was evidenced by the assignment of only two lawyers in the General Counsel's Office (who had other responsibilities as well) to work on Title IX.

While the administrative process was generating proposed regulations, Congress was still taking action on Title IX. In May 1974 Senator John R. Tower (R–Texas) introduced an amendment to the Education Amendments of 1974 that would have exempted revenue-producing intercollegiate sports from Title IX coverage. This amendment passed the Senate. Since this provision was not included in the House version of the education bill, the House-Senate Conference Committee was left to resolve this difference (and two hundred other differences in the bills, too). On June 18, 1974, HEW released the regulations to implement Title IX. They provided coverage for schools and colleges in admissions, treatment of students (in athletics as well as other areas), and employment. In July of 1974 the House-Senate Conference Committee rejected the Tower amendment and included substitute language proposed by Senator Jacob Javits (R–N.Y.) that "reasonable provisions" for female participation in intercollegiate athletic activities be provided by Title IX. This committee also proposed the provision for the review of regulations within forty-five days mentioned earlier.

[11] Andrew Fishel and Janice Pottker, *National Politics and Sex Discrimination in Education* (Lexington, Mass.: D.C. Heath, 1977), 106.

Although women had won in the conference committee, their battles were not over. They were caught unawares when, in October 1974, Representative Marjorie Holt (R–Md.) introduced an amendment that would have barred HEW from gathering data on sex and race discrimination in educational institutions. She was assisted by Representative Green, who by this time was upset by the less than rigorous interpretation of Title IX provided by HEW. The amendment passed the House by a vote of 200 to 169. When it reached the Senate Appropriations Committee, women's groups and civil rights groups were able to influence the committee members and the amendment was defeated in committee. Coalition contacts on the Hill used prepared questions and comments to support Title IX. Regulations for Title IX remained a volatile issue; HEW received nearly ten thousand written comments. There was, however, no consensus among the letter-writers. In November of the same year the Holt amendment was reintroduced as an amendment to an HEW supplemental appropriation. It passed the House by a larger margin than it had in October and again was defeated in the Senate.

Pressure began to mount on Congress to exempt social fraternities and sororities from Title IX coverage. Senator Birch Bayh (D–Ind.) introduced an amendment to exempt such groups. The amendment was carefully worded so that honor societies, recreational groups, and professional societies were not exempted from coverage. Women's groups did not actively oppose this amendment because Bayh had been supportive of women's issues and it was clear that social sororities and fraternities were as "American as apple pie." Two events followed these forays. First, women's groups, angered that HEW was not enforcing Title IX, in November 1974 filed a suit in U.S. District Court in Washington, D.C., against HEW and the Department of Labor (*WEAL* v. *Weinberger*).[12] In addition, in February 1975 the final regulations were sent to President Ford for his approval. They were sent with a memo. Both the regu-

---

[12] U.S. Dist. Ct. for D. of C. Civ. Act. no. 74-1720 (1974).

lations and the memo were secret. However, a source in HEW sent copies to a women's group leader, who in turn distributed copies to other women's organizational leaders. Because of this crucial disclosure, the exact nature of the regulations was known in advance of publication; the women's groups were aware of the weakened character of the regulations, and they could consider a strategy prior to their enactment. In particular, there was a provision that required a person complaining of sex discrimination to use the school's internal grievance procedure before HEW would act on the complaint. Eventually this provision was dropped from the regulations—a testament to the women activists' lobbying and monitoring efforts.

At the same time that the women's groups were involved in trying to change the proposed procedure they opposed, some members of Congress still were busy trying to restrict the scope of Title IX by law. Representative Robert Casey (D–Tex.) introduced an amendment to a supplemental appropriations bill that would have prohibited HEW from withholding federal money from schools not offering coeducational physical education. The House passed the amendment; the Senate did not approve it. Later in 1975 it went to a conference committee where this effort to weaken the law failed.

On July 2, 1975, the President signed the Title IX regulations, which were weaker than the original proposed regulations. However, a new problem arose for the women when, on the same day that the regulations were issued officially, HEW announced a proposed rule change that would have led to the consolidation of all statutory civil rights enforcement—including Title IX enforcement—thus potentially weakening the law. The rule that had been passed in 1974 mandating a period of review lasting forty-five days meant that Title IX regulations were now up for congressional approval or disapproval.

Despite some disappointment with the final regulations, the women's groups decided to lobby Congress to approve the regulations, since there was some fear that if Congress disapproved, schools might take it as a mandate to continue sex discrimination. The regulations were sent to the House Post-Secondary Education Committee chaired by Representative James O'Hara (D-Mich.). O'Hara introduced a disapproving resolution and an amendment to "railroad" it through his subcommittee without hearings and thus with considerable speed; the full House Education and Labor Committee rejected both measures. Women's groups worked hard—with the support of women congressional staffers—to defeat the proposals. On July 21, 1975, three years after the initial legislation was passed, the regulations to implement Title IX went into effect.

But the battle was not over. The 1976 education appropriations measure was to become the target of congressional forces opposed to Title IX. Casey's amendment (to prohibit HEW from withholding funds from schools not in compliance) was again introduced. The House barely accepted it by a vote of 212 to 211; the Senate rejected the amendment 65 to 29. The Senate would not budge from its position. The House leadership finally threw its support behind deletion of the Casey amendment, and it was rejected 215 to 178 in a later vote. In this fight women organized their most extensive lobbying effort ever on any congressional issue, with hundreds of volunteers working under the guidance of the various involved groups.

The opposition to Title IX has continued even after these defeats, but the regulations have remained relatively intact. Although HEW withdrew its proposal to consolidate civil rights enforcement the Office of Civil Rights never was vigorous in its enforcement efforts as related to Title IX.

IMPLEMENTATION OF THE LAW AND ITS REGULATIONS

As noted previously, the primary, though not total, responsibility for the federal role in implementing Title IX rested with the OCR in HEW. (When a separate Department of Education was established in 1980, the responsibility for Title IX moved with the OCR to the new department.) Insofar as the major federal responsibility for Title IX was granted to the OCR, only the role of that agency will be considered in this discussion of the federal administration of the law.[13]

It is important to recognize that ultimately all implementation of this law resides with school districts and college and university officers. The actual effect of the law has been therefore determined to a significant degree by the willingness of local officials to act in accord with the spirit as well as the letter of the law. It is well known that there is always significant variation in effects of a law when it reaches grassroots administration.[14] In the following pages, however, this phase of implementation will be given only cursory examination. We will focus our attention mainly on implementation at the federal level through the OCR.

The Office of Civil Rights must address two types of problems regarding implementation of laws: one is compliance and enforcement, and the other is policy. It is organized to take this division into account. The OCR is charged with the implementation not only of Title IX, however, but also of a variety of other civil rights and affirmative action policies. Its multiple responsibilities have tended to retard the OCR's effective implementation of Title IX policy. It was estimated by Cindy Brown, then Deputy Director for Compliance and Enforcement of the OCR (and previously a member of the Coalition for Women and Girls in Education), that only between one-third and one-half of staff time at the OCR was spent on cases of sex discrimination. The OCR office had a poor record in civil rights enforcement in general. With regard to Title IX there was limited coordination between the federal and regional offices, poor (almost nonexistent) record-keeping, turnover of personnel, and continual reorganization. According to Gary Orfield, the Title IX responsibility "was an extremely

---

[13] A good discussion of the role of other government agencies in the administration of Title IX is Nancy J. Balles, *The Unenforced Law: Title IX Activity by Federal Agencies Other than HEW* (Washington, D.C.: The National Advisory Council of Women's Educational Programs, 1978).

[14] George E. Hale and Marian Lief Palley, "Federal Grants to the States—Who Governs?" *Administration and Society* 2 (May 1979).

complex one for which few additional resources were provided."[15] (The 1975 regulations took up seventeen pages of small print in the code.) In addition, implementation of Title IX was complicated by disagreement among those people in the OCR charged with enforcement and compliance on just what the appropriate policy should be. There was limited interest by successive Secretaries of HEW in seeing the law administered effectively; hence no clear sense of priorities or mission was established. Furthermore, the OCR staff had more concern and involvement with implementing civil rights legislation as it affected nonwhites than with alleviating sex discrimination. The OCR staff in the 1970s was largely drawn from the black civil rights movement of the 1960s. In addition, it was mostly male, and seemed to be in questionable sympathy with the goals of women activists.

Despite these obvious roadblocks to active enforcement of the law, women's groups remained vigilant—as have groups in opposition to Title IX—in monitoring the effects on Title IX. In fact, given the counterforces they faced, they were remarkably agile in not losing ground prior to 1984. As noted previously, the major visible attacks on Title IX have been made by the male sports establishment, particularly the NCAA. The supporters of men's athletics have been successful in keeping equality of opportunity for women in sports as guaranteed in 1972 by Title IX from becoming a total reality. This is especially true in colleges and universities with NCAA Division I teams, somewhat less true in colleges and universities with NCAA Divisions II and III teams and in high schools. However, as compliance with Title IX regarding athletics increased in high schools, demands for better compliance in post-secondary institutions grew as well. In addition, as noted by an Assistant Deputy Director at the OCR, women's groups are rarely surprised by events since their representatives are always monitoring the system. Still, to date no funds were ever cut off because of noncompliance with Title IX, and Title IX

[15] Orfield, *Must We Bus?* 307.

never had the positive impact for which women activists hoped.

This fact, and the discussion of limited enforcement of the law, must *not* be taken, however, as indicative of either a total lack of effect of the anti-sex-discrimination provision of Title IX or of a failure by women activists in their continuing efforts to make Title IX's goals a full reality. It is essential to recall that success must be defined in terms of increments of change rather than total victory, although significant change may nevertheless be achieved. Also, though the sharpest attacks on Title IX are directed at equality in athletics, Title IX does affect many other aspects of the educational system. Admissions, course availability, student financial aid, counseling, housing and facilities, marital or parental status, scholarships, and employment practices all come under the purview of Title IX. Furthermore, sometimes changes have occurred in institutions because of multiple forces—internal pressures, influence of women activists, public opinion, the existence of Title IX— and not as a result of ongoing active enforcement by the OCR of the provisions of Title IX. Local-level monitoring by feminists, too, may make a difference in enforcement.[16] PEER's guide to ending local educational sex bias, *Cracking the Glass Slipper*, is one effort in this direction.

The extent of federal enforcement was quite constrained during the first years of Title IX's existence. In 1977, at least in part as a response to the PEER report, *Stalled at the Start*, some efforts were made to invigorate enforcement of the anti-sex-discrimination provisions of Title IX. The PEER report was specific in documenting claims by the OCR that it was under-

---

[16] June Petty, *Almost as Fairly: The First Year of Title IX Implementation in Six Southern States* (Atlanta: American Friends Service Committee, 1977). Despite a generally unfavorable picture, the author suggests that local-level monitoring does have some impact. A recent study of the Region X area makes similar points. See *Title IX Status in Region X: An Evaluation of Models and Barriers to Implementation of Title IX of the Educational Amend-Amendments of 1972, Government Region X of HEW* (Olympia, Wash.: Miller and Associates, 19781.

staffed and thus unable to address all of the problems brought to its attention and in compiling data on the limited response of the OCR to complaints of sex discrimination. PEER reported that during the first four years of Title IX's existence

> 871 complaints about elementary and secondary schools were received by HEW. Of these, 13 were lost within the agency. The remaining 858 charged discrimination within the institutions of every one of the 50 states. . . . HEW managed to resolve just 179 complaints. . . . Two- and three-year delays were not uncommon. More than a third of the complaints filed during 1973 were still unresolved three years later. . . . In more than four years, the agency completed independent checks on just 12 of the nation's 16,000 school districts. There was no follow-up on information it collected in several nationwide surveys which showed Title IX violations. . . . [F]rom 1973 to 1976, HEW received fewer than two Title IX complaints against public schools each year for each investigator on the payroll. Out of those, the agency managed to resolve an average of three-tenths of one complaint per investigator. Even when the agency's other civil rights responsibilities are added in . . . the total case load of complaints filed against public schools was just over six complaints per investigator each year.[17]

From the vantage point of what was gained from the investigations during the first four years of Title IX, the PEER report showed a rather dismal picture:

1. 18 of the nation's 16,000 school districts agreed to alter employment practices;
2. 21 districts agreed to upgrade sports programs;
3. 77 districts agreed to open traditionally male or female courses to both sexes;
4. 20 districts agreed to change sex-biased student rules; and

[17] PEER, *Stalled at the Start* (Washington, D.C.: NOW-LDEF, 1977).

5. 21 institutions agreed to miscellaneous other changes included in the law.[18]

As of 1980 the OCR had attempted to cut off funds in only 33 cases, and in only a relatively few of these did the OCR press its charges to the hearing stage. A 1979 study by the U.S. Commission on Civil Rights found that enforcement was "unduly slow," data collected very incomplete, and information about discriminatory practices disseminated to schools by the OCR quite inadequate.[19]

FEMINIST TACTICS TO
MAINTAIN TITLE IX ENFORCEMENT

In addition to the issuance of *Stalled at the Start* by PEER, feminist groups also sought to keep pressure on the federal government through *The Unenforced Law: Title IX Activity by Federal Agencies Other than HEW*, issued by the National Advisory Council of Women's Educational Programs in 1978 under the Women's Educational Equity Act. This study provided careful documentation of feminist allegations and directed public attention to nonenforcement. Feminists continued pressure for more vigorous enforcement and strengthened regulations through other techniques as well. A quarterly newsletter published by SPRINT, *In the Running*, has reported on the latest developments in athletic policy, while the *PEER Perspective* newsletter has provided interested feminists with detailed analysis of Title IX legislative and administrative activity. Feminists have held demonstrations and a marathon track meet to dramatize their continuing commitment to demands for favorable Title IX policy. They constantly pressed for meetings with HEW Secretaries (Richardson, Weinberger, Matthews, Califano, and Harris), OCR directors, and White House officials. The National Coalition has also lobbied members of Congress repeatedly, urging defeat of amendments that

[18] *Ibid.*, 7.
[19] *Chronicle of Higher Education*, Dec. 8, 1980, 11-12.

would cripple Title IX. With the change in Administration in 1981, many carefully nurtured contacts with members of the bureaucracy were nullified as numerous appointees hostile to the goals of the women's movement gained positions of prominence.

To gain compliance with Title IX, feminist activists have had recourse to the courts as well. The WEAL Fund, in conjunction with other feminist groups, took legal action against HEW's record of noncompliance with Title IX. Through the consent order entered against HEW in December 1977 in *WEAL* v. *Califano* and *Adams* v. *Califano*, HEW promised to meet specific timetables and move vigorously against sex-discrimination complaints. HEW also promised to eliminate its massive backlog of 841 complaints by October 1979 as well as investigate 120 new sex-discrimination complaints in 1978. HEW was obliged to schedule reviews for assessing institutional compliance with the law and to issue computerized information reporting enforcement every six months. In July 1979 women's groups led by the WEAL Fund went back to court to charge that HEW had not fulfilled its obligation to clear the backlog, respond to new complaints, and schedule reviews for assessing institutional compliance.[20] Although Judge John Pratt failed to find HEW and the OCR in contempt, the suit may have succeeded in its aim indirectly, since the agency issued favorable guidelines on athletic policy within the year.

Feminists won a significant victory, also in the judicial arena, when the Supreme Court ruled 6-3 in May 1979 in *Cannon* v. *University of Chicago*[21] that Title IX permits individuals the right to file private lawsuits against educational institutions to enforce the law. Given the OCR's sporadic record in responding to individual complaints and its failure ever to cut off federal funds to recalcitrant institutions, this ruling provided an alternative mechanism for enforcing Title IX and strengthening the law. On the other hand, the Supreme Court

[20] *Ibid.*, July 16, 1979, 7.
[21] 441 U.S. 677.

refused to review three lower court decisions holding that HEW does not have the authority to regulate employment practices under Title IX. This action leaves standing the lower court rulings that restrict Title IX's application to students only; the OCR indicated that it would continue to investigate employment bias in certain circumstances. The most recent judicial decision in the Grove City case presented a setback to feminist goals. Thus litigation efforts have met with mixed success.[22]

Pressure from feminist groups succeeded in gaining legitimacy in governmental circles for the National Coalition on Women and Girls in Education and the sixty-odd organizations it represents. Feminist groups gained access to the policy-making structure in Congress and to the OCR in the 1970s, although their legitimacy as a pressure group did not always guarantee a totally favorable outcome. When Cindy Brown was Deputy Director for Compliance and Enforcement of the OCR, she was representative of a new feminist influence within the policy-making structure. On the task force responsible for HEW's December 1978 policy interpretation of Title IX and athletics (to be discussed below) were two women sympathetic to the feininist movement, athletic directors Diane Wendt of the University of Colorado and Christine Grant of the University of Iowa. PEER was asked to help improve data collection and monitoring at HEW. Formal and informal associations within a feminist network, both on Capitol Hill and in HEW, that involve officeholders and staff helped to supply information and assess impact on Title IX. Feminist activists indicate that they have been approached frequently for information on Title IX, a significant measure of their credibility at the federal level.

TITLE IX UNTIL GROVE CITY

Largely because of *WEAL* v. *Califano*, there was some increased momentum in enforcing Title IX despite the continu-

[22] *Chronicle of Higher Education*, Dec. 3, 1979, 15.

ing opposition of the male athletic establishment. According to Cindy Brown, more compliance officers were assigned within HEW to examine charges of sex discrimination in education. However, although the size of the agency's staff trebled (with 898 new positions) only one-third of the new staff members' time was devoted to work on Title IX issues. HEW threatened (but did not follow through with these threats) to cut off funds to several districts and institutions that were resisting compliance.[23]

In the late 1970s, activity related to Title IX centered on athletic policy guidelines, in order to clarify what was meant by "reasonable provisions" for female participation in intercollegiate athletics pursuant to the Javits amendment of 1974. An April 1978 memorandum made public a directive from HEW Secretary Califano that reaffirmed the applicability to revenue-producing intercollegiate athletics of Title IX. A task force appointed to draft further policy guidelines to aid in implementing Title IX's application to intercollegiate athletics was established, as noted above, with representatives of women's interests as well as with representatives of the educational establishment and men's athletics. Despite extensive lobbying by the NCAA, major revenue-producing sports were included within the guidelines, although several potential loopholes were left open. The draft guidelines issued in December 1978 provided that "substantially equal per capita expenditures" be made for men's and women's athletics, including such things as scholarships, travel, and equipment. However, "unequal spending could be permitted if 'nondiscriminatory factors' were involved, viewed by some feminists as a back door approach to excluding big time college football from the constraints of Title IX."[24] While feminists generally supported the policy, which provided for a (two-stage) immediate and long-term program to upgrade women's athletics, they saw the proposals as "overly ambiguous and not going far enough toward

[23] *PEER Perspective* 4 (May 1978), 1.
[24] *Chronicle of Higher Education*, Dec. 18, 1978, 9, and *PEER Perspective* 5 (May 1979), 1.

equality."[25] Nonetheless, an attorney for the NCAA characterized the policy as having been written by representatives of
women's groups who had, in his view, "continuous and daily
input." He also indicated his perception of the dominant presence of feminist groups in Washington—eight women to every
NCAA spokesman. In his opinion, HEW staff members shared
the views and attitudes of the feminist lobbyists.

Although the guidelines sought to strike a balance between
feminists and the NCAA, during the period allowed for public
comment, which lasted until February 10,800 letters opposing
Title IX flooded both Congress and HEW. The NCAA again
sought to have Title IX amended to exclude revenue-producing sports and established a coalition of 300 colleges and universities to modify or eliminate the proposed guidelines. A letter submitted to HEW from Terry Sanford, President of Duke
University, and co-signed by presidents of several major college football powers called the equal per capita spending
standard "anathema" and asked that each institution be permitted to develop its own nondiscrimination plan. Holly
Knox, Director for PEER, retorted that this scheme was "little
like asking the fox to come up with a plan for guarding the
chickens."[26] Feminists countered the major university sports
plan through a Coalition alert that sought to mobilize phone,
mail, or personal visits to Congress to save the proposed policy
interpretation. Female athletes and coaches who were often
prevented from submitting comments through institutional
pressure demonstrated and lobbied in Washington to influence
Congress and HEW.[27]

At this stage feminists essentially prevailed in their three
goals: 1) to prevent Title IX from exempting revenue-producing sports, 2) to oppose riders to HEW's appropriations bill
that would inhibit HEW's ability to enforce Title IX in athletics, and 3) to persuade Secretary Harris to release the final pol-

[25] *On Campus With Women* 23 (Spring 1979), 1.
[26] *Chronicle of Higher Education*, June 18, 1979, 12.
[27] *Ibid.*, April 27, 1979, 19.

icy interpretation without submitting it to Congress for what might be weakening review.

The guidelines as finally issued in December 1979 called for colleges and universities to provide "proportionately equal" scholarships for men's and women's athletic programs. They also had to offer "equivalent" benefits and opportunities in other aspects of intercollegiate sports. Secretary Harris appeared to strengthen the Department's resolve to enforce compliance when she released a list of 62 colleges which had not complied with sex-discrimination regulations. The feminist community was generally supportive of the policy interpretation, considerably different from the 1978 draft, while remaining vigilant regarding the actual process of implementation. The NCAA indicated it was "very concerned" about the standard requiring "proportionately equal amounts of financial assistance" to be made available to male and female athletes.[28] The NCAA's Executive Director, stating his concern with what he termed the new policy's "sex dictated quota system," predicted that a legal test would be sought.[29] Secretary Harris stressed the flexibility inherent in the new policy, but promised that no sports, including those producing revenue, would be exempt. She indicated that 120 persons in the OCR would be responsible for enforcement, although ultimately the policy would come under the jurisdiction of the new Department of Education. Thus seven years after the initial passage of Title IX, clarification for the issue of athletics finally arrived.

In an earlier test of strength between the feminist movement and the NCAA, the politics of Title IX emerged at the United States Commission on Civil Rights as well as at HEW. The Commission held hearings in December 1978 on the Title IX proposals and urged HEW to exempt football from the requirement for equal spending, recommending instead a five-year "adjustment period" for equal football expenditures to be "phased in." Feminists countered by demanding a reanalysis

[28] *Ibid.*, Dec. 10, 1979, 1, 14.
[29] *New York Times*, Dec. 7, 1979, D19.

and rehearing (held on July 9) of the Commission's findings, In a reversal of its earlier position, the Commission in September 1979 urged that colleges be asked immediately to equalize their expenditures on athletic programs for men and women and recommended the same to HEW. The reversal was hailed by feminist groups, which had lobbied hard for the reheating and reconsideration, and denounced by the NCAA, in what had become a familiar political configuration.[30] Feminists were successful in gaining access and influence on this issue, a major priority for them.

The policy interpretation on athletics led to legal action by the NCAA, which contended that the new regulations were "arbitrary and capricious" and exceeded congressional intent. Failing to succeed in the legal and political arenas, the NCAA successfully sought the demise of the AIAW. The NCAA took over the field of women's athletics by setting up a competing program of women's championships and offering economic benefits (such as payment of travel expenses for teams going to championship meets) that AIAW could not match.[31] The controversy regarding Title IX and its precise meaning has therefore continued in several different arenas.

TITLE IX SINCE 1982

Title IX has had a profound impact on the patterns of participation of women and girls in school-related athletic programs since its enactment in 1972. Between 1972-73 and 1982-83, the number of girls participating in sports in public high schools grew by nearly 114 percent from 800,000 to nearly 1.8 million. During this same period, the number of boys participating in school-related athletics dropped by 11 percent.[32] Involvement in athletics is seen as a mechanism for developing

[30] *Chronicle of Higher Education* Sept. 17, 1979, 15.

[31] *On Campus With Women* 27 (Summer 1980), 3; *Chronicle of Higher Education*, Jan. 14, 1980, 1, 14; *Chronicle of Higher Education*, May 9, 1983, 17, 20, and May 30, 1984, 27.

[32] *New York Times*, April 5, 1985, Cl.

leadership. It has also been identified as a way to teach decision making and to facilitate the development of organizational skills. Moreover, athletic achievement bears directly on the emergence of self-confidence and self-esteem.[33] The success experienced by American women in the 1984 Olympic Games and in such intercollegiate sports as basketball has been partially attributed to the role of Title IX in creating awareness of possibilities among athletes and the general public.[34]

Numerous female athletes who participated in the 1984 Olympics traced their success to Title IX. The head of the Women's Sports Foundation was quoted as saying: "Thank Title IX for some of that Olympic gold. The whole world was watching women's success and the catalyst for growth was Title IX. It forced colleges to broaden their sports programs and women finally are reaching their potential as athletes."[35] Of the more than 200 women on the U.S. Olympic team, over 170 received their training at universities that complied with Title IX regulations. Before the implementation of Title IX there were only about 16,000 women participating in college athletic programs annually. By 1984 this figure had changed dramatically, and over 150,000 women were involved in these programs. By the mid-1980s more than 10,000 women were receiving athletic scholarships, whereas in 1972 such awards rarely if ever were given to women. The amount of money spent on women's sports programs increased during this period from 1 percent of total college athletic expenditures to 16 percent.[36] In addition to increasing opportunities for women athletes, opportunities for female coaches have increased, too.

Some of the positive effects of Title IX may prove to be mitigated by the Supreme Court's decision in *Grove City* v. *Bell*,[37] which set forth a narrow interpretation of the federal law barring sex discrimination in education. The case, brought by a

[33] *Ibid.*, B4.
[34] *Chronicle of Higher Education*, Dec. 5, 1984, 36, and Aug. 23, 1984, 31.
[35] *Ibid.*
[36] *Chronicle of Higher Education*, Dec. 7, 1983, 19.
[37] 103 S. Ct. 1211 (1984).

small Pennsylvania liberal arts college, directly concerned the scope of Title IX, in particular the issue of whether an entire educational institution or simply the actual program that is receiving federal money would be bound not to discriminate on the basis of sex. Whereas previous administrations had supported the broader interpretation of the law, the Reagan Administration supported the narrower or "program specific" approach to bias. In a 6-3 decision the Supreme Court held that the government does not have broad, institutionwide authority to enforce Title IX whenever schools receive federal money. The ramifications of the decision extended beyond Title IX alone because other laws including Title VI of the Civil Rights Act, Section 504 of the Rehabilitation Act, and the Age Discrimination Act all have similar language and are therefore affected as well.[38]

Since this decision had implications for groups other than women, a broad-based coalition, similar to that organized around the Pregnancy Discrimination Act, swung into action, with involvement by groups representing the civil rights community, the disabled, and the aged. They all worked under the aegis of the Leadership Conference on Civil Rights and the National Coalition for Women and Girls in Education in order to restore the concept of federal fund cutoffs from an entire institution guilty of bias in any program. At the outset approximately forty groups met to discuss the situation and to outline a strategy. It was decided immediately that any presentation had to move beyond Title IX and its effect on women and include all the other groups that were affected by the Grove City ruling. The goal that they set was the passage of a law by Congress that would restore the law to its pre-Grove City status. Furthermore, they decided to press their legislative supporters to put a proposed law on a "fast track" since it was already the second session of the 98th Congress. A subcommittee of the

[38] The following discussion about the 1984 campaign to enact the Civil Rights Act of 1984 relies heavily upon an interview with Ralph Neas, Leadership Conference on Civil Rights, Aug. 30, 1984.

steering committee of the coalition drafted a bill, within one week of the convening of the coalition. Members of Congress were lobbied in an effort to generate general support for the legislation. These efforts were especially directed toward the Senate. During March and early April 1984, the members of the Coalition focused their efforts on drafting and redrafting the bill and lobbying members of Congress. They also worked at the grassroots level on an effort to mobilize congressional co-sponsors, and in fact they were able to gain 63 Senate co-sponsors and 25 co-sponsors in the House of Representatives for the proposed legislation. They started very slowly in their relations with the press because they did not want to provide the opposition with lead time to set up a counter strategy.

On April 12, 1984, the Coalition held a press conference at which the bill was first introduced to the public. Several senators and representatives attended the presentation, including Senators Dole, Packwood, and Kennedy, the principal co-sponsors of the Senate legislation. At the press conference it was made clear that this was not being identified as a women's issue but rather as a broader-based civil rights issue to which women were a party. Moreover, the supporters of the bill gave notice that if only Title IX and women's grievances were addressed by Congress, the members of the Coalition—aged, disabled, civil rights, and women's groups—would actively oppose it.

At about this time right-wing groups, especially the Christian Broadcasting System, began to develop their own program to oppose the passage of what was to be called the Civil Rights Act of 1984. The opponents of the proposed law claimed that the bill was an attempt at a "big power grab" and that it would eliminate the distinctions between private and public sector activities. In the Senate the proposed legislation was sent to the Committee on Labor and Human Resources, which was chaired by Orrin Hatch (R-Utah), a staunch opponent of any omnibus legislation that would override the Grove City decision. Steven Markman, Director and Chief Counsel of the Constitution Subcommittee of the Senate Judiciary Committee, which Senator Hatch also chaired, suggested that what was wrong with the Civil Rights Act of 1984 was not only the blurring of boundaries between the public and the private sectors but also its possible effects on federal-state relations. Senator Hatch, he noted, actually supported the overruling of the Grove City decision; his opposition was to the omnibus legislation because of the potential for the expansion of federal power at the expense of the states.[39] Opposition to the Civil Rights Act, Markman averred, was reasonably broad-based and included the U.S. Catholic Conference, National Association of Counties, Chamber of Commerce, National Association of Governors, National Association of Small Businesses, the Baptist Convention, and a variety of smaller organizations. Working with Senator Hatch in his opposition to the passage of this bill were the White House, William Bradford Reynolds, Assistant Attorney General for Civil Rights, the Civil Rights Commission, and the Office of Management and Budget.[40]

Some efforts were made to develop a compromise, and staff members from Reynolds's staff and from Senator Kennedy's and Senator Packwood's staffs met to try to come to some mutually acceptable agreement regarding a legislative solution to the Grove City decision. The talks, however, amounted to nothing.[41]

The proposed Civil Rights Act of 1984 would have forbidden discrimination by any recipient of federal money, with "recipient" defined as any organization that received federal money directly or indirectly, or "transferee" to whom federal aid was shifted.[42] The legislation as it was passed in the House of Representatives by a vote of 375-32 provided for the overturn of the Court decision and for the restoration of the full

[39] Interview with Steven Markman, Director and Chief Counsel, Constitution Subcommittee of the Senate Judiciary Committee, Sept. 24, 1984.

[40] *Ibid.*

[41] Interview with Carolyn Ossonlinick, staff member, Office of Senator Edward Kennedy, Aug. 30, 1984.

[42] *New York Times Magazine*, May 6, 1984, 1.

range of enforcement powers, including the sanction of federal funds cut off to an entire institution even if just one program was not in compliance with the law. However, in the Senate, the legislation was stalled by opposition from the Reagan Administration and conservative senators led by Senator Hatch.[43]

Delaying tactics were employed by Senator Hatch, who promised to "fight the bill with everything I've got unless its language is substantially altered."[44] Numerous, and nongermane, amendments were introduced to prevent the bill from coming to a vote. In the end, Senator Packwood tabled the bill he had co-sponsored owing to the parliamentary impasse occasioned by successful filibustering. Senator Hatch and other opponents of the legislation threatened to attach over 1,300 amendments to the continuing resolution on federal funding if the Senate voted to attach the civil rights measure to it.[45] The parliamentary stalemate threatened to delay the Senate's adjournment and created intense pressure to break the deadlock. Supporters of the measure, who felt they had at least 40 votes with which to pass it, were angered by Majority Leader Baker, who agreed to schedule the measure for debate only if a compromise agreement could be worked out beforehand.[46]

Efforts continued in the next session of Congress to pass the Civil Rights Restoration Act of 1985, in order to broaden the narrow interpretation of federal anti-bias laws. The proposed legislation, sponsored again by a bipartisan group of senators and representatives, would have applied not only to education but also to hospitals, social service agencies, housing, and transportation.[47] At the same time Senate Majority Leader Dole introduced a measure that would have applied only to educational institutions that received federal aid. The new bill carefully sought to define what a federally assisted program or

[43] *Chronicle of Higher Education*, Aug. 29, 1984, 31.

[44] *Chronicle of Higher Education*, June 20, 1984, 11.

[45] *Chronicle of Higher Education*, Oct. 10, 1984, 22.

[46] *Ibid.*

[47] *Chronicle of Higher Education*, Jan. 30, 1985, 23.

activity means, in order to eliminate problems some senators had with the language in 1984.

By the end of the second session of the 98th Congress, legislative efforts to overturn the Supreme Court's Grove City decision were still stymied by efforts to retain the narrow language of the Court ruling that aimed at dividing the allies who had been united on a broad approach to civil rights enforcement. In the House amendments on abortion language and exemptions for church-related institutions were added.[48] In the absence of legislation similar to that which resulted in the Pregnancy Discrimination Act, the Court decision still holds. It is not clear how significant the impact of the Supreme Court ruling has been or will be. However, the Education Department has put numerous complaints about discrimination on college campuses "on hold." A law suit filed in June 1984 by the National Women's Law Center charged that the agency was closing or suspending cases without issuing any rules or spelling out precise changes in enforcement policies required by the Supreme Court ruling.[49] In response, "initial guidance" in the form of a memorandum to regional civil rights offices was issued, but no followup ever appeared. Harry Singelton, head of the Department of Education's Office for Civil Rights, indicated that in the wake of Grove City he felt the OCR did not have jurisdiction to investigate a complaint on sex discrimination in Penn State's athletic program.[50] At least 23 investigations were closed and over 50 others reviewed by the OCR. Nonetheless, numerous college administrators and lawyers have indicated that the decision may have little practical effect and that they would continue the anti-discriminatory policies already put into practice after 1972.[51]

Until early 1984, when the Supreme Court handed down its decision in *Grove City* v. *Bell*, the women's movement was able to forestall any attempts to alter the intent of Title IX de-

[48] *Chronicle of Higher Education*, May 15, 1985, 1.
[49] *Chronicle of Higher Education*, April 3, 1985, 22.
[50] *New York Times*, June 3, 1984, 36.
[51] *Chronicle of Higher Education*, March 14, 1984, 27.

spite numerous attacks. Although coalition efforts have been mounted with considerable congressional support to overturn the Grove City decision, by mid-1986 they had not proved successful. In large measure the failure to override the Court decision with a new law has been stalled by a well-organized minority that has the endorsement of the Administration and key conservative members of Congress, especially Senator Hatch. While opposition to the Civil Rights Act of 1984 was forthcoming from a number of groups, this alone might not have prevented easy passage of the act. It was the ongoing antipathy of the Reagan Administration, which had submitted an *amicus curiae* brief in behalf of the narrow restrictive interpretation of the law, along with Senator Hatch's strategizing, that led to its ultimate failure to be enacted in 1984 and 1985.

CONCLUSION

In the years since the initial enactment of Title IX of the Education Amendments of 1972, there have been many attempts to alter the intent of the law, both by amendment and by regulation. Even before 1984 actual enforcement was clearly uneven. The role of women's groups in influencing the writing of regulations and enforcement of the law has been difficult because of the resistance stemming from the personal values of members of Congress and the bureaucracy (especially regarding sports) and the existence of organized counterpressures.

Feminists used a variety of strategies including litigation, publicity, and monitoring in order to influence the policy-making process. Through the use of a highly effective coalition, the Coalition for Women and Girls in Education, they shared information, effectively divided responsibility, and presented a united political front and the image of broad-based political support. The maintenance of this effective single-issue group, which drew on the resources of mass membership groups, specialized research and legal organizations, and staff and elected officeholders in federal office, gained credibility for feminist interests in education. Feminists gained access to the policy-making process both in Congress and in HEW. In Congress they beat back repeated efforts to weaken Title IX through riders and modified appropriations. At the Office of Civil Rights they were viewed as "the most assertive, viable, and well-organized group," according to one long-time observer. They gained a consulting role, were able to place feminists in positions of influence within the agency, and won access to Secretary Califano, and then to Secretary Harris, pressuring them to move toward issuance of long-desired rules clarifying the relationship between Title IX and intercollegiate athletics. But they were not able to influence the outcome of the Court decision in *Grove City* v. *Bell*. Nor as part of a larger civil rights coalition have they been able to win prompt reversal of this ruling.

While most policy makers viewed the feminists as persuasive and often highly effective, this opinion is not universally shared by all the involved actors. One high-level HEW administrator referred to the feminist constituency as "the most vocal, not necessarily the most effective" group pressuring for policy change at the OCR. A member of the U.S. Commission on Civil Rights referred to the adversarial relationship feminists have had with the Commission; she commented that they did little to maintain ongoing relationships with the Commission's staff. (The reason may be the limited attention the Commission has paid to most women's issues and the feminists' need to conserve their resources and energy.) Another OCR policy administrator commented that "although feminists yell the loudest, Title IX is the worst enforced law." Nonetheless, he suggested that when feminists were successful, it was because they were good politicians who "understand, compromise—would help us as soon as beat us over the head." This policy maker also indicated that feminists were justified in their concern over the slowness with which the agency had dealt with policy implementation. In his view, although feminists sometimes squandered their resources on "unimportant" issues such as hair and dress codes, without them there would be no policy on athletics. He averred that feminist lobbying on Capitol Hill was particularly potent—"they came in with facts and neutralized the opposition effectively." At the administrative level, the use of the marathon track meet mentioned above and constant pressure on Secretary Califano led to a belated but ultimate acceptance not necessarily of feminist views but of their influence and tenacity.

The issue of athletics is one particularly challenging to values regarding the place of women in society and moves from the more easily resolved role equity issues to those of role change. Despite this characteristic, and the existence of formidable adversaries in the NCAA and among prominent college and university presidents, feminists have held their own. It should be noted that on several occasions—in 1975, when the regulations were reviewed by Congress, and in 1979, when the athletics guidelines representing a compromise between feminists and the athletic community were issued—women's groups were in the position of defending policies with which they were not entirely comfortable. But they felt that the realities of politics required a philosophy of pragmatism and have worked to gain acceptance for such policies.

Reversing the *Grove City* decision has become a goal for civil rights activists generally. The women's movement represents one component of the coalition that has been trying to influence Congress to enact legislation that would overturn the ruling. As the arena of politics has broadened, with the changed scope of the issue, there are now new opponents with different agendas. As a result, the scope of conflict has been expanded and resolution of the issue has become more difficult. The role change/role equity scheme is no longer as clearly applicable to this case as it was prior to the change in the issue's scope.

Nevertheless, despite efforts to stall enforcement of Title IX, especially regarding athletics, and more recently to limit its impact by judicial action and legislative inaction, substantial changes have taken place. Increasingly, women's sports are receiving additional institutional funding; scholarships are being made available to women athletes; more options in sports are open to women; and physical education classes are integrated. Because feminist groups have been united and have played by the "rules of the game," they have succeeded where a more shrill and less organized approach might have led to a different outcome. Furthermore, by constantly monitoring the political process, they have not been caught unawares when a new effort to water down the law or the regulations has been attempted. In the absence of feminist pressure before 1984, Congress would most probably have vitiated Title IX while HEW would have ignored it. The continuing dynamics of Title IX will focus on the strength of opposition groups, politics at the Department of Education, problems of maintaining financial resources for feminist groups, and continuing efforts to monitor policy at the local as well as federal level.

CHAPTER 6

WOMEN DIVIDED
AMONG THEMSELVES:
"THE RIGHT TO LIFE" VERSUS
"FREE CHOICE"

INTRODUCTION

More than any other area of policy considered here, the issue of free choice in abortion appears to involve questions of fundamental role change for women. Peter Skerry has argued that "the defense of traditional moral and sexual values underlies the resistance to abortion reform."[1] Abortion is seen as a technique for preventing or postponing families, hence as a threat to the traditional family structure. Others have found that anti-abortion attitudes are correlated with opposition to premarital sex, divorce, contraception, and sex education.[2] Thus the issue of women's control of their reproductive capacity seems to touch the core of sexual politics and to challenge basic values about appropriate sexual and social behavior. There appears to be a deep-seated anxiety about the consequences if and when women are freed from the restraints of biological motherhood.[3] The essence of power relationships in society may be at stake in the abortion issue.

[1] Peter Skerry, "The Class Conflict Over Abortion," *Public Interest* 52 (Summer 1978), 52, 70, 79.

[2] Donald Granberg, "Pro Life or Reflection of Conservative Ideology," *Sociology and Social Research* 62 (April 1978), 414-29.

[3] Barbara Hayler, "Abortion," *Signs* 5 (Winter 1979), 322-23.

BACKGROUND

Abortion was widely accepted in the United States until the middle of the nineteenth century. Prior to the nineteenth century the legal status of abortion followed the traditional British common law. For hundreds of years before 1800 the governing principle regarding abortion was tied to quickening. Quickening is the first sense of fetal movement felt by the mother. Such fetal movement usually occurs late in the fourth month or early in the fifth month of pregnancy. The common law did not recognize the existence of a fetus in criminal cases until such quickening had taken place. In addition, destruction of a fetus in the second half of a pregnancy was punished less harshly than the destruction of other human life. Before quickening the termination of a pregnancy was not considered criminal in England or the United States. The moral question whether or not a fetus is a living being had been debated for thousands of years. In fact, the British common law doctrine, tied as it was to the quickening doctrine, apparently arose out of the medieval disputes over whether an ovum possessed a soul.[4]

During the nineteenth century abortion began to be proscribed and punished by criminal law in virtually every state in the Union. Between 1821 and 1841 ten states and one territory enacted laws that made certain kinds of abortion violations of statutes, rather than leaving common law practice as the governing doctrine.[5] The trend to enact anti-abortion laws continued unabated until the end of the nineteenth century. The laws became harsher as the years wore on. Every state except Kentucky had an anti-abortion law by 1900. In Kentucky the state courts outlawed the practice.[6]

A recent analysis of these stringent anti-abortion laws suggests that the radical reversal of previous customs was linked in part to efforts by the "regular" physicians to regain control

[4] James Mohr, *Abortion in America 1800-1900* (New York: Oxford University Press, 1978), 3-4.

[5] *Ibid.*, 20.

[6] *Ibid.*, 229-30.

over medical practice and to nativist prejudice that feared the dominance of immigrant populations in the absence of a prohibition against abortion. Hence criminal abortion statutes were not motivated primarily by concern for the physical dangers of abortion to women, despite rhetoric that sometimes emphasized such concern.[7]

Physicians dedicated to the principles of scientific medicine, known collectively as "regulars," tended to be graduates of the country's better medical schools or to follow the lead of those who were. As a group they believed in such principles as rational research and cooperative exchange of information. These regulars organized and maintained state and local medical societies, published journals, and worked to maintain high educational standards at the nation's medical schools. Other physicians, known as "irregulars," who were not committed to the same principles as the regulars, were entering the medical profession in unprecedented numbers. They were in competition with the regulars for patients. The regular physicians often were in moral opposition to abortion—related in part to their roles as "social and intellectual modernizers in a world that still took for granted the assumption that a widespread and routine destruction of life was part of the human condition," or perhaps their desire "to find secular absolutes to replace spiritual ones."[8] Furthermore, the regular physicians perceived that abortion was a medical procedure that gave their competition, the irregulars, a competitive edge and also undermined the unity of their own ranks. As more and more irregulars began to advertise their willingness to perform abortions, especially after 1840, the regulars began to grow more and more concerned about losing their practices. If a woman went to an irregular for an abortion, she might continue using that doctor for other medical needs, thus affecting the size of the clientele of the regular physicians over the long term.[9]

[7] *Ibid.*, 255-56.
[8] *Ibid.*, 36.
[9] *Ibid.*, 36-38.

The regulars' triumph over their competition in getting restrictive legislation passed ushered in an era when abortions became increasingly difficult to obtain legally, an era that lasted until 1973. In that year, in its decision in *Roe* v. *Wade*,[10] the Supreme Court struck down restrictive anti-abortion laws in the United States. According to one analysis of the abortion struggle, "feminist organizations adopted the cause of abortion reform or repeal as a rallying point. In the social history of the movement, abortion may have been as significant a unifying goal . . . as the movement was to changing abortion attitudes."[11] In *Roe* v. *Wade* the Supreme Court held that the "right of privacy" includes the decision to have an abortion, but that the state's compelling interest in regulating abortion increased after the first trimester of pregnancy. The Court rejected the view that an unborn fetus has a constitutional "right to life."

The Court's decision effected nationwide changes of significant magnitude. In 1973 a total of 745,000 legal abortions were performed in the United States; by 1977 the number had grown to 1.3 million. However, it has been estimated that 600,000 women who wanted abortions in 1977 were still not able to obtain them. Poor women, teenagers, minority women, and rural women were most affected by the inaccessibility of abortion procedures due to distance, lack of funds, or lack of knowledge regarding availability.[12]

In response to the decision, two opposing trends emerged and soon came into direct conflict. The feminist movement through coalitions and other efforts coalesced behind the decision, and even groups such as WEAL that had initially opposed "free choice" for abortion rallied in support of this issue. At the same time the judicial decisions helped generate a vigorous organized opposition that sought legislative and con-

---

[10] 410 U.S. 113.

[11] Malcolm Potts, Peter Diggory, and John Peel, *Abortion* (New York: Cambridge University Press, 1977), 357.

[12] *Abortions and the Poor: Private Morality, Public Responsibility* (New York: Alan Guttmacher Institute, 1979), 5.

stitutional amendments restricting access to abortion. These efforts have continued and have limited implementation of the 1973 Court ruling, even leading to modifications of it. A highly mobilized anti-choice movement, which calls itself the "right-to-life" movement, with considerable grassroots support and the backing of the Catholic Church has been unremitting in its efforts to limit access to abortion in every way possible.

This is the context in which the politics of abortion must be considered: the expansion of conflict, changing societal values, highly mobilized supporters and opponents, and political activity relating to abortion at numerous points in the political process. Like Title IX, implementation of abortion reform involves activity at the federal level as well as local discretion.

This issue, unlike others examined in this study, pits women against one another. Powerful political symbols have been manipulated by both sides in the struggle to attempt to sway public opinion their way. Conflict has escalated, drawing larger numbers into active or peripheral participation. Succinctly, "pro-choice" activists may be said to hold the view that the reproductive decision is possibly the most important a woman can make; it is a fundamental issue of self-determination. In contrast to this position emphasizing *women's rights*, "right-to-life" activists are concerned with the *rights of the fetus*, whom they believe to have a soul and the same rights as any other human being. Although not all the political decision makers who have eroded the blanket *Roe* v. *Wade* pro-choice decision justify their positions in theological and moral terms, many do. The ideological underpinnings of the pro-life movement itself rest on theological and moral grounds. It is the belief of pro-lifers that life begins at conception and thus the aborting of a fetus is equivalent to murder. Most pro-choice supporters of the feminist movement adhere to the view that life begins with viability of a baby out of its mother's body and thus the termination of a pregnancy in the early months is not the ending of a human life. Advocates of free choice sometimes question at what point a fetus is viable, but most agree that this is reached in the last trimester. Medical opinion varies on the question of viability, though scientific support exists for the viability of a fetus out of the mother's womb in the last half of pregnancy.

In the remainder of this chapter the major participants—both in government and among interest groups—will be identified and analyzed. In addition, their interactions in coalitions and in strategies pursued will be examined in relation to legislative activity and judicial decisions. In particular, we will look closely at the political decision making surrounding the Hyde amendment to the HEW annual appropriation. Because of the role change aspects of "free choice," feminists have met stiffer opposition to their goals on this issue than they have on role equity issues. Increasingly, pro-choice forces have been forced to seek alternative routes to the legislative process. They have pursued legal strategies and have turned to grassroots organizing and active campaigning for pro-choice candidates for public office in order to recoup their earlier position that seemed so promising in 1973.

Abortion Politics

The 1973 Supreme Court decision in *Roe* v. *Wade* was seen as a major advance in women's rights. However, in the aftermath of the decision, the right-to-life movement has worked to weaken its impact by influencing members of Congress to pursue legislative countermeasures. In addition to gaining passage of the Hyde amendment to the annual appropriations bill for HEW and the Labor Department, which restricts government funding of abortions for poor women, right-to-life strategists have sought to get anti-abortion amendments attached to many significant appropriation bills. This is a short-term tactic inasmuch as their long-term goal is to secure an anti-abortion amendment to the Constitution.

Though divided on specific aspects of the credit law, women's groups were all in agreement that a legislative solution was necessary in order to eliminate credit discrimination against women. No strong counterpressures to the intent of a law were generated, and no strong moral or cultural opposition to equal credit existed. In fact, equal credit was a reasonably clear case of a demand for role equity and thus easily gained legitimacy. In contrast, feminist activists have confronted strong countermobilization on the issue of "free choice" and have emerged with varying degrees of success.

Since 1974, in an attempt to limit the impact of *Roe* v. *Wade*, which denied states the right to interfere with a woman's decision to have an abortion during the first trimester of pregnancy, Representative Henry J. Hyde (R–Ill.) annually has introduced an amendment to the appropriations bill for HEW and Labor banning the use of Medicaid funds to pay for abortions. The original Hyde amendment essentially denied Medicaid funding for abortion except in very restrictive circumstances (1) where the mother's life is endangered, (2) where she would suffer "severe and long-lasting health damage" as certified by two physicians, and (3) where pregnancy is due to rape or incest as reported promptly to a law enforcement agency or public health service.

Congressional debate has centered on the language of the amendment, with feminists seeking the vaguest language possible and right-to-life advocates striving to obtain the most restrictive wording possible—abortion only when the mother's life is endangered. During the annual confrontation the House has proven to be more prone to accept anti-abortion appeals while the Senate until 1979 held out for a pro-choice perspective. The inconsistencies between bills passed by the two houses were resolved by conference committee. In 1974 and 1975 the Congress failed to approve the Hyde amendment. In 1976 the House easily approved the amendment, but the Senate refused to ban federal funding of abortions for the poor. On August 25, 1976, the Senate voted 35-53 to reject the Hyde amendment and sent it back to the conference committee, where the Senate conferees had previously compromised and accepted it. Senators Birch Bayh (D–Ind.), Edward Brooke (R–Mass.), and Robert Packwood (R–Ore.) led the "free choice" forces in the Senate, which were adamant in their pro-choice position, while in the House support for the Hyde amendment was increasing. As a result, conferees from each house were locked into their differing positions on the issue. Representative Silvio Conte (R–Mass.) offered a compromise proposal that finally proved acceptable to the conferees. The substitute amendment barred the use of federal funds to pay for abortions "except where the life of the mother would be endangered if the fetus were carried to term." The language used was intentionally vague, and Conte was quoted as saying that "it will be up to HEW to interpret this." The appropriations bill with the modified Hyde amendment was approved by both houses of Congress and was sent to President Ford for his signature. The President vetoed the bill. At that time liberals were placed in the uncomfortable position of wanting to vote to override the veto because of the funding for human resource needs that were included in the bill. Members of Congress who were opposed to the Hyde amendment, such as Representative Bella Abzug (D–N.Y.), who called the anti-choice amendment "unconstitutional, illegal and discriminating," felt obligated to vote to override because they supported the spending levels in the bill. The House voted to override the veto by a vote of 312 to 93. The Senate followed suit with a vote of 67 to 15. The ban on the use of federal funds to pay for abortions thus became law in part as a result of votes by liberal, pro-choice members of Congress.[13]

Additional review of this issue is useful in order to understand the problems women confronted in this area. The ban was enacted into law for FY 1977; however, it was not implemented at that time because a federal injunction, resulting from a legal challenge, was initiated in the Federal District Court for the Eastern District of New York. In fact, the pro-choice groups under the direction of the National Abortion Rights Action League had laid plans for a court test of the

[13] *Congressional Quarterly 1976 Almanac* (Washington, D.C.: Congressional Quarterly, 1976), 802-804.

modified version of the Hyde amendment as soon as the bill became law, and both they and their congressional allies were less insistent on a favorable bill for FY 1977 because of their certainty of reversal in the Supreme Court.[14] To the surprise and chagrin of women activists, the Supreme Court ruled on June 20, 1977, in *Maher* v. *Roe*[15] that it is not a violation of constitutional "equal protection" for a state participating in a Medicaid program to refuse to pay expenses incident to non-therapeutic abortions. A second decision, *Beal* v. *Doe*,[16] found that exclusion of nontherapeutic abortions under Title XIX of the Social Security Act (Medicaid) was not "unreasonable."

Subsequent legislative debate in the summer and autumn of 1977 dealt primarily with the issue of whether Congress would vote an absolute ban on use of federal funds for all Medicaid abortions or whether language adopted in the Senate on June 30, 1977, to ban federal funds except when the mother's life is in danger, when the cause of pregnancy is rape or incest, or when it is considered "medically necessary" would prevail. On December 7, 1977, a partial ban was approved and written into the law, when the House of Representatives finally approved compromise language by a vote of 191 to 167. The FY 1978 amendment provided for federally funded abortions if the mother would suffer "severe and long-lasting health damage" in the event of the birth, and also provided for the funding of "medical procedures" in cases of rape or incest promptly reported to relevant law enforcement or health authorities. The Secretary of HEW was instructed to promulgate directives for implementation.[17]

Joseph Califano, Secretary of HEW during the early years of Jimmy Carter's presidency, was, like the President himself, firmly opposed to free choice. (It should be noted here that President Carter, though opposed to abortion, never favored a

[14] *New York Times*, June 2, 1977, 22; *Congressional Quarterly 1976 Almanac, ibid.*

[15] 97 S. Ct. 2376.

[16] 97 S. Ct. 2366.

[17] *New York Times*, Dec. 8, 1977, 1.

constitutional amendment to ban it.) Although HEW statistics showed that, as a result of the initial Hyde amendments and the implementing regulations, Medicaid abortions had decreased by about 98 percent in 21 states, Califano approved amended regulations effective August 1978 that further tightened the implementation of the Hyde amendment. The amended regulations require a victim of rape or incest who seeks an abortion to disclose her address, the date of the incident, and the date of the report. If another person reports the incident, he or she must give a name and address. The initial regulations required only the name of the victim. NARAL leadership feared that the changed regulations would pose a question of privacy for the woman and would make it more difficult for a woman to report such a crime when her address would become known to law enforcement officials and the press. Also, physicians certifying severe and long-lasting physical damage must include the patient's address. The two physicians who certify such "damage" must, moreover, be "financially independent" of each other; that is, the income of more than one of the doctors must not be affected by the abortion fee.[18] These regulations have remained in place for all subsequent Hyde amendments. The pro-choice coalition was unable to effect any loosening of the regulations during Califano's tenure at HEW.

The pro-choice groups continued to lobby on the Hill for an end to subsequent Hyde amendments or at least for a loosening of the anti-choice language. But the 1977 experience was repeated in both 1978 for the fiscal 1979 budget and in 1979 for the fiscal 1980 budget, though the results for the pro-choice coalition were considerably more devastating for fiscal 1980 than they had been in the earlier years. On June 27, 1979, Representative David Obey (D–Wis.) introduced an amendment in the House of Representatives that would have continued the Medicaid funding restrictions that had been law for the prior two fiscal years. The amendment was defeated

[18] *NARAL Newsletter* 10 (Aug-Sept 1978), 1.

241-180 because anti-choice forces argued that the language was "too liberal" and was tantamount to providing "abortion on demand." On July 27, 1979, the Senate voted 57-42 to continue to use the language of the existing amendment (that is, the same language as the Obey amendment).[19] This was a weakening of the Senate position of previous years when they had supported funding for all "medically necessary" abortions. Next, when the House of Representatives voted out its version of the HEW-Labor appropriations bill, it included an amendment that would have funded abortions only when the life of the mother is endangered. The Senate, as just noted, in its version of the appropriations bill included the less restrictive amendment. The Senate and House conferees could not reach any mutually acceptable position on the abortion amendment, and thus in FY 1980 the Departments of HEW and Labor were funded under a continuing appropriations resolution. This resolution, however, prohibited abortion funding except when the life of the mother is endangered or pregnancy results from rape or incest. This is stricter language than the 1978 amendment, which provided funding for abortions when the life of the mother is endangered, when pregnancy results from rape or incest, or when severe and long-lasting physical health damage is certified.[20]

In fact, 1979 was not a very good year for the pro-choice forces in Congress in part because of the electoral defeats of such strong pro-choice advocates as Senator Edward Brooke (R–Mass.). The right-to-life strategy of chipping away everywhere seemed to gain new adherents. Whereas the FY 1979 Department of Defense appropriations bill allowed some funding for abortions, the FY 1980 Defense appropriations bill was more restrictive, with abortion funding for Department of Defense personnel limited to life endangerment, rape, or incest. For the Foreign Assistance appropriations bill, the Senate as well as the House agreed to prohibit any money to be

[19] *NARAL Newsletter* 11 (Sept. 1979), 5.
[20] *NARAL Newsletter* 12 (Jan.1980), 6.

used for abortions for Peace Corps volunteers even in cases of life endangerment. And in 1979 the FY 1980 District of Columbia appropriations bill became the target of anti-choice forces. Representative Robert Dornan (R–Calif.) introduced an amendment that would have prohibited the use of all D.C. funds, including those raised by local tax sources, to pay for abortions except in cases of life endangerment. However, the Senate D.C. Appropriations Committee Chairman, Senator Patrick Leahy (D–Vt.), and the ranking minority member, Senator Charles Mathias, Jr. (R–Md.), had records supporting abortions under the Medicaid program and thus backed modifications in the Dornan amendment. They facilitated a loosening of the anti-choice language in response to both D.C. home rule pressure and pro-choice forces.[21] Whereas the House of Representatives supported the Dornan amendment by a vote of 217-210,[22] the Senate, led by Senator Leahy, defeated the same amendment, offered in the Senate by Senator Jesse Helms (R–N.C.), by a vote of 55-34.[23] As the D.C. appropriations bill was enacted, federal funds to the District of Columbia could fund abortions only in cases of life endangerment, rape, or incest. However, any and all abortions could be funded with locally raised money.[24] Also, and of potentially more serious consequence to pro-choice forces, the House of Representatives on December 6, 1979, supported by a vote of 217-169 an amendment introduced by Representative Harold Volkmer (D–Mo.) to the Child Health Assurance Program (CHAP) that would prohibit Medicaid funding for abortions except when necessary to save the life of the mother.[25] Such an amendment would change Title XIX of the Social Security Act, which is the Medicaid statute. This would have a more lasting impact than the yearly amendments to the appropriations bill to restrict Medicaid-funded abortions since an amendment to

---

[21] *Washington Post*, July 19, 1979, B1 and B17.

[22] *Washington Post*, Sept. 24, 1979, C1.

[23] *NARAL Newsletter* 11 (Sept. 1979), 5 and 8.

[24] *Ibid.* and *NARAL Newsletter* 12 (Jan. 1980), 6.

[25] *NARAL Newsletter* 12 (Feb. 1980), 11.

CHAP would be included in the authorization language and authorizations, unlike appropriations, are not subject to yearly review and approval. Moreover, this amendment, if enacted, would interfere with court orders to fund abortions because the court orders are based in part on what is included in the Medicaid statute.[26]

Women's groups and the coalition lobbying to protect choice had learned to be satisfied with "fuzzy" language as a compromise between some choice and no choice at all. In 1979 they were clearly unsuccessful in maintaining even loose anti-choice language. Their congressional lobbying efforts failed, especially in the Senate where the language of the original Hyde amendment was the language approved and sent to conference committee.

At the state level, all legislatures have felt the continuing pressure of anti-abortion lobbyists, since the Hyde amendment deprives states of matching federal funds for Medicaid abortions except under Hyde criteria and thus leaves it up to states whether or not to continue funding on their own. As a result, state after state has curtailed public funding of abortion, eliminating the access of lower-income women to legal abortion. By 1980 fifteen states had supported a constitutional amendment limiting abortion rights.

It should be noted that a *Congressional Quarterly (CQ)* analysis of 25 roll calls on the abortion issue found that lobbying had little impact; 415 representatives never wavered on their position. What the study did find was that religion was the key predictor of voting, with two-thirds of Catholic representatives taking a staunchly anti-abortion position, though some Catholics, such as Father Drinan (then Democratic Representative from Massachusetts), have been in the forefront of congressional pro-choice forces. Senate Catholics were less nu-

---

[26] *NARAL Newsletter* 12 (Jan. 1980), 6. Other congressional restrictions included a prohibition on consideration of abortion issues by the U.S. Commission on Civil Rights, exclusion of abortion cases from coverage by federally funded legal services, and the anti-abortion (Beard) amendment of the Pregnancy Discrimination Act.

merous and more divided on abortion. Blacks generally opposed limits on abortion, as did 12 of the 18 women in Congress, thus fragmenting the congressional women's caucus on this issue. Although voting on abortion-related issues crosses partisan lines, the CQ analysis reveals a degree of issue congruence apparent in voting on abortion. A substantial majority of abortion opponents voted against welfare measures, too, suggesting that while this is not strictly a liberal/conservative issue, elements of ideology play a considerable role.[27] Despite CQ's finding that lobbying per se does not necessarily influence individual congressional voting on abortion, many members of Congress perceive the existence of a highly mobilized, single-issue-focused anti-abortion constituency and vote accordingly. As John Kingdon has shown, when constituency positions are perceived as intense, as on racial matters, and are viewed as having high salience, a member of Congress will vote with his or her constituents.[28] Kingdon also adds that interest-group activity is likely to be of concern in congressional decision making insofar as it is connected with a strong constituency base and accords with preexisting values.[29] A recent article has contended that "the abortion issue has produced the most highly charged lobbying since the contentious days of the Vietnam war."[30]

Anti-abortion views are internalized for many members of Congress through deeply held religious and ideological values. Hence overt lobbying tactics may not always be necessary. In addition, pro-life groups have "hit lists" of people in Congress to defeat and, through effective focusing of resources, may have had an intimidating effect on voting in this matter. The widely publicized defeat of pro-choice Senator Dick Clark of Iowa in 1978, mobilized through massive telephone surveys, pro-life mailings, and leaflets distributed to thousands of state

[27] *CQ Weekly Report*, Feb. 4, 1978, 258-60.

[28] John Kingdon, *Congressmen's Voting Decisions* (New York: Harper and Row, 1973), 41.

[29] *Ibid.*, 57-60.

[30] *New York Times*, June 26, 1977, Sect. IV, 10.

residents may have served notice on numerous other members of Congress to "vote right"—against funding for abortions.

The Pro-Life Action Committee, which singled out Clark as a target, distributed 300,000 pamphlets through churches at a total cost of less than $10,000. Senator Clark's pro-life opponent won by 26,000 votes; a *Des Moines Register* election-day survey found that 25,000 people voted against Clark because of his position on abortion, thereby *almost* providing the margin of defeat.[31] The defeat of Representative Donald Fraser in Minnesota in 1978 also turned in part on the right-to-life issue, as well as on questions of continued welfare-state liberalism with which abortion is often associated (as did Senator Clark's Iowa race).

The 1980 Senate elections saw a concerted effort by abortion opponents to defeat pro-choice candidates. Their widely publicized efforts were successful in aiding in the defeat of Birch Bayh (D–Ind.), George McGovern (D–S.D.), Frank Church (D–Idaho), and other liberals. The right-wing National Conservative Political Action Committee (NCPAC), working in conjunction with the Life Amendment Political Action Committee (LAPAC) and the Moral Majority, poured millions of dollars (an estimated 5 million) into the campaign against incumbents they had targeted for defeat. In contrast, NARAL could raise only $250,000 for candidates it supported.[32] As a result, in the 98th Congress the Senate Appropriations, Budget, Finance, and Judiciary Committees all had anti-abortion rather than pro-choice leadership.

There is a well-developed network of conservative activists—including Catholic and some fundamentalist and Mormon church groups as well as several traditional right-wing organizations—that have focused on the abortion issue and have sought to persuade members of Congress that voters are single-issue oriented and that a pro-choice vote would spell cer-

[31] *New York Times*, Nov. 13, 1978, 18.

[32] *NARAL Newsletter* 12 (Dec. 1980), 1, 4-5. See also *New York Times*, Nov. 7, 1980, A16, and Richard Cohen, "Congressional Focus," *National Journal*, Nov. 18, 1980, 1960.

tain electoral defeat. This belief is widely held despite the fact that the feminist groups have shown that this is not the case.[33]

THE GROUP ACTORS

Pro-Lifers

In the wake of the Supreme Court decision in *Roe* v. *Wade* and the congressional debates on the Hyde and other anti-choice amendments, an angry and highly organized group of women (and men) have mobilized against abortion rights. At the state conventions in 1977 held under the auspices of the International Women's Year as well as in other public forums, such as the 1980 White House Conference on the Family, opposition to state ratification of the ERA and to abortion on demand surfaced and demonstrated conflict among women at the grassroots level regarding abortion policy (although at the White House conferences, pro-choice groups generally prevailed). Ellen McCormack ran for President in 1976 on a right-to-life platform, and in 1978 in New York State the Right-to-Life Party gained sufficient voters to qualify automatically for inclusion on the ballot in future years.

In January 1980 some fifty leaders of right-to-life groups met in Washington for three days to plan their strategies of political activism and to prepare for their "March for Life" on the Capitol, held yearly on the anniversary of the Supreme Court's decision in *Roe* v. *Wade*. The conference was cosponsored by the Life Amendment Political Action Committee and Christian Family Renewal. One particularly interesting point was made at this meeting by Paul Weyrich, Director of the Committee for the Survival of a Free Congress, a conservative political action group. He noted: "It doesn't matter what the majority of the American people think on a poll. What matters is the perception members of Congress have about your issue

[33] Interview with Linda Lipson, Congressional Clearinghouse for Women's Rights, Sept. 1, 1977.

and their future."[34] Pro-choice forces have had difficulty in dealing with this problem. In part they have because pro-choice groups are often unable to compete with the right-to-life groups that are organized around a single issue and that employ tactics appealing to fear and emotion. The belief that an intense minority may prevail even against popular opinion thus gains credence. Consider for a moment the statement of Carolyn Thompson, Chairperson of the Pro-Life Action Committee' the political arm of Iowa's anti-abortion movement. In discussing the 1980 Iowa caucuses to elect delegates to the national convention, she noted: "Most people are going to sit by the fire that night and not bother to go out. That's why a special interest group like ourselves can be so effective, because if we make any effort at all to turn our people out, we can take the delegation."[35]

In addition, the right-to-life groups are deeply involved in the use of the language of morality and religion and present themselves as the defenders of moral righteousness acting against the pro-choice groups that, in contradistinction, are represented as the forces of anti-morality, anti-religion, and anti-God. Robert Moffett, administrative assistant to Representative Robert Dornan (R–Calif.), suggested that the anti-choice movement, by identifying itself as the "Right-to-Life Movement," has absorbed the moral tenets of Judeo-Christain faith. Further, he noted that if anti-choice is identified as "right-to-life," pro-choice becomes identified to many people as "anti-life." He drew some parallels between the contemporary pro-life movement and the anti-war movement in the late 1960s and early 1970s. The anti-war movement was identified as morally good and supportive of life and thus, by extension, if you were not against war, you were identified as for war and therefore for killing, death, and destruction.[36]

The National Right to Life Committee, an umbrella organ-

---

[34] *New York Times*, Jan. 21, 1980, 22.

[35] *New York Times*, Jan. 12, 1980, 22.

[36] Interview with Robert Moffett, U.S. Congress, Oct. 10, 1979.

ization, is the largest on either side of the abortion controversy; claiming 11 million active supporters in 3,000 chapters,
with formidable grassroots strength and a $3 million annual
budget. The Catholic Church has been a major institutional
and financial force behind right-to-life activities, although
Mormons, Orthodox Jews, and Protestant fundamentalists
have also been active.

The right-to-life position of the Catholic Church is rooted
initially in the 1869 prohibition of all abortions by Pope Pius
IX. The 1968 papal encyclical *Humanae Vitae* reaffirmed
Church opposition to abortion. In 1975 the Catholic Bishops
of the United States approved unanimously a "Pastoral Plan
for Pro-Life Activities." This Pastoral Plan "seeks to activate
the pastoral resources of the Church in three major efforts: (1)
educational . . . ; (2) a pastoral effort . . . ; (3) a public policy
effort directed toward the legislative, judicial and administrative areas so as to insure effective legal protection for the right
to life."[37]

An interview with Rev. Bryce, head of the Committee for
Pro-Life Activities of the National Conference of Catholic
Bishops, revealed that abortion is seen as an issue that serves
to mobilize Church activists and is therefore an issue of unusual—and more than strictly spiritual—importance for the
Church hierarchy. The Church's political activities are, of
course, tax exempt.[38]

It should be noted that despite the organized effort of the
Catholic Church to ban all abortions, Catholics as a group are
not opposed to abortion; differences between Catholics and
Protestants on this issue are relatively slight and continue to
narrow.[39] A 1977 CBS News and *New York Times* poll asking
"Should the right of a woman to have an abortion be left entirely to the woman and her doctor?" was repeated in 1979
(see Table 7). To a second query, asking whether the govern-

---

[37] "Pastoral Plan for Pro-Life Activities," *The Wanderer* 108 (Dec. 14,
1975).

[38] Interview with Rev. Edward M. Bryce, Sept. 18, 1978.

[39] Skerry, "The Class Conflict over Abortion," 74.

TABLE 7
Should the Right to Have an Abortion Be Left Entirely to the Woman and Her Doctor?

	Disagree		Agree		No Opinion	
	1977	1979	1977	1979	1977	1979
Protestants	21%	27%	76%	69%	3%	4%
Catholics	26%	32%	68%	64%	5%	4%

SOURCE: *New York Times*, Nov. 11, 1979.

ment should help a poor woman with her abortion bills, 47 percent of Protestant respondents and 43 percent of Catholic respondents answered "yes." A 1977 Gallup Poll found 53 percent of Catholic respondents agreeing with 58 percent of Protestant respondents that abortion should be legal "under some circumstances."[40]

Despite this apparent split in Catholic opinion, Church support of the right-to-life position remains unyielding. As the executive director of the National Right to Life Committee put it: "The only reason we have a movement in this nation is because of the Catholic people and the Catholic Church. The rest of us would hardly make a ripple." It is possible that Catholic domination of the movement should be seen as a consequence of the sheer organizational power of the Church—the most centralized church bureaucracy in the United States, catering to the single largest denomination.[41]

In addition to the right-to-life activities of the National Conference of Catholic Bishops, there are groups of lay Catholics such as the National Committee for a Human Life Amendment. William Cox, director of this committee, claims that his group is separate from the National Conference of Catholic Bishops but does receive money from dioceses and the Na-

[40] NARAL, "Polls on Abortion," Jan, 1978; and *New York Times*, Nov. 11, 1979, 43.

[41] Skerry, "The Class Conflict over Abortion," 74.

tional Conference. The primary goal of Cox's group and other anti-choice groups is to secure an anti-abortion amendment to the Constitution.[42] The secondary goal of this group is to secure right-to-life legislative amendments such as the Hyde amendment. These two goals are shared by virtually all right-to-life groups. There is some overlap between this lay Catholic organization and other right-to-life groups such as the National Right to Life Committee, which is nonsectarian, American Citizens Concerned for Life, and the Catholic League for Religious and Civil Rights.[43] They are organized into a loose coalition known as the "Life Lobby."

Some of the techniques utilized by "Right to Lifers" have already been indicated above. The 1975 Bishops' Pastoral Plan calls for a sophisticated network of parish committees to carry out anti-abortion work. These are organized along congressional district lines to facilitate mobilization of political action groups each with an assigned pro-life political coordinator.[44] Activists have been organized to work in electoral and party politics and to lobby at the state and national level. Money is raised on such occasions as "Respect Life" Sunday and through Catholic Charities. William Cox likened the techniques used by the Church in what is probably its most sophisticated political effort to date to those employed by Common Cause and the anti-war movement.[45]

In addition to traditional political techniques, right-to-life activists have also organized demonstrations including the annual March for Life to protest the anniversary of the 1973 Supreme Court decision. The January 1979 March attracted 60,000 people to Washington.[46] In recent years some right-to-

---

[42] Interview with William Cox, Director, National Right to Life Committee, Sept. 29, 1978.

[43] *Ibid.*

[44] *Women Under Attack: Abortion, Sterilization Abuse and Reproductive Freedom* (New York: Committee for Abortion Rights and Against Sterilization Abuse, 1979), 32.

[45] Interview with William Cox.

[46] *New York Times*, Jan. 23, 1979, C10.

life forces have expanded their activities from the legislative and electoral arenas to conduct a campaign of harassment and violence against abortion clinics. For example, Joseph Scheidler, director of a Chicago group called Friends for Life, has criticized a public view, prompted by fire bombings of abortion clinics in several states, that "pro-life is violent." However, though he does not personally advocate violence to achieve anti-abortion goals, he has noted that "I don't cry real hard when I hear about one of their fire traps burning down."[47]

The conflict over abortion pits women against one another. The Ad Hoc Committee in Defense of Life, an anti-abortion group that publishes a biweekly newsletter, *Life-letter*, counts numerous women as members, as do other similar groups. A study of anti-ERA activists, who often have overlapping memberships in right-to-life groups, has found that these women are formidable adversaries for the women's rights groups. They often are middle to upper class in background, educated, motivated to activism by traditional social values and religious beliefs, and they are active political participants with a strong sense of efficacy.[48]

An interview with Anne O'Donnell, director of the National Right to Life Committee, revealed a somewhat different perspective. In her view abortion politics involves a "class struggle" owing to the predominantly lower- and middle-class character of right-to-life activists, who are also engaged in intensive religious activity.[49] Again, despite their reputation as single-issue groups, Right to Lifers have alliances and linkages to anti-ERA and conservative, anti-government, anti-gun control, and other right-wing forces. Increasingly, some students of abor-

[47] *Ibid.*

[48] David Brody and Kent Tedin, "Ladies in Pink: Religion and Political Ideology in the Anti-ERA Movement," *Social Science Quarterly* 56 (March 1976), 72-82.

[49] Interview with Anne O'Donnell, Director, National Right to Life Committee, Sept. 28, 1979. See also Skerry, "The Class Conflict over Abortion," who suggests the relevance of the class conflict model as well.

tion politics have come to view pro-life activists as those who would "reprivatize" a whole set of policy issues, including Medicaid, health care, and abortion. Such reprivatization of social welfare functions would have as its ultimate goal the dismantling of the entire welfare state.[50]

The Feminist Response

Women's groups including the Women's Lobby, NWPC AAUW, and NOW began to work together in June 1977 as part of a pro-choice coalition along with NARAL, Planned Parenthood, and the ACLU belatedly to influence the legislative process. A coalition of twenty-seven women's groups did, for example, urge President Carter to reconsider his opposition to Federal funding for abortions—with no tangible results. In addition, a group of twenty organizations have joined together into the Abortion Information Exchange, and for several years they have met biweekly to plan strategy. Their efforts are buttressed by local groups such as CARASA (Committee for Abortion Rights and Against Sterilization Abuse), oriented toward community-based efforts to gain and expand reproductive freedom. But, unlike the "other side," many feminist groups have been forced to devote their limited resources and leadership to other issues as well.[51]

Third-party support has been notably absent. Neither the NAACP, the Leadership Conference on Civil Rights, labor unions, Common Cause, nor the powerful medical community have been willing to be extensively involved in this controversial issue—though the American Medical Association has endorsed the pro-choice view on abortion. Analysis of the politics of reproductive freedom by social historians suggests that physicians and other health professionals have traditionally

[50] Rosalind Petchesky, "The Courts, the State and the Medical Model of Abortion: Rethinking the Feminist View Since Harris v. McRae" (paper presented at the Northeast Political Science Association convention, New Haven, Conn., Nov. 21, 1980), 50-53.

[51] *New York Times*, Aug. 3, 1977, 9.

been reluctant to cede control over reproductive self-determination solely to women.[52] Until recently, traditional groups such as the League of Women Voters have sought to remain aloof from the abortion issue. Among civil rights allies, support has been forthcoming on the abortion issue from Jesse Jackson's "Operation Push" and the Congressional Black Caucus, which under the aegis of Congressman Louis Stokes (D–Ohio) issued a pro-choice letter.

Organizations such as NARAL, which is probably the most active group in the pro-choice movement, have grown dramatically in recent years as they have sought to counter the grassroots efforts of the Right to Lifers. NARAL has grown from 20,000 to 100,000 members; a self-survey reveals a membership that is white, female, urban, disproportionately Jewish, and relatively young (25-44). A large number of members come from the Middle Atlantic states, and many are professionally educated and professionally employed. Members consider themselves liberals, and there is a substantial overlap between NARAL membership and that of other feminist groups including NOW and pro-choice groups such as the ACLU and Planned Parenthood.[53] The NARAL survey lends credence to the view the pro-choice activists represent a far different women's constituency than the Right to Lifers.

NARAL derives virtually all of its resources from its membership; these now total over one and a half million dollars annually. A tax-exempt (501) (c) (3) foundation funded in part by Stewart Mott aids in public relations and media-related activities. NARAL itself, however, does not have tax-exempt status; it must derive virtually all of its funds from membership dues and contributions. Also, although by the end of the 1970s NARAL began to organize state and local affiliates more dili-

---

[52] See Hayler, "Abortion," 312, and Linda Gordon, *Women's Body, Women's Right* (New York: Grossman, 1976). Hayler quotes studies suggesting physicians' negative artitudes toward abortion, unless performed for strictly medical reasons (315).

[53] Robert Cameron Mitchell, John D. McCarthy, and Kathy Pearch, *Report on a Membership Survey* (Washington, D.C.: NARAL, April 9, 1979).

gently, the right-to-life movement had started much earlier and had a substantial headstart on grassroots organizations via the Church. Nonetheless, NARAL and other groups have recognized the importance of moving beyond the national legislative arena and building local organizations. Such efforts appear essential, as a *New York Times* thirteen-state survey revealed that "in nearly every state, abortion rights advocates have failed to equal the opponent's network of dedicated and steady if often modest contributors or, more often than not, cannot turn out equivalent busloads of demonstrators."[54] In addition to NARAL's local efforts, the Religious Coalition for Abortion Rights (RCAR) and the ACLU-RFP have hired field coordinators, are recruiting state and local coordinators, and are reordering priorities and resources.[55] Groups such as Planned Parenthood, interested in family planning in general, have a substantial community affiliate base (183 affiliates in 43 states) and have become increasingly active in pro-choice, reproductive freedom issues.

Feminists have made other attempts to remain vigilant and counter the backlash against reproductive rights. Among these has been electoral politics. The NARAL Political Action Committee claimed that, of nineteen candidates to whose campaigns it contributed in 1978, 71 percent were elected. NARAL also successfully fought an anti-abortion ballot in Oregon in that year.[56] In 1980 NARAL adopted the strategy of electoral "hit lists" used successfully by the other side and organized a Political Action Committee (Impact 80) to support pro-choice candidates for public office, including Presidential candidate John Anderson.

A group called Voters for Choice, financed by contributions, was organized to "target" anti-abortion members of Congress in 1980 as well. Despite the general inability of pro-choice groups to positively affect election results, NARAL claimed

[54] *New York Times*, Oct. 23, 1977, 24.

[55] Jeanne Bell Nicholson and Debra Stewart, "The Supreme Court, Abortion Policy and State Response," *Publius* 8 (Winter 1978), 176.

[56] Letter from Karen Mulhauser, Executive Director, NARAL.

victory in two primary races in Massachusetts, with the selection of two pro-choice candidates for Congress (notwithstanding a widely circulated letter from the local Cardinal opposing them). A pro-choice candidate was also chosen to succeed Representative John Anderson in Illinois.

And, though unsuccessful in influencing the outcomes of the 1980 and 1984 Presidential races and several key senatorial races, feminist delegates to the Democratic national convention were able to gain platform support for a pro-choice plank including federal abortion funding (as well as for support of the ERA) by utilizing their numerical strength and group cohesion to advantage. The Republican platform took an opposing view on abortion and the ERA, even advocating selection of pro-life federal judges, thus providing voters with a clear-cut issue choice. (The results of the 1980 and 1984 votes, which demonstrated a women's vote distinct from that of men, will be considered in Chapter 8.)

Feminists have also sought to litigate abortion-related issues. The ACLU announced abortion as a priority concern in 1978. Its RFP joined with Planned Parenthood and the Center for Constitutional Rights (all groups active in litigating on behalf of reproductive freedom) to bring *Harris v. McRae*,[57] a class-action suit, into Federal Court, representing the interests of lower-class women who had been denied Medicaid abortions. The suit alleged a violation of separation of church and state and infringement of the rights of privacy, due process, and equal protection.

On January 15, 1980, some thirty-nine months after the *McRae* case was introduced, Judge John F. Dooling, Jr., of the Federal District Court of Brooklyn, New York, ordered government officials to resume authorizing the expenditure of federal Medicaid funds to help pay for "medically necessary abortions provided by duly certified providers." Judge Dooling held that not to provide such services was "to violate the pregnant woman's First and Fifth Amendment rights." He further

[57] 429 U.S. 129.

held that a decision to have a medically necessary abortion was an exercise of a woman's "most fundamental of rights, nearly allied to her right to be, surely part of the liberty protected by the Fifth Amendment, doubly protected when the liberty is exercised in conformity with the religious belief and teaching protected by the First Amendment."[58]

However, on June 30, 1980, the Supreme Court (by a vote of 5-4) refused to reinstate the obligation of states to finance abortions for poor women. The Court upheld the Hyde amendment's curtailment of federal funding at any stage of pregnancy, for any reason other than to save a woman's life. The decision concluded that "abortion is inherently different from other medical procedures, because no other procedure involves the purposeful termination of a potential life." This marks a retreat from the *Roe* v. *Wade* position, which seemed to suggest a woman's fundamental right to abortion, at least until the third trimester.[59] Other judicial efforts by women's rights groups have been able to limit further the erosion of "free choice" by preventing parents or husbands from vetoing the right to have an abortion (*Bellotti* v. *Baird*[60] and *Planned Parenthood of Central Missouri* v. *Danforth*[61])—though in *Hil* v. *Matheson*[62] the Court upheld parental consent for abortions performed on dependent minors who lived with their parents.

Rights groups have been divided regarding strategies on how to proceed. The question has been raised as to whether it would be more effective to counter the pro-life advocates and their emotional appeals with demonstrations showing photos of women who have died as a result of self-induced abortions or to work through the traditional political process. Right-to-life groups are willing to make any appeals to aid their cause. In general, as is true for the feminist movement as a whole pro-

[58] *New York Times*, Jan. 16, 1980, A1 and B2.
[59] See Petchesky, "The Courts, the State and the Medical Model of Abortion."
[60] 428 U.S. 132 (1976).
[61] 1428 U.S. 52 (1976).
[62] L.W. No. 79-5903 (1981).

choice groups have adhered to traditional political techniques (at least since the early 1970s) and have not resorted to protest or "guerilla theatre." Pro-choice advocates in a rare demonstration did deliver 200 coat hangers to Representative Daniel Flood (D–Pa.), then chair of the Labor and Health, Education, and Welfare Subcommittee of the House Appropriations Committee, as a reminder of old methods of abortion.[63] Still, even the name "pro-choice" is designed to present a moderate, nonthreatening tone to this branch of the feminist movement.

In the pro-choice community NARAL is the major single-issue membership group that has abortion rights as its sole focus. Other groups such as Planned Parenthood, the ACLU, and NOW serve other constituencies as well and differ in singularity of purpose. Only the Religious Coalition for Abortion Rights shares NARAL's exclusive interest in the abortion issue. The coalescence of pro-choice groups with feminist groups provides additional strength; at the same time money and activism, already in short supply, are diffused into numerous policy areas. However, the existence of a separate pro-choice coalition has freed the larger feminist movement from continual focus on this issue and has also served to separate the controversial abortion issue from other feminist goals in the minds of policy makers. This has had the effect of preventing defeats on abortion from causing a general anti-feminist spillover —different feminist issues appear to be separable in the congressional political psyche.

The vast majority of the American public certainly seems to support "free choice." A 1980 poll by the New York City firm of Dresner and Tortorello commissioned by NARAL found that 88 percent of registered voters believe in the right to choose abortion depending upon circumstances that relate to a woman's life, health, or victimization by rape or incest.[64] These results are not at variance with other survey findings. Thus the June 1979 issue of *Redbook* magazine carried the re-

[63] *New York Times*, Sept. 8, 1979, Sect. III, 11.
[64] *NARAL Newsletter* 12 (Feb. 1980), 1.

sults of a poll it commissioned from the Gallup organization in which 80 percent of Americans are shown to believe that abortion should be legal at least under some circumstances.[65] It should be noted, however, that support for "free choice" varies with the circumstances involved and with the period in which the abortion is sought. In addition, a small majority of the population appears to oppose federal funding for abortions, perhaps motivated as much by opposition to welfare spending as to abortion.[66] Hence the abortion issue is one in which significant counterpressures have been generated in a political climate hostile to continuing or even sustaining abortion reform but in which the vast majority of people support some aspects of "free choice."

POST-1982 DEVELOPMENTS

As suggested above, the significance of *Roe* v. *Wade* lay both in its broadening of rights to choose to have an abortion and in its mobilization of two sets of political activists, one group pro-choice, one group pro-life or anti-abortion.

During the 1980s, activists on the anti-abortion side pressed their efforts to rescind all pro-choice legislation and judicial rulings. The contest for control of moral, social, and symbolic values continued in the legislative arena, the courts, and even the streets, as the right-to-life activists turned increasingly to harassment of women seeking abortions and to violent attacks, including arson, on clinics providing abortion services. The new Christian right, comprised of such groups as the Moral Majority, Christian Voice, and the Religious Roundtable, has often joined forces with single-issue, anti-abortion groups such as the National Right to Life Committee, National Pro-Life Political Action Committee, and the American Life Lobby in efforts to achieve its goals. These efforts, like those of all interest groups, have been aided by the Federal

[65] Reported in *NARAL Newsletter* 11 (May-June 1979), 16.
[66] *New York Times*, July 29, 1977, 1, and April 21, 1979, 49.

Election Campaign Act Amendments of 1974 legitimizing political action committees (PACs) that operate independently of political parties and of the candidates themselves. In 1976 the Supreme Court's decision in *Buckley* v. *Valeo*[67] permitted unlimited expenditures by groups so long as they are formally independent of candidate's campaign organizations. The new right has seized upon this wedge in the political system and exploited it to the fullest. By 1980 their organizations headed the list of biggest spending PACs. In addition, new right groups have made excellent use of direct mail and other advanced political technologies for mobilizing and building a mass constituency.[68] Grassroots lobbying has been employed effectively by pro-life groups, too. The 1980 electoral successes, together with the cooptation of the Republican party's agenda by conservative interests, appeared to herald a new political ascendancy for the anti-abortion movement.

Recent analysis of the social makeup of the anti-abortion forces contends that the right-to-life groups represent the politicization of a new group in American politics: high-school-educated married women with children who are not employed in the labor market. Such women avow an active belief in the significance of motherhood, the distinctiveness of male and female roles, the importance of religion in their lives, and the use of sex for procreative purposes. In contrast, pro-choice women, as suggested earlier, are more likely to be participants in the labor force with good incomes and college educations, to have small families, and to view sex as an expression of intimacy rather than simply as a means for producing babies.[69] To the degree that this analysis of the disparate socioeconomic bases of the forces supporting and opposing abortion is accurate, the relevance of abortion to role change issues is again made evident.

[67] 424 U.S. I (1976).

[68] Jerome Himmelstein, "The New Right," in *The New Christian Right*, ed. Robert C. Liebman and Robert Wuthnow, (New York: Aldine, 1983), 29.

[69] Kristen Luker, *Abortion and the Politics of Motherhood* (Berkeley: University of California Press, 1984), 137, 160, 194.

Despite the increased political activism of pro-life groups and the continuing controversy over abortion rights, pro-choice groups have been able to hold the line on many issues. This success is particularly notable in view of the increased salience of abortion rights as an issue in the 1984 presidential campaign, when President Reagan reiterated his support for a constitutional amendment forbidding abortion and Catholic Church leaders criticized Vice Presidential candidate Geraldine Ferraro, herself a Catholic, for rejecting the concept of a national ban on abortion.

Internal divisions within the anti-abortion movement have helped limit its effectiveness. In 1982 a dispute between Senators Jesse Helms (R-N.C.) and Orrin Hatch (R-Utah) led to the failure of the right-to-life movement to achieve its legislative goals. In 1983 the Judiciary Committee approved Senator Hatch's amendment to restrict abortion via constitutional amendment, but it was never considered by the full Senate. It became caught up in Hatch's conflict with Helms who sought to bar abortion by statute rather than amendment; Helms's bill fell victim to a protracted filibuster and was killed on a procedural vote.[70] In 1983 Senator Thomas Eagleton (D-Mo.) proposed a return of abortion law to pre-1973 status, by returning jurisdiction to the states, via constitutional amendment. This measure was opposed by Senator Roger Jepsen (R-Iowa) and others who wanted a ban on all abortions. Despite President Reagan's endorsement of the all-encompassing bill and the introduction of a bill similar to Jepsen's in the House, the legislation died. The vote of the Eagleton-revised Hatch amendment was 50-49, with Helms voting present but not supporting the amendment. This represented a significant legislative rout for anti-abortion forces, one reflecting a split on strategy regarding amendment versus statutory approaches.[71] Efforts to restrict abortion rights by calling for state legisla-

[70] *Congressional Quarterly 1983 Almanac* (Washington D.C.: Congressional Quarterly, 1984), 308.
[71] *Ibid.*, 309.

tures to restore the *status quo ante* on abortion rights have also failed.

Nonetheless, Congress has prohibited funding of abortions under the Federal Health Employment Benefit Program, and annual Hyde amendments continue to limit federal funding of abortions to "life-endangering" pregnancies. The impact of the Hyde amendments has been to eliminate 90 percent of Medicaid abortions, although fifteen states and Washington, D.C., continue to fund them.

A victory for freedom of choice and the decision in *Roe v. Wade* came in the courts in 1983, in *City of Akron v. Akron Center for Reproductive Health Inc..*[72] In a 6-3 decision the Court ruled unconstitutional several ordinances that restricted access to abortions, including a 24-hour waiting period, mandated hospitalization for second trimester abortions, "informed consent" requirements, and parental or minority consent.

Other attacks on abortion rights have been made upon Title X of the Public Health Service Act of 1970. Although legislative attempts to weaken the act, which provides for abortion counseling, have failed, efforts to reorient bureaucratic policies in line with anti-abortion views have often been successful. The appointment of Marjorie Mecklenberg, former president of the Minneapolis-based American Citizens Concerned for Life, as Title X Administrator has led to a reduction in the program's effectiveness. Another noted anti-abortion figure, Dr. Everett C. Koop, was named Surgeon General. Furthermore, presidential rhetoric continues to decry abortion rights, even welcoming Joseph Scheidler of the Pro-Life Action League (which supports anti-abortion violence) to the White House. Anti-abortion groups, especially the American Life Lobby and National Right to Life Committee, have been particularly active in seeking to undermine family planning programs that provide abortion counseling, either through cutting funds or killing the programs. The Reagan Administration was prod-

[72] 456 U.S. 988 (1983).

ded by these groups to block foreign aid that is channeled to organizations providing abortion-related services. This newly articulated policy applies to governments, the United Nations, and privately funded agencies.[73]

Pro-choice groups in reaction have moved to mobilize support at the grassroots level, and they have expanded their use of PACs in electoral campaigns as well. Groups such as NARAL have increased their membership considerably in the wake of the attacks on free choice, and contributions to Planned Parenthood have risen from $2 million in 1980 to $12 million in 1985. In 1985, largely as a result of bombings of abortion clinics, membership in Planned Parenthood grew by 15 percent.[74] Despite the escalation of violence by anti-abortion forces, support for freedom of choice continues to be favored by a majority of Americans, in specific circumstances, and NARAL and the *New York Times*/CBS polls continue to find a large majority of Americans (63 percent) opposing a constitutional amendment that would ban all abortions.[75]

CONCLUSION

At the outset of this analysis it was hypothesized that feminists have been most successful in the political process when they are able to "contain" a political issue, stress its technical aspects over which they may present a monopoly of information, and limit the degree to which debate becomes public. Abortion fits none of these criteria. In addition, it was postulated that the broader the issue and the more threatening to prevailing values—the more it represents role change as opposed to role equity—the more difficult will be efforts to contain conflict and prevent countermobilization.

We have suggested that the issue of abortion choice appears to threaten traditional family values and lifestyles; it is an issue

[73] *Congressional Quarterly Weekly Report*, Sept. 1, 1984, 2146.

[74] *Newsweek*, Jan. 14, 1985, 23, and Planned Parenthood Federation of America, *PPFA Fundraising Growth*, mimeo, April 9, 1985, 1-3.

[75] *New York Times*, Oct. 14, 1984, IV, 3.

that portends fundamental change in women's role in society, for reproductive freedom provides an alternative to compulsory motherhood and family life. Thus it is the most difficult type of issue on which to gain change. The feminist movement has sought to counter the immense power of the Catholic Church in partership with the right-to-life movement that it supports monetarily and spiritually. Feminists have endeavored to reorder their priorities and focus, though limited by lack of resources and personnel. Through continued legislative lobbying, bringing court suits, building grassroots strength, and engaging in electoral and campaign activity, feminists are seeking to regain the ground they have lost. It is likely that they will succeed in preventing an anti-abortion constitutional amendment, owing to the difficulties associated with the amendment process. Nonetheless, abortion remains an issue that tears the women's constituency apart with conflict, that has stirred deep-seated moral and religious values, and that remains highly controversial.

CHAPTER 7

THE PREGNANCY DISCRIMINATION ACT AND COALITION POLITICS

INTRODUCTION

The campaign to reverse the Supreme Court's 1976 decision in *General Electric* v. *Gilbert*[1] and to amend Title VII of the Civil Rights Act of 1964 to prohibit sex discrimination on the basis of pregnancy seemed at the outset to reveal political patterns similar to those which existed for equal credit opportunity. Pregnancy disability is a relatively narrow role equity issue that involves no public outlay of funds and that deals with matters of potential benefit to all women. However, since the issue deals with pregnant women and therefore the potential role of women as mothers and homemakers, it was fraught with more controversy than the Equal Credit Opportunity Act had been, especially since the question of funding abortions under disability plans received particular attention from opponents of "free choice."

Unlike the credit issue, the Pregnancy Discrimination Act, which at the outset of the congressional deliberations seemed likely to gain speedy approval with only limited opposition, foundered under attacks from anti-abortion forces. However, the time elapsed from the moment the Supreme Court handed down its decision to the final passage of the law was just under two years. The act, as finally passed, does contain the anti-abortion amendment introduced by Representative Edward Beard (D–R.I.). Nonetheless, the successful effort to overturn the Supreme Court's *Gilbert* decision marked a coalitional re-

[1] 429 U.S. 125.

sponse by an unusually broad-based cross section of groups including feminist and other women's organizations, labor and civil rights forces, and some right-to-life groups as well.

The issue of pregnancy disability has taken on a role of increased significance for the feminist movement as labor force participation by women has grown. Pregnancy has been used as a rationale for providing different and inequitable treatment for women in the work force, and thus the relatively narrow issue of pregnancy-disability insurance has ramifications of both a symbolic and practical nature—particularly in an era when five times as many mothers are working as in 1950, and when more than 60 percent of women in the 25-54 age range are in the work force, triple the percentage in the years immediately following World War II.[2]

BACKGROUND

Prior to World War II and the domestic manpower shortage that accompanied the national military mobilization, it was assumed that women, when they worked outside of the home, did so only until marriage or childrearing responsibilities removed them from the work force. In other words, women belonged in the home. There were several consequences for the labor force that emerged in the 1920s and 1930s as a result of this belief.[3] Often women were barred from employment or dismissed when they became married. A 1930-31 National Education Association (NEA) study indicated that 77 percent of surveyed districts would not hire wives and 63 percent dismissed female teachers if they married. During the 1920s there was a movement to provide workers with fringe benefits. The idea behind the fringe-benefit movement was that a company

[2] Peg Simpson, "A Victory for Women," *Civil Rights Digest* 11 (Spring 1979), 17.

[3] This discussion relies heavily upon the testimony of Wendy M. Williams before U.S. Senate, Committee on Labor and Human Resources, Labor Subcommittee, *Discrimination on the Basis of Pregnancy*, 1977 (Washington, D.C.: U.S. Government Printing Office, 1977), 122-47.

could attract and then hold good workers by generating security and loyalty. Thus fringe benefits that would benefit the employee would ultimately benefit the employer as well. Inasmuch as women were identified as being marginal workers whose primary roles were those of wives and mothers, limitations were imposed on the benefits made available to them. Some companies just allowed women fewer benefits, but other companies excluded women totally from being eligible for benefits.

As noted previously, during World War II many women— 4.5 million—entered the work force. Although there was a need to reassess employment policies and practices, and both the War Manpower Commission and the Children's Bureau issued studies recommending change, women's jobs were terminated once the war effort ended without regard to seniority or employment aspirations, and for the most part pre-war patterns of discrimination in employment reemerged. The author of the Children's Bureau study contended that although protection of mother and fetus as well as fear of liability for miscarriage was the justification given for termination of a pregnant women from employment, often there were aesthetic and moral reasons at the root of these practices—it was "not nice" for pregnant women to work and it had a "bad effect" on male workers.

In 1964, when Title VII of the Civil Rights Act was enacted, conditions for women in the work force were such that 40 percent of all employers did not even provide unpaid maternity leave—pregnant women were just fired. Among those employers who did provide maternity leave, over 50 percent required women to go on leave before their seventh month of pregnancy. Only 6 percent permitted female workers to use sick leave for pregnancy-related illness or disability.

Title VII's impact upon employment discrimination against women was considerable, and regarding pregnancy in particular, it was dramatic: 73 percent of female workers by 1973 were entitled to maternity leave and reemployment rights; 26

percent could use sick leave for pregnancy-related disability of illness.

When the Supreme Court, in *General Electric* v. *Gilbert*, decided that denial of benefits for pregnancy-related disability and illness is not discrimination based on sex, several questions regarding employment opportunities for women emerged onto center stage. It is estimated that approximately 80 percent of all women become pregnant at some point in their working lives. Even women who do not become pregnant are viewed as potentially pregnant by their employers until they pass childbearing age. As Wendy Williams observed in her testimony at hearings before the Labor Subcommittee of U.S. Senate Committee on Labor and Human Resources: "Thus, all women are subject to the effects of the stereotype that women are marginal workers with the multifaceted consequences this has for hiring, job assignment, promotion, pay, and fringe benefits."[4] When women have been forced to take unpaid leave, they have often lost their benefits—including accrued retirement benefits, vacation leave, and sick leave—as well as their seniority. Thus, if promotion opportunities are to be based upon time spent in a position, women who have lost their seniority owing to unpaid leaves often have been locked into low-paying positions.

The entire question of rights for working women had become crucial to labor market considerations by the time the Supreme Court issued its decision in the *Gilbert* case. Whereas in 1950 women comprised 29.6 percent of the labor force and 33.8 percent of all women were employed, by 1977 women comprised 41 percent of the labor force and nearly one-half of all women were working outside of their homes.[5] Also, women were clustered in low-paid, low-status positions. If pregnancy-disability benefits were to be denied women, their status would have been further worsened at a time when more and more

[4] *Ibid.*, 130-31.
[5] U.S. Department of Labor, Bureau of Labor Statistics, *Handbook of Labor Statistics*, 1978 (Washington, D.C.: U.S. Government Printing Office, 1978).

women found it necessary to work, because they were either supporting their families as heads of households or helping keep their families, with another employed member, out of conditions of poverty.

THE CAMPAIGN TO OVERTURN THE GILBERT DECISION

The effort to define pregnancy as a disability for insurance purposes is similar in some ways to the anti-abortion Hyde amendment, in that it has involved a legislative attempt to overturn a Supreme Court decision, albeit from the opposite side of the political spectrum.

The Equal Employment Opportunities Commission (EEOC) was established by the Civil Rights Act of 1964 to implement Title VII prohibiting discrimination by employers on the basis of sex. But the role of the EEOC has been a limited one to date.[6] Not until 1972 did the EEOC issue guidelines requiring that pregnancy and related conditions be treated as disabilities for employment purposes. And, even then, the EEOC was known to be understaffed, weak, inefficient, and deluged with complaints. Hence feminists and other relevant interest groups turned to the federal courts for enforcement of rights. (The EEOC did participate in *Gilbert* and other related cases as *amicus* because of its concern with the validity of pregnancy guidelines.)

In December 1976 the Supreme Court held in *General Electric* v. *Gilbert* that refusal to extend disability benefits to pregnant women is not discrimination based on sex. The Court's decision was not entirely unexpected, following as it did the 1974 decision in *Gudulig* v. *Aiello*,[7] which upheld California's refusal to pay pregnancy disability benefits to female workers.[8]

---

[6] Carol Greenwald, "Women's Rights, Courts and Congress: Conflict Over Pregnancy Disability Compensation Policies" (paper presented at the American Political Science Association convention, Sept. 3, 1978), 24-25.

[7] 417 U.S. 484.

[8] The Court's record with regard to maternity and pregnancy cases has been, to say the least, prone to inconsistency. In another 1974 case, *Cleveland*

The Supreme Court's majority opinion in *Gilbert*, written by Justice Rehnquist, found that the exclusion of pregnancy and pregnancy-related disabilities from coverage under an otherwise comprehensive temporary disabilities plan was not a violation of Title VII's prohibition of discrimination "against any individual with respect to his compensation, terms, conditions or privileges of employment because of . . . race, color, religion, sex or national origin."[9] According to Rehnquist, General Electric's policy was "facially neutral"; since the nature of exemption was pregnancy and not pregnant women, there was no sex discrimination.

The *Gilbert* case arose from a suit brought by the International Union of Electrical, Radio, and Machine Workers (IUE) and argued by its attorney, Ruth Weyand, although *amicus* briefs were submitted by several feminist groups including the Women Rights Project (ACLU), WLDF, and WEAL. Weyand's filing of a lengthy set of briefs, totalling 250 pages, apparently incurred the wrath of the jurists, perhaps limiting the impact of the case presented by feminists.[10]

The Court's decision in the *Gilbert* case engendered the development of a coalition of groups in support of women's interests in pregnancy disability. In this instance, a widespread network was activated within days of the adverse Court decision of December 1976, and a coalition with over three hundred groups participating was developed. Labor union backing was especially strong on this issue. Church groups and even some Right to Lifers were among the original members of this broad-based coalition, known as the Campaign to End Discrimination Against Pregnant Workers (Campaign). Because the original court case was brought by the International Electrical, Radio, and Machine Workers Union, the IUE, AFL-

---

Board of Education v. *La Fleur* (414 U.S. 663), a law requiring teachers to leave their positions when five months pregnant was declared unconstitutional.

[9] *General Electric* v. *Gilbert*, 429 U.S. 125 (1976).

[10] Karen O'Connor, *Women's Organizations' Use of the Courts* (Lexington, Mass.: D.C. Heath, 1980), 144-45.

CIO, UAW, and other union groups were prominent in this struggle, although the issue was of paramount importance for women's activist groups such as NOW, WEAL, NWPC, and the WRP of the ACLU. The coalition's leadership was drawn from the original litigating groups; Ruth Weyand of the IUE, who had argued the case before the Supreme Court, and Sue Ross of the ACLU-WRP were elected co-chairs.

The Pregnancy Discrimination Act (S. 995), to amend Title VII of the Civil Rights Act of 1964 to include pregnancy-related disability, was introduced in Congress by Senator Harrison Williams in March 1977. A "Fact Sheet" distributed by the Campaign set "the parameters of legislative debate. Little time was spent discussing the logic of the *Gilbert* decision. Congress began to deal directly with the circumvented issue."[11]

The intent of the Act was to prohibit discrimination against pregnant women in all areas of employment including hiring, firing, seniority rights, job security, and receipt of fringe benefits. It also required employers who offered health insurance and temporary disability plans to provide coverage to women for pregnancy, childbirth, and related medical conditions.

Feminist groups were opposed more overtly on this issue than they had been on credit by some industry groups including the U.S. Chamber of Commerce, National Association of Manufacturers, National Retail Merchants Association, American Retail Federation, and insurance companies. Nonetheless, industry did not present monolithic opposition to pregnancy-related disability insurance. Businessmen's objections, as expressed in hearings, centered on the view that pregnancy is a "voluntary condition," not an illness, hence not liable to the same coverage as other disabilities. In addition, they cited the potential for increased costs. Even so, the business community was clearly not unanimous in its opposition to this bill since such leading corporations as Xerox, Polaroid, and IBM already provided pregnancy-disability coverage for

[11] Greenwald, "Women's Rights," 28.

their employees. Also, as in the case of equal credit opportunity, some business groups were reluctant to go on record against the feminist community, particularly on an issue involving "motherhood." The Supreme Court winners—General Electric, Liberty Mutual, AT&T, and others—did not testify, although invited to do so, at the Senate hearings held in April 1977.[12]

At both the House and Senate subcommittee hearings held in April and June 1977, feminist groups and their allies provided testimony stressing the importance of change. Several women who had been personally victimized by discriminatory insurance plans offered dramatic commentary on the necessity for remedial legislation. The proposed legislation enjoyed unusually broad-based support even from pro-life forces (specifically the American Citizens Concerned for Life) who welcomed the proposed legislation as a "matter of social justice" and supported rights of pregnant "mothers" as a logical extension of their concern for life. Conflict began to occur when the Bishop's Committee for Pro-Life Activities sought the addition of language eliminating elective abortions from the definition of covered conditions, as part of their broader strategy to generate anti-abortion support in every way possible. In the Senate Thomas Eagleton (D–Mo.) introduced an anti-abortion amendment to the Pregnancy Discrimination Act. Feminists were especially dismayed because they had thought incorporation of pro-life groups in the Campaign's coalition would prevent such action. Nonetheless, the bill passed the Senate in September 1977 by a vote of 75-11, with its initial definition of covered pregnancy-related conditions intact. Senator Eagleton's anti-abortion amendment was defeated.

The issue of pregnancy disability then moved to the House where controversy regarding anti-abortion language continued and was heightened. Representative Beard (D–R.I.) introduced the anti-abortion amendment in the House. At this time issues such as extension of the ERA and the Humphrey-Hawk-

12 *Ibid.*, 30.

ins Full Employment Bill occupied the attention of many Campaign coalition members. Nonetheless, coalition action and cohesion were maintained. Member organizations were asked to visit key legislators during home recesses. A postcard campaign in support of the bill was launched. Action/information pieces were distributed by the Campaign and by NOW-LDEF. Wide media (television and newspaper) exposure was obtained to focus attention on the bill.

In February 1978 the House subcommittee chaired by Representative Augustus Hawkins (D–Calif.) marked up H.R. 6075 rejecting the Beard anti-abortion amendment by two votes; on March 13, 1978, the full committee overruled the subcommittee, adopted the Beard amendment by seven votes, and then voted 25-6 to report out the bill to the floor of the House as amended. During the next five months the Campaign maneuvered to remove the amendment or obtain a floor vote under a "suspension of the rules." Eventually, the House leadership decided to bring H.R. 6075 up under "suspension of the rules," a procedure normally used to expedite noncontroversial legislation. Bills called up under this procedure may have no amendments from the floor and must be passed by a two-thirds vote.[13]

The House leadership and leaders of the Campaign supported this strategy as a way to move the bill to conference committee where they hoped it might be possible to eliminate the anti-abortion amendment. This strategy created an unusual split among pro-choice forces; NARAL, NOW, and the Religious Coalition for Abortion Rights opposed this tactic, wishing to put supporters and opponents "on the record," although they muted overt disagreement. The ACLU and NWPC and other women's rights groups favored "suspension" in an effort to prevent a floor fight that they felt they would surely lose and that would result in a damaging symbolic defeat. The *New York Times*, editorializing at the time, said: "We recommend, albeit sadly, a vote for the amend-

[13] *Ibid.*, 35.

ment" because of the necessity to gain passage of the legislation rectifying abuse against pregnant women.[14]

In the House roll-call vote on the issue, some "no" votes were registered in opposition to the anti-abortion language as well as to the pregnancy-disability act itself. The bill with the anti-abortion Beard amendment passed the House by a vote of 376-43. The bill then went to conference committee where pro-choice forces were reunited and where conferees were deadlocked all summer over the language of the bill.

House conferees voted consistently in favor of the Beard amendment provisions and against Senate conferees' compromise language, supported by pro-choice forces, which would allow religious institutions to deny abortion coverage to their employees.[15] House conferees rejected Senate conferees' efforts to broaden the so-called conscience clause language to include sole proprietors with religious or moral objections to abortion. Finally, on October 12, 1978, a compromise emerged. Pro-choice forces agreed to compromise by including some anti-abortion provisions, in order to gain the larger objective of securing the passage of the Pregnancy Discrimination Act.

The final language approved by the conference committee and sent back to the House and the Senate for approval allows employers to exempt elective abortions from medical coverage, except if the life of the mother is threatened or if medical complications result from abortion. But, in a minor weakening of the original House anti-abortion provisions, employers were required to provide disability and sick-leave benefits to women recovering from abortions. The Act does not specify an absolute ban on employer provision of abortion benefits; employers may provide all health benefits related to abortion if they wish. Both houses of Congress passed the bill and the President signed it. The law took effect immediately upon passage, on October 31, 1978, with the exception of fringe and

[14] *New York Times*, July 18, 1978, 16.
[15] *CQ Weekly Report*, Oct. 21, 1978, 3073.

insurance benefits, which took effect 180 days after enactment.

Pro-choice and feminist groups welcomed the passage of the Act as a milestone for the women's movement, but pro-choice groups in particular remained bitter over what they viewed as the "betrayal" of Representative Augustus Hawkins (Chair of the House Subcommittee), who had orchestrated the original compromise on suspending the rules. Pro-choice forces felt that Hawkins's efforts to strike the Beard provisions proved less than zealous and that House and Senate conferees had sought continuing approval from the United States Catholic Conference on various compromise proposals.[16]

The law applies only to employers who offer other disability coverage, and most do not. Fewer than 40 percent of employed American women receive paid disability leave of six weeks or more after they give birth.[17] Since the enactment of the 1978 law, the Supreme Court, in *Newport News Shipbuilding and Drydock* v. *Equal Employment Opportunities Commission*,[18] ruled in a 7-2 decision in June 1983 that employers must cover the pregnancy costs of employees' wives as comprehensively as they do other dependents' medical expenses.[19] This decision was seen as having a significant impact in that universities and other institutions will have to bring their health benefit packages into compliance with the Pregnancy Discrimination Act.

CONCLUSION

The passage of the Pregnancy Discrimination Act after twenty-two months of Congressional debate contains within it several paradoxes. Feminists, pro-choice groups, and their allies in the unusually broad-based Campaign to End Discrimination Against Pregnant Workers achieved their goal of the Act's passage, overturning a Supreme Court decision within a relatively

[16] *Ibid.*, 3074.
[17] *New York Times*, Dec. 25, 1983, 48.
[18] 103 S.Ct. 2622 (1983).
[19] *Chronicle of Higher Education*, June 29, 1983, 23.

short period of time. Even the Court itself may have responded to pressure generated by feminist groups. In a related case, *Nashville Gas Co. v. Satty*,[20] the Supreme Court seemed to adopt a position somewhat different from that in *Gilbert* when it held that employer policies of denying accumulated seniority to women returning from maternity leave violated Title VII of the Civil Rights Act of 1964, although the Court did hold that a policy of not awarding sick-leave pay to pregnant employees was not prima facie evidence of sex discrimination. Nonetheless, the Campaign almost faltered, but not because of opposition from the business community whose interests were most directly at stake, as might have been anticipated. In fact, business groups were split on the issue, despite the fact that no industry groups actually testified in support of the bill. The Act almost failed because of the activities of pro-life groups, who threatened to divide the members of the Campaign and weaken their unity, thus destroying the coalition and chances for the bill's passage.

The efforts of pro-lifers did not succeed, but there was disagreement within Campaign ranks over appropriate strategies and even over ultimate worth of the bill. Pro-choice groups, especially NARAL, which has a single-issue mission, of necessity see their interests as somewhat different on such a policy controversy from those of broader-based feminist groups. Although their focus on this issue differed considerably, the feminist/labor strategy of compromising in order to win what they saw as the larger issue prevailed. The final bill, other than the anti-abortion language, does represent a sweeping victory for feminist forces; even an earlier section of the bill, delaying implementation of the Act for smaller companies, was deleted from the final version. In addition, the broad language of the original bill, which contains a sweeping definition of areas of employment in which discrimination is outlawed, prevailed. It should be recalled that the compromise version of the abortion language in the Act does permit optional provision of abortion

[20] 98 S. Ct. 347 (1977).

coverage by employers and also requires that the costs of complications arising from abortions in all cases be covered. This represents a softening of the initial Beard amendment language. The National Conference of Catholic Bishops, understandably, was not pleased with the law and the EEOC guidelines issued to enforce it and brought suit in Federal Court challenging the Pregnancy Discrimination Act. The suit was dismissed by Judge John Pratt of the U.S. District Court on the grounds that no new issue suitable for adjudication had been presented.[21]

The Pregnancy Discrimination Act broadens equal opportunity protection for millions of working women, while serving as a reminder of the price of compromise that had to be paid in order to obtain this important victory. Although it is still too early to assess compliance with the Act, it provides a legislative mandate that guarantees that women are paid for their period of disability and that they have a comparable job upon their return to work.

[21] *Chronicle of Higher Education*, Feb. 4, 1980, 16.

CHAPTER 8

ISSUES OF ECONOMIC EQUITY

INTRODUCTION

The failure of 35 states to approve the Equal Rights Amendment to the Constitution by June 30, 1982, despite the fact that the majority of Americans supported the amendment, both frustrated and angered many people. This development along with the effects of the Reagan Administration's policies that have accelerated the feminization of poverty while ignoring the "workplace gap" have made women's movement activists and their supporters more determined than ever before to influence the public policy process in the United States.

In the Bible, in Leviticus 27:3-4, it is written that women of working age were valued at 30 silver shekels, whereas men were valued at 50 silver shekels. This ratio remains virtually unchanged today despite the women's movement, the laws that mandate equal pay for equal work and outlaw sex discrimination, and the many centuries of gradual change during which women have moved from hearth and home into the paid work force. Most women today work in the low-paying "pink collar" ghetto. Moveover, pension benefits and insurance coverage tend to maintain women in an economically inferior position relative to white men. Women who have dedicated their lives to caring for their husbands and children at home, as well as women who have chosen to join the paid work force, often have not fared too well economically—especially in terms of pay scales but also in the areas of insurance and pension benefits.

Women are represented disproportionately among the nation's poverty population. Thus, in 1984, 80 percent of all families that received Aid to Families with Dependent Children

(AFDC) were maintained by single women; 73 percent of the elderly poor were women; and, of the almost 10 million women-headed households, 36.3 percent survived near or at the poverty level.[1]

The combined effects of the failure to ratify the ERA and Reagan Administration policies that seem to have had a disproportionately negative economic impact on women have shifted the attention of the women's movement toward economic issues. In particular, passage of the separate titles of the omnibus Economic Equity Act (EEA) has sparked the interest of feminist groups. The issue of equal pay for jobs of comparable worth, often referred to as "pay equity," is also in the forefront of movement concerns. This issue has been addressed primarily at the state and local levels, rather than at the level of national decision making. In this chapter attention will be focused mainly on the activities of the women's movement in relation to economic equity issues that are included in the Economic Equity Act.

The Economic Equity Act includes provisions for equity in pensions, unisex insurance, equal apportionment of economic responsibility between divorced parents, and more extensive day care coverage for working parents. Of these provisions, two—retirement equity and collection of child support payments—were passed by the 98th Congress. This chapter will discuss the reasons for the success of the pension efforts, while contrasting this case with the failure of Congress to enact a unisex insurance bill, H.R. 100. The analysis suggests the continuing significance of relatively narrow "role equity" questions particularly in an election year in which the "gender gap" appeared to be a major factor. It stresses the degree to which organized opposition can be a factor in influencing legislative outcomes. The chapter also will demonstrate how patterns of political advocacy that utilize methods of coalition politics and specialization of function have been maximized by feminist lobbyists active in the 1980s.

[1] *WEAL Facts*, March 1, 1984, p. 1.

The mid-1980s saw much of the earlier emphasis on civil rights legislation translated into new interest in economic needs.[2] There was a heightening of political consciousness among women and feminist-oriented men. Republican senators and representatives felt guilty over their party's opposition to the ERA and other feminist issues, such as abortion. They were concerned that these positions might have negative consequences for their electoral prospects. The Republican legislative leadership saw in the various sections of the Economic Equity Act—particularly those segments of the Act that provided for limited equity-oriented gains, with little direct cost—a chance "to do something for women."

THE ECONOMIC EQUITY ACT: BACKGROUND

The Economic Equity Act was introduced by Senator Dave Durenberger (R-Minn.) in the 97th Congress, and has been reintroduced into each successive session of Congress. The EEA is a legislative package of several disparate measures that would have profound economic benefits for women if they are enacted. Although it was introduced as a "package," its supporters knew it would be dealt with piece by piece. Initially the legislation was proposed as an implementing tool for the Equal Rights Amendment and not as a replacement for the amendment, although with the defeat of the ERA its significance became even more apparent. The strategy that supporters of women's rights in the Congress have followed regarding the passage of the EEA has been to separate the titles of the Act into individual pieces of legislation and then introduce separate bills. In the 97th Congress provisions dealing with pensions for military spouses, estate taxes, and sliding child care tax credits were enacted. In the 98th Congress legislation was enacted based on Title V, enforcement of child support payments, and on one portion of Title I, reform of pension sys-

[2] Interviews with Pat Reuss, Legislative Director, WEAL, and Maxine Forman, Director of Policy Analysis, WEAL, Washington, D.C., June 21, 1984.

tems. Other portions of Title I that address taxes and retirement have been defeated, including a displaced homemakers tax credit and refundability of the child care credit for low-income families. Efforts have been made to effect changes in the provision of insurance as outlined in Title III, but to date passage has not been realized. Legislative endeavors regarding Title II, which address care for dependent children, have been considered for at least the past decade and a half without success. Child care provisions in the Economic Equity Act, which have not been passed but are under congressional consideration, include an increase in the child care tax credit, provision of tax-exempt status for nonprofit day care centers, creation of information and referral centers related to day care services, and care before and after school for children of working parents.[3]

On March 14, 1983, Representative Patricia Schroeder (D-Colo.) introduced the Economic Equity Act of 1983 (H.R. 3909) into the House of Representatives. An identical piece of legislation (S. 888) was introduced in the Senate by Senator Dave Durenberger on March 23, 1983. In the House, H.R. 3909 had 134 co-sponsors; S. 888 had 32 co-sponsors in the Senate, suggesting its widespread support.

FAIR INSURANCE

It is not possible to discuss the insurance industry without differentiating its major component parts. The insurance industry provides two major types of insurance: life and health insurance, and property and casualty insurance. At the present time the only criteria that are employed to differentiate fees and payment scales in the insurance industry are age and sex. Differentials such as financial status, habits (such as drinking, smoking, or the use of dangerous drugs), occupation, condi-

[3] Telephone interview with Anne Radigan, Congressional Caucus for Women's Issues, Sept. 10, 1985. Congress has authorized, but not appropriated, funds for day care information and referral services and care before and after school for "latch key" children to be merged into a child care block grant.

tion of health, and the like are not used to determine either insurance fee or payment schedules. Life insurance and health insurance are provided to people both individually and as members of groups.

Differential fee and payment schedules for women and men were instituted by the insurance industry in the 1950s as more women began to enter the work force and more women began to purchase insurance. The use of unisex tables has been focused on insurance that is based on individual contracts and not group contracts. Life, automobile, and disability insurance policies are most often purchased by individuals rather than groups. Hence it is these sectors of the insurance industry that are involved in the conflict regarding the use of unisex tables to determine insurance premiums and benefit levels.[4]

Nondiscrimination in insurance is a role equity issue whose supporters have not had to contend with the kinds of opposition generated by opponents of role change issues. In fact, the major barriers that have been set in the way of passage of a fair insurance law are economically based and address redistribution of resources and government regulation of industry. The insurance industry claims that a ban on the use of sex to determine rates and benefits would be financially disastrous for the insurance companies and would not benefit women.[5] Also, because historically the insurance industry has been subject to states' oversight and controls, federal intervention and regulation are viewed with some fear.

Support for legislation that would mandate unisex insurance has existed since the late 1970s. In fact, the Nondiscrimination in Insurance Act (H.R. 100) was introduced in every session of Congress since 1978, though there was no significant activity in behalf of the proposal until 1983. In 1983, when H.R. 100 was introduced in the House of Representatives, a companion bill, S. 372, was introduced in the Senate by

[4] Interview with Representative James Florio (D-N.J.), Cherry Hill, N.J., July 3, 1984.

[5] Nancy L. Ross, "Both Sides Find Support in GAO Study of Unisex Coverage," *Washington Post National Weekly Edition*, Feb. 13, 1984, 22.

Senator Robert Packwood (R-Ore.). For the first time there was momentum generated in both the Congress and in the women's movement for the passage of the proposed law.

The proposed legislation would have prohibited discrimination in both the setting of insurance fees and the payment of benefits on the basis of race, color, sex, and national origin. The original legislative proposal would have made this coverage retroactive to cover people who were already recipients of insurance benefits and people who are currently paying premiums.

Legislative efforts related to pension and insurance equity were in part stimulated by Supreme Court decisions. The issue of eliminating sex as an insurance rating factor had first been considered in 1978 by the Supreme Court in its decision in *Manhart* v. *City of Los Angeles*.[6] In the Manhart decision the Court ruled that Title VII of the Civil Rights Act of 1964 "precludes treatment of individuals as simply components of a racial, sexual or national class."[7] In 1983, in its decision in *Arizona Governing Board* v. *Norris*, the Court in a 5-4 decision used this Manhart precedent and outlawed sex discrimination in those employer-sponsored insurance policies where payments are deducted from take-home salary.[8] Only future contributions to pension plans are affected, because of the costs involved in equalizing benefits retroactively. In response to the Norris decision companies have had to convert employer-purchased pension plans to unisex standards. However, individual policies were not covered by the Norris decision or by Title VII of the Civil Rights Act of 1964. The proposed fair insurance legislation would extend the Norris coverage to individual as well as group policyholders.

Hearings were held on H.R. 100 in 1982. Initially the insurance industry was not too concerned about the legislation and thus did not direct many of its resources to combating the pro-

---

[6] 434 U.S.815 (1978).

[7] Daniel Froomkin, " 'Easy Vote' on Insurance Gender Gap Turns Out to Be a Tough Political Call," *National Journal* 15 (July 23, 1983), 1545.

[8] 102 S. Ct. 3492 (1983).

spective law. Its nonaction was due in large measure to disbelief that there were sufficient votes in the Congress to pass unisex insurance legislation. When the Senate committee began to work up S. 372, the insurance industry began to take the proposed legislation and its supporters in the women's movement seriously. It became apparent to the insurance companies that there might after all be sufficient votes to enact a law. Thus they garnered their very considerable resources to fight the passage of a law.[9]

As discussed earlier, the basis for the industry's opposition to unisex legislation appears to be twofold. First, the industry estimates that the administrative costs of switching to unisex tables will be $1 billion. (The women's movement points to a GAO study stating that this figure represents just 4 percent of one year's administrative costs.) Also, there is opposition to federal regulation of the insurance industry; insurance traditionally has been regulated by the states.[10]

The issue of unisex insurance led to the mobilization of the insurance industry in an effort to protect the existing system. The major insurance companies as well as their agents have been the primary opponents of any unisex insurance legislation. The umbrella organization for the life insurance industry, the American Council of Life Insurance (ACLI) representing 575 companies, has been particularly active in opposing legislation. Also involved in active lobbying against unisex insur-

[9] Interview with Daniel Case, Actuary, American Council of Life Insurance, Washington, D.C., Sept. 24, 1984. Actually, the use of unisex insurance tables would bring the insurance industry full circle back to its pre-1950s' status when it did in fact utilize unisex tables. It was not until the decade of the 1950s that insurance companies moved to sex-based tables to determine insurance premiums and payments. This alteration in policy was propelled by several factors. First, insurance companies saw an increase in the potential market among women—both in the work force and among housewives. Also, given the longer life expectancy of women, it was determined that there was a need for differentiated premium and payment scales. At the present time, between 20 and 25 percent of individual life insurance contracts are purchased by women. In the 1940s and 1950s the comparable figure was much lower.

[10] *Washington Post National Weekly Edition*, Feb. 13, 1984, 22.

ance legislation has been the Committee for Fair Insurance Rates, a coalition set up specifically to combat the passage of H.R. 100. Members of this coalition include insurance companies that sell various types of insurance. Thirty-four companies have been involved in this coalition, including most of the very largest.[11]

The insurance industry mounted a million dollar campaign to defeat the legislation, running full-page ads in 64 newspapers, including the *Wall Street Journal* and the *Washington Post*, suggesting that sex discrimination in this case was fair and necessary and produced lower life insurance rates for women, whereas a change in the law would create significant financial hardship. Pro-insurance industry advocates also pointed to the fact that women under 25 paid lower premiums than men for auto insurance. Insurance lobbyists directed a major direct-mail campaign to over 500,000 people, using personalized letterheads and printed letters for recipients to return to the appropriate members of Congress.[12] The campaign provided for a toll-free number that people could call to indicate their support for the insurance companies' position on unisex insurance. The companies would then send an anti-unisex insurance message on the individual's behalf to his or her representative at no cost. What began as an equity issue, championed by a coalition of civil rights and feminist forces, engendered significant opposition based on purported costs to women and insurance carriers.

Most notable among women's groups lobbying in this foray were WEAL, the National Federation of Business and Professional Women, and AAUW. Also very actively involved in this campaign has been the Leadership Conference on Civil Rights. LCCR has directed considerable resources toward efforts to enact unisex legislation, which is viewed as a civil rights issue because it is one of the last vestiges of legal discrimination allowed. Coincident with the insurance industry's commitment to fighting the passage of H.R. 100, 175 organizations that fa-

[11] Interviews with Pat Reuss and Maxine Forman.
[12] *New York Times*, May 20, 1983, I-18.

vored passage of a unisex law, including women's groups, unions, civil rights groups, religious organizations, and consumer groups, joined together in the Task Force on Insurance Discrimination of LCCR to lobby for passage of unisex legislation.[13] The Executive Director of LCCR, Ralph Neas, has been intimately involved with this issue from the time he helped draft the initial Economic Equity Act legislation as a member of Senator Dave Durenberger's staff. Most of the participants in the lobbying efforts to enact legislation credit Neas with being a prime mover in the process of bringing the issue into the legislative limelight. Support for unisex insurance legislation has been forthcoming from several labor unions and professional organizations. The American Federation of State, County, and Municipal Employees (AFSCME), the International Union of Electrical, Radio, and Machine Workers, and the nursing association have been particularly active in lobbying for a law.[14]

In the Congress itself, legislative support has been reasonably widespread. In the House of Representatives the legislative prime movers have been Representatives Barbara Mikulski (D-Md.), James Florio (D-N.J.), and John Dingell (D-Mich.). In the Senate, Senators Dave Durenberger (R-Minn.), Mark Hatfield (R-Ore.), who introduced similar legislation in 1980, and Robert Packwood (R-Ore.), whose committee has been considering the insurance legislation, have been especially supportive.

The support that the women's movement had in Congress initially was considerable and unusually active. For example, Representative Florio conducted a seminar for women's groups to educate them about the intricacies of insurance issues so that they would have all the facts and expertise necessary to combat the insurance industry.[15]

In 1982-83, when the unisex insurance issue first came into

---

[13] Interview with Judy Schub, Director of Public Policy, The National Federation of Business and Professional Women, Washington, D.C., June 20, 1984.

[14] *Ibid.*

[15] Interview with James Florio (D-N.J.), Cherry Hill, N.J., July 3, 1984.

legislative prominence, some efforts were made to meld a compromise between the insurance industry and LCCR's Task Force on Insurance Discrimination. Though insurance industry people were unhappy about the prospects of any national unisex legislation being enacted, they were prepared to talk with representatives of the task force. In particular, the industry was concerned about the retroactive provisions of the proposed law, since it estimates very high costs for implementing such a provision. There were some attempts to work out a compromise between the insurance industry and the Task Force, but they all failed. On one occasion NOW took a strong position in favor of retroactivity and objected to efforts to delay implementation,[16] which had been proposed in an effort to allay industry concerns about solvency. NOW was also unwilling to budge on the issue of "topping up" of women's lower pension payments to higher levels to match men's. NOW adopted a hard-line position and would not compromise at all on the unisex principle. Other groups in the coalition were willing to discuss the issue. However, NOW had enough support on the Task Force to be able to carry the vote and thus prevent any discussion of compromise.

Compromise efforts finally came to a halt in May 1983 when industry representatives on the American Council of Life Insurance withdrew from further negotiations after a tumultuous (and unusual) meeting, at which membership was polled on the issue, and they rejected the compromise-oriented stance initially endorsed by the board under the leadership of the Prudential Insurance Company.[17]

On March 28, 1984, H.R. 100 was considered by the entire House Energy and Commerce Committee. This bill, proposed by Representatives Dingell, Florio, and Mikulski, represented a compromise in response to some of the articulated concerns, especially regarding retroactivity. The bill would have:

a) eliminated retroactivity by removing the need to increase the benefits of those already receiving them (all

[16] *Chronicle of Higher Education*, June 22, 1983, 13.
[17] Interview with Daniel Case.

future retirees/beneficiaries, however, would be en-
sured equal benefits when payment begins);
b) eliminated the requirement that future benefits be
equalized by raising the female benefit to the level of
the male benefit ("topping up");
c) extended the effective date from 90 days to one year
after enactment.[18]

Rather than adopting this compromise, the Committee
voted 24 to 18, with all of the 15 Republicans supporting the
majority[19] (and with some of the co-sponsors of the initial legislation—such as Normal Lent (D-N.Y.) and William Richards (D-N.M.)—voting with the majority) to approve an
amendment that gutted the fair insurance principle as set forth
in H.R. 100.[20] The amendment that "killed" H.R. 100 was introduced by Representative Billy Tauzin (D-La). It provided
for:

a) exclusion of sex discrimination in individual insurance
contracts from coverage of the bill;
b) exclusion of pregnancy discrimination from the definition of sex discrimination under the bill;
c) undermining federal enforcement of the legislation.[21]

Once the vote was cast on Tauzin's amendment, H.R. 100
no longer had any real meaning since individual contracts were
excluded from coverage of the law. Initial supporters of the bill
opposed its further consideration in the amended form. In the
Senate Commerce Committee a vote was not taken to consider
the GAO report assessing the financial impact on the industry
requested by Packwood, owing to the adverse political climate. Consequently, the amended version of H.R. 100 was not
brought to the floor of either house of Congress for a vote.

The effort to enact the law failed, though the expectation of
most of the congressional and interest group participants in

---

18 WEAL, *The Economic Equity Act of 1983* (June 22, 1984), mimeo.
19 Interview with Judy Schub.
20 Interview with Representative James Florio.
21 WEAL, *The Economic Equity Act of 1983.*

the process is that it is only a matter of time before there are changes in the insurance laws that will render discrimination against women by the insurance industry illegal. Most agree that, as with other efforts, political education was one result of the Campaign. Ultimately, it may be suggested, the insurance industry was able to raise the level of conflict and determine the parameters of debate by calling into question (through massive resource expenditure and astute public relations) the Act's potential harm and cost.

Ralph Neas, the LCCR's director, has suggested that a national insurance law is simply "a matter of time,"[22] a view concurred with by Representative James Florio (a member of the House Energy and Commerce Subcommittee that considered H.R. 100), who maintains that within five years all insurance fees and benefits will be based on unisex tables.[23]

Additional interim strategies are being utilized by feminist groups to pressure the insurance industry into recognizing the principle of unisex insurance, particularly litigation and efforts at the state level. In Pennsylvania, NOW-LDEF won a ruling from the State Supreme Court finding that the state ERA prohibits insurance companies from basing auto insurance rates on sex.[24] Four other states—Hawaii, North Carolina, Massachusetts, and Michigan—also outlaw sex-based and marital status criteria in auto insurance pricing. Montana, in 1983, enacted legislation that requires insurance companies not to treat men and women differently. This act was the subject of an intensive repeal effort by insurance company lobbyists in 1985, and both in Montana and Pennsylvania industry lobbyists have attempted to delay implementation of unisex laws.[25] NOW has filed a class-action suit on behalf of the organization's 10,000 District of Columbia members, contending that health insurance provider Mutual of Omaha has vio-

---

[22] Interview with Ralph Neas, Director, Leadership Conference on Civil Rights, Washington, D.C., Aug. 30, 1984.

[23] Interview with Representative James Florio.

[24] *National NOW Times*, Nov.-Dec. 1984, 9.

[25] *New York Times*, Feb. 17, 1985, 33.

lated the District's 1977 Human Rights Act. Feminists have also sought to induce individual insurance companies to "break ranks" with regard to the unisex issue in order to weaken unity. Women's groups were successful in bringing pressure to bear on American Express to have its Fireman's Fund establish unisex tables and in persuading this group to withdraw from the Committee for Fair Insurance Rates.[26] Other companies that have adopted unisex tables include Aetna, Allstate, and Travellers, as well as the Hartford Insurance Company. Through multiple efforts, it is likely that at some point in the not too distant future there will be a national law mandating a system of unisex insurance.

PENSION EQUITY

Whereas the proposed unisex insurance legislation met with strong opposition from the affected industry, pension reform legislation encountered little conflict and almost no articulated opposition. Pat Reuss and Maxine Foreman, both of WEAL, suggested that in part this lack of resistance may be explained by the fact that pension costs can be passed on to the pensioner. Also, the Internal Revenue Service can monitor pension provisions whereas the insurance industry envisions high change-over costs.[27] It is true, too, that this was a case in which the legislation and the political symbols were successfully manipulated so as to make a strong argument for equity adjustments. Even the name of the law was selected well. The Retirement Equity Act has a sex-neutral title that makes no reference to women.[28] The new law lowers the age for enrollment in pension plans from 25 to 21, and the age at which employees begin to earn credit toward vesting from 22 to 18, as well as providing maternity and other leave provisions without sacrifice of pension credit. Coverage for surviving and divorced spouses is

[26] Interview with Daniel Case.
[27] Interviews with Pat Reuss and Maxine Forman.
[28] Interview with Judy Schub.

also included. Thus Representative Geraldine Ferraro (D-N.Y.), who was a sponsor of the original legislation, contended that "this legislation is a key piece in the efforts to remove handicaps and barriers to the full participation of women in our nation's economy."[29] Representative Olympia Snowe (R-Me.) further observed that the "bipartisan support. . . demonstrated . . . the widely recognized and urgent need to redress the lack of financial security and the inadequacy of our pension laws with respect to women."[30]

The conditions to which Representatives Ferraro and Snowe were referring clearly showed women to be at a disadvantage vis-a-vis men regarding pension rights. Older women have tended disproportionately to experience the inequities of the nation's private pension system owing to the disregard of their roles as housekeepers and workers. In 1981, almost 60 percent of all people over 65 were women. More than half of these women were widows. Single women over 65 living alone represented 85 percent of all older people whose incomes fall below the poverty threshold. Moreover, in 1983 the average Social Security benefit for a woman 65 or older was $4,476 per year; for a man the comparable figure was $5,724. In 1981, 10.5 percent of all women over 65 were receiving private pensions that averaged $2,427 a year; 27.7 percent of all men over 65 were receiving private pensions or annuities that averaged $4,152 a year. Of single women over 65, 60 percent depended solely on Social Security benefits for their income. Finally, only 5 to 10 percent of surviving spouses received their spouses' pension benefits.[31]

Private pension plans are regulated by the Employee Retirement Income Security Act (ERISA) of 1974. The 1974 legislation did not provide any protection for women as wives, divorced spouses, or widows of men who participated in company pension plans. Furthermore, it failed to take into ac-

[29] Congressional Caucus for Women's Issues, *Update* 4 (May 31, 1984), 1.
[30] *Ibid.*

[31] Congressional Caucus for Women's Issues, *The Economic Equity Act*, D.C., undated, 3.

count the unique work patterns that women often experience owing to their childbearing and other household roles.[32] For example, ERISA regulations failed to credit women fully for their early participation in the work force or to allow for childbearing and childrearing responsibilities. ERISA also allowed for a total forfeiture of spousal survival benefits in various situations despite the fact that the worker may have been fully vested in a pension plan before his death. ERISA also failed to recognize the contribution of a wife/homemaker to a worker's pension. No provision was made for the allocation of these benefits in the event of divorce.[33] Thus there was considerable concern regarding pension rights for women.

The campaign to enact pension equity legislation was spearheaded by several advocacy groups. In particular, women from WEAL, the Women's Pension Project of the Pension Rights Center, and AAUW were involved at the outset. They were joined in their efforts by lobbyists from other women's organizations. Groups such as the Older Women's League (OWL) founded in 1983, which specializes in issues of particular concern to older women, the National Federation of Business and Professional Women, and NOW worked in close cooperation to get pension equity legislation enacted. Representatives of the women's groups met together, ironed out conflicting interests, and then presented a united front on the pension issue[34] (in contrast to dissension with regard to unisex insurance). Several members of Congress were particularly active in the early stages that led to passage of the law: Senators Robert Dole, David Durenberger, and Robert Packwood and Representatives Pat Schroeder and Geraldine Ferraro. It was toward the end of 1982, after the failure of sufficient states to ratify the ERA, that Senator Dole realized that Republicans should provide some leadership role in the enactment of pension equity

[32] *Ibid.*

[33] Congress of the United States, Congressional Caucus for Women's Issues, *The Economic Equity Act of 1983*, Washington, D.C., June 22, 1984, 2.

[34] Interview with Ann Moss, Director, Women's Pension Project of the Pension Rights Center, Washington, D.C., June 21, 1984.

legislation. Public opinion polls at this time showed clearly that there was sympathy and support for legislation that would provide more equitable conditions for women. Senator Dole introduced S. 19 in the Senate. The proposed legislation was sent to the Finance Committee, which together with the Labor and Human Resources Committee has joint jurisdiction over all pension laws. This pension reform act was much simpler than the law that ultimately was enacted. Some of the other titles of the Economic Equity Act were identified by the Republican leadership as quite worthwhile, but programs such as dependent care were believed to be too expensive. Thus the pension issue was selected by the Republican leadership as *the* women's issue on which to concentrate, partially so they "could go home and say they did something for women."[35] The staffs of Senators Dole, Durenberger, and Packwood joined with the staff people from key Democratic offices, including Senator Edward Kennedy's (D-Mass.) and Senator Russell Long's (D-La.), to draft the legislation. Staff personnel from the office of Senator Orrin Hatch—since he is a key member of the Labor and Human Resources Center—worked on the legislative proposal as well. What emerged from this process was a clearly bipartisan piece of legislation.[36] The Senate bill was the one that was voted out of the Finance Committee. The Labor and Human Resources Committee approved their version with no controversy at all.

In the House of Representatives the pension equity issue was considered by both the Ways and Means Committee and the Education and Labor Committee. Both of these committees initially reported out different versions of the bill. What was passed ultimately by the House and sent to conference committee was primarily the Ways and Means Committee bill.[37]

As with credit and pregnancy discrimination, there was very little opposition in the Senate or the House to the legislation

[35] Interview with Ann E. Moran, Tax Counsel, U.S. Senate Finance Committee, Washington, D.C., Aug. 31, 1984.

[36] Interview with Ann Moss.

[37] Interview with Judy Schub.

that was drafted. Many opponents of unisex insurance supported the pension equity legislation, which passed both houses unanimously. The only problems that did arise regarding enactment were related to the amending process in the Senate. At the very end of the Senate session in the fall of 1983, when the Pension Equity Bill was being discussed on the Senate floor, numerous amendments were added to the bill. These amendments were not being attached to generate opposition to the proposed legislation. Rather the bill was seen as a convenient vehicle for many "pet projects." By virtue of successful lobbying efforts the women's groups were able to have the amendments removed. The senators who introduced the amendments deleted them as a result of constituency-generated pressures fostered by the women's groups.[38] In part, the ease with which the legislation passed both houses of Congress is due to the fact that key business organizations, such as the Chamber of Commerce, had been convinced that no increased costs would be incurred as a result of the passage of pension equity legislation.[39]

On November 18, 1983, the Senate passed H.R. 2769/S. 1978. On May 22, 1984, the House of Representatives passed H.R. 4280, the Retirement Equity Act.[40]

Both the Senate and the House versions of the bill provided for:

a) a lowering of the minimum wage for vesting from 22 to 18, for participation in pension plan from 25 to 21;

b) protection of pension benefits during maternity/paternity leaves (there is a liberalization in break-in-service rules, too);

c) a requirement that there be automatic joint and survivor benefits unless both spouses consent to waive them;

[38] Interview with Ann Moss.
[39] Interview with Judy Schub.
[40] Congressional Caucus for Women's Issues, *Update*, 1.

d) a clarification of state court authority to distribute pension benefits between spouses upon divorce.

The primary differences between the bills concerned the loss of survivor benefits in two separate situations.

1) If an employee died before attaining the early retirement age (55), the spouses's survivor benefits were forfeited. The Senate bill amended this provision so that if a worker had worked for ten years, is vested in the plan, and reaches age 45, the survivor benefits are secure. The House bill rejected any arbitrary age limit and provided that once the employee is vested in the plan survivor's benefits are guaranteed.
2) If an employee died of natural causes within two years of electing survival benefits, these benefits were forfeited. The Senate bill retained this rule whereas the House bill eliminated it.[41]

After differences in the Senate and House versions were worked out in conference committee, compromise legislation passed both houses of the Congress with no difficulty and President Reagan signed the Retirement Equity Act into law in August 1984. The new law:

1) lowers from 25 to 21 the age at which employers must enroll most workers in pension plans;
2) lowers from 22 to 18 the age at which employees begin to earn credits toward vesting;
3) prevents counting a one-year maternity or paternity leave as a break in service and permits workers to stay away from their jobs for five years without sacrificing pension credits;
4) prevents employees from waiving coverage for survivors without the written consent of their spouses;
5) gives state courts the authority to treat pensions as joint property in divorce cases;

[41] *Ibid.*

6) grants death benefits to the spouse of a worker who is fully vested even if the worker dies before the company's early retirement age.[42]

The pension law that was enacted is not all inclusive, but it was seen by women's groups as a "foot in the door" for the protection of women in the provision of pensions. The new act meets criteria outlined regarding costs—these may be passed on to the pensionee. In fact, because of the limited nature of this legislation, any costs would be moderate. The legislation was "incremental," not vast or sweeping, and does not deal with numerous issues such as integration and vesting.

There are other problems that activists concerned with pension reform wish to address. First, most people do not receive any private pension benefits at all.[43] Also, when dealing with the area of pension equity legislation, many different committees are involved and thus lobbying becomes a very complicated process. For example, wives' rights for military pension benefits must be reported out of the defense committees; public pension provisions must be reported out of government operations committees; and private pensions, as was the case with the Retirement Equity Act, must be considered in the Senate by the Finance Committee and the Senate labor and Human Resources Committee and in the House by the Ways and Means Committee and the Education and Welfare Committee. Congressional simplification would facilitate reform.

Efforts to overhaul the private pension system are not completed. In fact, preliminary work to expand coverage for women commenced almost immediately after passage of the 1984 law. Any additional pension equity legislation will address issues relating to vesting, integration, and portability. Geraldine Ferraro, who drafted additional pension reform legislation in the fall of 1984, when she was still a member of the House of Representatives, suggested that these are "the three

[42] David A. Vise, "The Next Pension Bill Could Cost Companies Money," *Washington Post National Weekly Edition*, Nov. 19, 1984, 22.

[43] Interview with Judy Schub.

areas in which ERISA is in the greatest need of reform if it is to be fair to all workers and flexible enough to accommodate modern-day working patterns."[44] Her proposed legislation was referred to as the VIP Bill. The "V" in the bill would reduce from ten to five the minimum number of years of work necessary for an employee to be eligible for the vesting of pension rights. The "I" in the bill refers to integration. Integration is the practice of offsetting pension plan participants' benefits by the amount of the Social Security benefits an employee is eligible to receive. The proposed law would mandate that all integrated pension plans provide some minimum benefit above the Social Security benefit. The "P" in the bill refers to portability. This proposal would let workers take vested benefits and invest them in portable pension accounts to accumulate higher retirement benefits. There is some expectation that these proposals will engender industry opposition, especially to the vesting provision since this would cost companies more money.[45]

Though it has not been discussed in this chapter, it is significant that a second piece of the Economic Equity Act package, the Child Support Enforcement Act, also was passed by the 98th Congress. It provides for a 70 percent federal government contribution to the states for improvement of child support enforcement, interstate enforcement, the interception of tax refunds in child support cases in arrears, and expedited administrative and collection procedures. Moreover, it requires that, at the conclusion of a thirty-day period, withholding on wages and property liens will begin without further recourse to court proceedings. The legislation reforms an ineffective 1975 measure and extends coverage to non-AFDC mothers.[46]

[44] Quoted by Vise, *op. cit.*

[45] *Ibid.*

[46] Judy Mann, "Why Women Should Vote for Women," *Washington Post National Weekly Edition*, Aug. 27, 1984, 24; *1984 Congressional Quarterly Almanac*, 464.

COMPARABLE WORTH

A final aspect of economic equity to be considered in this chapter is not part of the proposed Economic Equity Act. This is the issue of "pay equity" or "comparable worth."

While the Equal Pay Act of 1963 makes it illegal for employers to pay employees of one sex higher wages for "equal work than the other sex—involving equal skill, responsibilities and efforts for work performed under the same conditions," and Title VII of the Civil Rights Act of 1964 explicitly forbids discrimination on the basis of sex, women's wages continue to lag at an average of 62 cents of each dollar earned by men.[47] This issue has come to the fore in the 1980s and may mark a change in direction for some women activists who realize that all women cannot be integrated into male-dominated jobs.[48] The emergence of this issue may also respresent a recognition that while many discriminatory laws have been eradicated, numerous economic problems remain for women. The salience of "pay equity" was sparked by a landmark federal court decision in Washington State in the fall of 1983 (*County of Washington* v. *Gunther*)[49] that found the state guilty of "direct overt and institutionalized discrimination" aginst 15,000 female employees. Judge Jack Tanner ordered the state to make salary adjustments and payments retroactive to 1979. The potential cost was estimated at between $500 million and $1 billion.[50] In September 1985 the Ninth Circuit U.S. Court of Appeals reversed the lower court decision, holding that the wage gap itself did not demonstrate intentional discrimination by the state against women.[51] Should the case eventually come before the Supreme Court, the outcome is uncertain, since the Court has

[47] *Public Administration Times*, May 5, 1984, 2; *New York Times*, Sept. 4, 1984, B9.
[48] Interview with Diane Doughty, Legislative Liaison, and Mary Jean Taylor, Vice President, NOW, Washington, D.C., Jan. 23, 1985.
[49] 452 US 161.
[50] *Chronicle of Higher Education*, June 11, 1984, 21-22.
[51] 449 US 950.

articulated no clear-cut position on related issues. (Nonetheless, the state has moved toward pay equity in the absence of clear judicial direction. A 1986 settlement between the State of Washington and the Washington Federation of State Employees ended a twelve-year dispute—providing for 350,000 workers to receive pay raises set at $482 million.[52]) In 1981 the Supreme Court ruled that prison matrons could sue the State of Oregon on the grounds that they were victims of discrimination because their jobs as matrons were similar to those of male prison guards, although they were lower paid. The Court in this instance made no judgment regarding comparable worth.[53] In *Spaulding* v. *University of Washington* the Supreme Court refused to review a similar decision involving nursing instructors at the University of Washington.[54]

The issue of equal pay for jobs of comparable worth has been endorsed by a coalition of women's groups, including the National Commission on Pay Equity (representing some 150 groups), and unions, such as AFSCME of the AFL-CIO. AFSCME has been a party to litigation in Washington State and in other states. However, it is important to note that some women's groups, in contrast to their attitudes on many other issues of concern to the women's movement, are ambivalent about the feasibility of achieving national legislation. There is also some concern that it might be a mistake to propose amendments to the Equal Pay Act and Title VII of the Civil Rights Act.[55] Even among those activists who share this view, though, the question of comparable worth is seen as an issue that can be used to "scare" decision makers and thus be exploited as a "tactical wedge" to achieve other movement goals.

Spurred on by Representative Mary Rose Oakar (D-Ohio),

[52] *New York Times*, Jan. 2, 1986, I, 5.

[53] *New York Times*, Sept. 4, 1984, B9.

[54] Marilyn Marks, "State Legislators, Judges and NOW Congress Examining 'Comparable Worth,' " *National Journal*, Sept. 8, 1984, 1666-7.

[55] Interviews with Marilyn De Poy, Women's Rights Coordinator, AFSCME, Sept. 1, 1984, and Pat Reuss and Maxine Forman, WEAL.

Chair of the House Subcommittee on Compensation and Employee Benefits, the 1984 Omnibus Civil Service Bill requested a GAO report on how a comparable worth study of the federal civilian work force should be conducted. The GAO study showed that there was on the average a $9,000 pay differential between federally employed women and men.[56] The Senate also has held hearings on the issue. Further congressional efforts relating to a potential "pay equity" analysis of government employees are pending.

Oakar's original pay equity legislation called for a comparable worth study of the federal pay system and was passed in the House by a 413-6 vote. But as an issue that involved a likely redistribution of economic resources from men to women, the legislation has met with major opposition. In particular, it is strongly opposed by the Reagan Administration (including outspoken U.S. Civil Rights Commission Chair Clarence Pendleton, as well as Assistant Attorney General for Civil Rights William Bradford Reynolds). Many congressional Republicans and the Office of Personal Management, fearing greatly increased costs, have objected to legislation in this area. Groups such as the National Association of Manufacturers oppose the extension of the concept to the private sector, while conservative think tanks such as the Heritage Foundation have urged that the issue be defeated. Issues of cost, intrusive government regulation, and problems of implementation, as well as the potential absence of unity among the feminist community, threaten to make this issue a difficult one to address.

Nonetheless, even in the absence of federal policy related to comparable worth, numerous states and municipalities, under pressure from women's groups and unions, have been dealing with the issue. Thirty states are currently studying the issue, while San Jose, California, and the State of Minnesota have en-

[56] *New York Times*, Nov. 1, 1984, 4, and phone interview with Anne Radigan, Sept. 10, 1985.

acted pay equity laws, with the letter setting aside funds to implement it.

Conclusion

Changes in the pension law, improved mechanisms for the collection of child support payments, and potential modifications in the provision of insurance benefits should improve conditions for many women. These are equity issues that have stirred up some debate and opposition but no ideological fervor. Comparable worth, an issue that is not addressed by the Economic Equity Act, concerns an equity matter that affects women in the work force. The current concern is for equal pay for comparable work. Though this is a basic equity issue, it is meeting strong opposition wherever it is raised. This opposition is based on the widely held belief that wages should be based on the operation of the free market. Any changes in the way that wages are determined thus generates considerable ideological conflict among both lawmakers and representatives of industry. Moreover, the costs of implementation are assumed to be very high. This is a role equity issue that because of its redistributive implications for women and the economy appears to be close to the role change end of the continuum suggested in Chapter 1, at least at the national level. It seems most likely that comparable worth will continue to be addressed most effectively through collective bargaining, court action, and state legislation.

CHAPTER 9

THE FEMINIST MOVEMENT: THE PAST AND LIKELY FUTURE

INTRODUCTION

Our analysis has suggested that when issues are perceived as affecting role equity rather than role change, the opportunities for favorable impact on the political system have been maximized for feminist groups. It has further been proposed that when the feminist movement has experienced success in attainment of policy goals, this has been due in large measure to keen understanding of the realities of the American political system and adherence to the four rules outlined in Chapter 1.

We have argued that several factors are crucial to attainment of goals in the American political system. These include an issue with the image of broad-based support; an issue narrow enough not to challenge basic values or divide supporters; a policy network with access, and capability of providing information, to decision makers; the willingness to compromise with constituent groups and in the political process; and, finally, the ability to define success in terms of increments of change rather than total victory.

In this final chapter we will evaluate the utility of the distinction between role equity and role change as two poles of a continuum and the validity of the four rules proposed. In addition, we will venture a look at the prospects for continued feminist participation in politics.

THE POLITICS OF CHANGE

Perhaps the most sweeping change created by the activity of women lobbyists in the policies considered bere occurred in the Equal Credit Opportunity Act, which operating in a policy vacuum created new policy in an area potentially affecting millions of women. However, although women did succeed in broadening the political agenda, they did so only by conforming to the system's "mobilization of bias." The issue was relatively noncontroversial, involving distributed costs and distributed benefits. While business may incur greater costs, they will be passed on indirectly to the consumer, and both women and men may profit, for example, from the extension of mortgage credit to a two-income family. Issue demands were specific and challenged no fundamental societal values. Though ultimately a redistributive issue in the sense that it transfers economic power to women, this policy was perceived as one of equity or equal rights and as such had no formal opposition. The issue did not involve mass publics and was resolved at the leadership levels of politics. The absence of a national precedent to rely upon facilitated possibilities for innovation.

The Pregnancy Discrimination Act was similarly a relatively narrow issue, one involving no public outlay of funds. Like the Equal Credit Opportunity Act. this legislation dealt with equitable treatment for women—in this instance, clarifying the precise meaning of sex discrimination against women under Title VII of the Civil Rights Act of 1964. However, since the issue dealt with pregnant women and therefore the potential role of women as mothers and homemakers, it was fraught with more controversy than the Equal Credit Opportunity Act, particularly since the question of funding abortions under disability plans received vociferous attention from opponents of "free choice." Nonetheless, backed by a coalition of over three hundred groups, from labor unions to Right to Lifers, and even some business groups, the legislation enjoyed broad-based support. No doubt some supporters of pregnancy discrimination legislation view this policy area as encouraging procreation and family development and, therefore, as being consistent with "pro-family" politics. The demands were highly specific and narrow and, like the credit issue, involved little intervention from outside the federal policy-making structure itself. Thus it is not surprising that women enjoyed success on this issue—although they did have to compromise on the issue of abortion as a pregnancy-related disability.

The Retirement Equity Act, like the Pregnancy Discrimination and Equal Credit Opportunity acts, engendered little opposition from the affected industry during the legislative process. An equity issue, it involved limited cost and stirred little controversy. However, it is a "first step" in an incremental process aimed at the reform of the American pension system. In contrast to the easy passage of the pension law, efforts to enact unisex insurance legislation have been obstructed by the major lobbying campaign mounted by the insurance industry.

For Title IX, banning sex discrimination in schools, the issue of role change was more clearly involved. More overt disagreement arose regarding the degree to which the federal government should go on prohibiting policies and practices that treated the sexes differently in educational institutions. A major controversy arose around the issue of intercollegiate sports for women, which involved the maintenance of traditional sex roles for women. Other issues seemed to have strong sexual overtones, related to fears of potential invasion of privacy, and created hostile reactions from members of Congress and administrative officials including then HEW Secretaries Casper Weinberger and Joseph Califano. In contrast to the speed and ease with which the Equal Credit Opportunity Act moved through the political rulemaking process, Title IX took seven years, and even at that, compliance with the Act is uneven and challenges continue to occur in the political arena, in courts, and on campuses.

Of all the issues considered here, abortion is the one that most involves role change, because it is perceived as having the most impact on women's roles as wives and mothers and most appears to threaten traditional societal patterns. Because of the ideological nature of the abortion issue, feminists have suffered several defeats in the legislative process. Abortion is perceived to have consequences at the ballot box. Virtually all members of Congress and lobbyists agree that the most mobi-

lized pressures come from the pro-life groups, who have created the impression that they represent single-issue voters who
can cause electoral defeat for legislators who oppose them.
Senator Robert Packwood of Oregon, who opposes the ban on
federal funding for abortion, has called abortion a single issue
that could destroy a congressman's career because of the
strong feelings it generates.[1] An important question for the
women's movement is whether erosion of support on such issues as abortion will cause a spillover and create a negative atmosphere in which to sustain and add to gains made in
the more narrow role equity areas. However, as our analysis of
responses from those we interviewed has suggested, feminist
issues are perceived as separable by legislators, largely owing
to the specialized, issue-focused orientation of the feminist
movement, and for this reason it is likely that defeat in one policy area will not result in defeat on other, narrower issues.

The Relevance of the Pluralist Rules

In the preceding pages it has been suggested that a number of
variables have helped determine the success or failure of feminist women acting through interest groups in the federal policy-making process.

A major factor that influences success is the image of broad-
based support. On each of the issues considered, women have
established coalitions with different but overlapping membership bases—in order to maximize resources and effectiveness.
Examples include the pro-choice caucus, the Campaign to End
Discrimination Against Pregnant Workers, and the National
Coalition for Women and Girls in Education. Coalitions with
unions and civil rights groups, particularly under the aegis of
the Leadership Conference on Civil Rights, have gained significance as well.

Another factor is the selection of narrow issues that do not
challenge basic values or divide potential supporters. We have

[1] *New York Times*, Oct. 6, 1977, 16.

seen that on issues that are narrow and that focus on role equity, activity by women's rights groups has found considerable support. Since the congressional passage of the ERA, Congress has been receptive to those women's issues that have little organized opposition in order to appeal to feminist constituents who may play a role in members' reelection.

When more dominant values are in question and role change issues regarding women's family and dependent status are at stake, the possibilities for success become severely limited. The media and congresswomen—to cite two groups generally supportive of women activists on the Equal Credit Opportunity Act, the Pregnancy Discrimination Act, and the Economic Equity Act—have been split, as has society generally, on such issues as federal funding for abortions.

The existence of a policy network, which has internalized the values of feminist lobbies and includes within its ranks members of the decision-making system, is supportive of women activists. The policy network that has been formally institutionalized in Washington includes representatives from the legislative and administrative sectors of government and the media, as well as legal and professional women in the nation's capital. As a result of this network, crucial information (feedback) regarding the status of proposed policies has clearly enhanced the position of feminists in policy making.

Receptivity to feminist issues has been aided by the stronger role that has developed for the Congressional Caucus for Women's Issues. The group was first founded in 1977, and it opened its doors to men in 1981. By 1984 it had 131 members and was one of the largest caucuses in Congress.[2] The impact of the caucus could be stronger but for the fact that only 4 of the 13 Republican women representatives and neither of the two women senators belong. All but two of the Democratic women representatives are members, giving the group a somewhat partisan cast. Nonetheless, the presence of sympathetic male group members placed on key committees and subcom-

[2] *Congressional Quarterly Weekly Report*, April 23, 1983, 786.

mittees seems to help compensate for the lack of unified support among women. At its best, the caucus highlights issues, helps develop alternative strategies for specific policies, gathers information on implementation of policies, and maintains contacts with numerous interest groups.[3] It also functions as an informational resource, a role aided by its bimonthly publication *Update,*and as a support system.[4] Although the caucus's role is constrained by its limited budget, which permits only two paid staff members (thus producing reliance on interns), it has created a new and positive congressional force for feminist concerns.

Another indication of the growing influence of women in politics is evident within the political structure itself, particularly with regard to the increased influence of women in Congress. For the first time, women representatives have gained some seniority and now have representation on key appropriations committees (Kennelly, on Ways and Means, and Boggs, on Appropriations).[5] These positions on key committees have proven invaluable to new legislative efforts, as was clear in Representative Kennelly's major role in obtaining passage of strong child support legislation.

Congressional aides and administrators in bureaucratic roles contribute to group effectiveness as well. In the administrative policy-making sector, as one recent study has pointed out, well-organized groups that monitor an agency and mobilize expertise in support of policy change may sometimes "counter-balance the considerable financial resources of industries and well-established groups."[6] In the case of the Equal Credit Opportunity Act and Title IX, the impact of monitoring

---

[3] Joan Hulse Thompson, "The Congressional Caucus for Women: One Hundred and Thirty Feminists in the House" (paper presented at the Midwest Political Science Association convention, April 11-14, 1984), 3.

[4] *Congressional Quarterly Weekly Report*, Jan. 26, 1985, 146.

[5] *New York Times*, May 6, 1984, E24.

[6] Paul Sabatier, "Social Movements and Regulatory Agencies: Toward a More Adequate and Less Pessimistic Theory of Clientele Capture," *Policy Sciences* 6 (1975), 320.

by newly mobilized and active organizations contributed to success. The Equal Credit Opportunity Act demonstrated the ability of women's organizations to influence the regulatory process in a new policy area.

Internally, women's groups have made more effective use of limited resources by developing specialized interests and dividing areas of specialization and by being flexible in choosing what strategy to employ in specific instances. Although several groups, such as NOW and WEAL, tend to be multi-issue organizations, we have seen that different groups have specific policy predispositions (such as NARAL in its coordination of activity on the abortion issue). High-level research and legal expertise are available to women activists from such groups as CWPS, ACLU-WRP, NWLC, NOW-LDEF, and WLDF, and these groups have provided vital assistance to activist women on all the policy issues considered here, though constrained in lobbying activity because of their tax-exempt status. Personal lobbying of sympathetic and interested legislators and bureaucrats has been increasingly utilized as newly sophisticated women's groups are involved in making "head counts" of supporters and opponents' strength. Constituency pressure, in the issues studied here, has also been used as a backup resource, to be mobilized in order to demonstrate adverse women voters' reactions to recalcitrant legislators and administrators.[7] Increased efforts by women's rights groups and their allies to maintain records on legislative voting for specific issues and disseminate information to constituents in order to defeat antifeminist elected officials may prove effective in future electoral campaigns. Litigation also is used in conjunction with traditional lobbying techniques in order to influence the outcome of national policy.

Successful groups also serve to provide informational resources to bureaucrats and members of Congress. In each of

---

[7] It should be noted that neither partisanship nor traditional support for liberal civil rights legislation necessarily is predictive of legislative voting on most women's issues. Republicans—including Brock, Packwood, and Brooke—have been active in supporting various women's rights policies.

the policies considered here, women have concentrated primarily on providing technical expertise through testimony in Congress and written comments in the regulatory process. For example, during the formulation of the Equal Credit Opportunity Act, legislators and administrators called upon women activists to legitimize their own support of a given decision as well as to supply political intelligence and to provide important data. According to a recent analysis of politics at the Office of Civil Rights: "To this day, the most detailed and comprehensive public record of OCR rulings under the Title IX regulations is not a government publication but the newsletter of the National Organization of Women (NOW) Project on Equal Educational Resources (PEER)."[8]

In each of the policies under consideration here, the women activists showed themselves ready to accept less than total victory. With regard to the Equal Credit Opportunity Act and the Pregnancy Discrimination Act, women compromised in their legislative demands and, regarding the ECOA, in their regulatory demands.[9] Women activists involved in Title IX lobbying accepted compromise on several notable occasions, too, by acceding to narrow exemptions to the law in order to forestall greater limitations.[10] On the abortion issue, activist women have been willing to concede the near impossibility of "victory" in releasing federal funds for abortions; they have concentrated their efforts instead on seeking the vaguest, fuzziest legislative language possible in order to permit the largest number of poor women to gain funded abortions, on working through the judicial process, and increasingly on building grassroots support.

[8] Jeremy Rabkin, "Office of Civil Rights," in James Q. Wilson, ed., *The Politics of Regulation* (New York: Basic Books, 1980), 329.

[9] Although as of March 1977, owing to legislative lobbying, primarily from other "rights" groups, many original feminist demands relating to the ECOA were met.

[10] Rabkin also makes this point with specific reference to exemptions for father/son, mother/daughter events from Title IX ("Office of Civil Rights," 335).

Success is usually defined as incremental, and both group tactics and image must be perceived as legitimate. In none of the cases examined here was confrontation the chosen strategy. The tactics of women's groups have been centrist and traditional, conforming to the system's "mobilization of bias." In evaluating the tactics adopted by women, an analysis of abortion politics in Hawaii seems relevant: "The appeal was reasonable, low key and essentially conservative," despite the radical degree of change entailed. Tactics appealed to reason, assuming legislators would decide on the merits of the issue, and stressed traditional middle-class values.[11]

Similar findings are reported by Janet Boles, who found in her study of the ratification process for the Equal Rights Amendment that, for the most part, ERA "proponents excelled in traditional interest group politics" and were particularly successful at the Congressional level, where they were able to discuss the issue in legalistic terms and present its abstract and technical meaning.[12]

Several concluding observations about the movement itself seem necessary. The women's movement has become professionalized and bureaucratized in the past several years. However, despite these developments, which often can lead to organizational rigidity, the groups that are involved with feminist political activity have not ossified. Quite to the contrary, the feminist movement has gained momentum and has engaged in new initiatives and strategies. The early emphasis of the movement on the concept of "sisterhood" has remained a unifying force, with the result that *inclusivity* remains an operating principle. Disparate groups have been accepted into movement politics.[13] The commitment of feminist activists remains movement oriented, negating the role of "media stars"

[11] Patricia Steinhoff and Milton Diamond, *Abortion Politics: The Hawaii Experience* (Honolulu: University Press of Hawaii, 1977), 210.

[12] Janet Boles, *The Politics of the Equal Rights Amendment* (New York: Longman, 1979), 123, 171.

[13] Carolyn Teich Adams and Katherine Teich Winston, *Mothers at Work* (New York: Longman, 1980), 133.

or charismatic leaders, as has occurred in some other types of reform groups, and preventing organizational demise with the departure of key individuals. We have suggested that women activists possess limited resources but relatively high status. They are professional activists who relate to mass constituencies that may be mobilized to demonstrate electoral (political) clout. Leaders and members are largely white, middle-class women[14] who possess significant levels of technical competence.

THE PARAMETERS OF CHANGE: THE LIMITS OF FEMINIST IMPACT

This book has sought to demonstrate the importance the newly mobilized feminist movement has come to assume in several key policy areas dealing with the role of women in contemporary society. Nonetheless, it should be emphasized that not all benefits—legislative and other—for women have emanated from pressure brought by organized groups. The passage of the Equal Pay Act of 1963, although it represented the enactment of a demand made by women's groups for decades, predates the onset of an organized feminist movement. The anti-sex discrimination clause of the Civil Rights Act of 1964 was inserted as a "joke" by a Southern representative who hoped that its frivolous inclusion would weaken the entire bill's credibility.[15] And, although the case for feminist impact may be made most convincingly for the period beginning in 1970, not all gains in this period reflect massive pressure-group activity by feminists. Occasionally other factors, including the lack of opposition and the narrowness of an issue, have

[14] Both Maren Lockwood Carden and Jo Freeman have stressed this aspect of the women's rights movement. See Maren Lockwood Carden, *Feminism in the Mid 1970's* (New York: Ford Foundation, 1977), 99-121, and Jo Freeman, "Women and Public Policy" (unpublished manuscript), 27-28.

[15] See Adams and Winston, *Mothers at Work*, 121, for elaboration of this point.

been sufficient to gain passage of needed legislation. Such success without massive expenditure of resources is a testament to the degree of acceptance feminists have gained in politics.

It must be emphasized that by 1980 the feminist movement had gained widespread acceptance as a legitimate pressure group. A wide cross-section of Washington activists perceive the feminist community as a continuing effective force, with no sign of abated influence. Even a leading opponent of most feminist demands, Steven Markman, an aide to Senator Hatch (R-Utah), indicated that "although feminist groups are not representative of all women, they are a force that's listened to." He perceives the feminist lobby as a "cohesive, intelligent, and effective."[16] Support for this view was provided by the federal government's funding of the Houston Women's Conference in honor of the International Women's Year, held in 1977, and by the unprecedented congressional extension of the period for state ratification of the ERA for another three and a half years. By 1980 the Virginia Slims American Women's Opinion Poll revealed a heightened perception of sex bias in economic-based activities and substantial increase in women's holding of mortgages, credit cards, and other financial arrangements in their own right.[17] It would appear that recognition of the equity-related issues is growing, and this reflects both an awareness of the impact of the feminist movement and a base for its continued political activity.

The impact of any movement for social change is difficult to gauge. On the one hand, as we have suggested, numerous sex-related barriers for women in society had eroded by 1980. Several signs, on the other hand, indicate how far the feminist movement still has to travel. Among the key problems remain-

[16] Interview with Steven Markman, Director and Chief Counsel, Constitutional Subcommittee of the Senate Judiciary Committee, Washington, D.C., Aug. 31, 1984.

[17] *1980 Virginia Slims American Women's Opinion Poll* (New York: Roper), 15, 96-97. A 1973 Redbook poll revealed 66 percent of readers favoring the women's movement; quoted by Carl Degler, *At Odds* (New York: Oxford University Press, 1980), 448.

ing are several that are economic in nature, including wage differentials and continuing sex-related occupational segregation.[18] In 1955 women on the average earned 63.9 percent as much as men, and in 1985 their average earning capacity was still approximately 62 percent of men's. Moreover, this unchanging relative pay differential occurred during a time when women in increasing numbers were joining the nation's work force and men's and women's educational attainment levels were the same. In 1955, of all women over the age of 16, 35.7 percent were in the labor force; in 1984 the comparable figure was 53 percent. In 1955 women represented 31.6 percent of the total labor force: in 1979 our nation's work force was 43 percent female. Occupational discrepancies explain some of the income differentiation. Although 43.3 percent of all professional and technical workers in the United States were women, only 14 percent of relatively well-paid lawyers and judges were women. As recently as 1980, 96.8 percent of all registered nurses and 84.3 percent of all elementary teachers—notoriously poorly paid professions—were women. Furthermore, although over 84 percent of elementary teachers were women and 50.7 percent of secondary teachers were women, only 37.5 percent of school administrators were women. If this latter figure is disaggregated among the more prestigious and well-paid positions—especially secondary school principals—there are an insignificant number of women.[19]

Another measure of the continuing necessity for change is that despite increased social acceptance of work for women, the role of women in home and family has remained much the same. Numerous writers have pointed to the dual—economic and domestic—roles shouldered by most women and to the

[18] See Adams and Winston, *Mothers at Work*, 2-3; and Ronnie Steinberg Ratner, *Equal Employment Policy for Women* (Philadelphia: Temple University Press, 1980), 12-23.

[19] U S. Department of Labor, Women's Bureau, Office of the Secretary, *Employment Goals of the World Plan for Action: Developments and Issues in the United States* (Washington, D.C.: U.S. Government Printing Office, 1980), 10-11, Appendix A, and Table 10; *Washington Post National Weekly Edition*, Aug. 6, 1984, 9.

limited change that has taken place in primary responsibility for the family, which still rests largely with women. The passage of equal employment legislation and litigation efforts by feminists have thus far resulted in only a limited government effort to aggressively alter patterns of sex bias that might significantly change economic roles for masses of women. In any event, even guaranteeing equal employment practices may have no impact on family roles, which often mirror in microcosm women's subordinate societal roles. Hence key problems for the future remain in the policy areas we have described as *role change* issues, which clearly redistribute power and resources to women, often in a highly politicized, conflict-laden political setting. Recognition of the nature of these problems suggests the accuracy of the view that only narrow, *role equity* issues may gain ready acceptance in the contemporary political system.

The politics of the ERA, an issue that appeared at the congressional level to be the very apotheosis of role equity, engendered profound opposition and massive counterpressures from those who feared its broader implications. As the anti-ERA groups linked to anti-abortion and other conservative forces and joined with "pro-family" groups, continued confrontation took place. It is interesting to ponder the likely effects of the failure of the pro-ERA forces to garner enough support in the states for the ultimate inclusion of the Amendment in the Constitution. Though failure to win approval of the ERA was demoralizing for the women's movement, the organizational diffuseness of the movement has served to maintain its viability. Thus the multiple activities and successes related to equity questions keep the movement alive. In addition, as more laws affecting equity roles are enacted and as more rights for women are protected by the law, sufficient momentum will be sustained to keep the movement a viable force in American politics. The cumulative effects of role equity changes at some future time may well have the effect of creating role change.

To date, the women's movement has made limited use of the courts, in part because of the uneven response of the judiciary to questions dealing with sex discrimination. However, during

211

the past two decades there have been some positive responses by the judiciary on issues dealing with women's equality. Gender-based classifications were found to be unconstitutional in several cases—*Reed* v. *Reed*[20] and *Frontiero* v. *Richardson*.[21] In *Taylor* v. *Louisiana*[22] automatic jury exemptions based solely on sex were declared unconstitutional. Several provisions of the Social Security Act were held invalid, when they differentiated on the basis of sex in the provision of benefits, in *Weinberger* v. *Weisenfeld*[23] and *Califano* v. *Goldfarb*.[24] The Supreme Court held unconstitutional mandatory termination of employment for pregnant women in *Cleveland Board of Education* v. *La Fleur*.[25] Title VII's sex-discrimination provisions were the subject of considerable litigation in the federal courts. In *Phillips* v. *Martin Marietta Corporation*[26] the refusal of employers to hire women with pre-school-age children was held unconstitutional. In *Dothard* v. *Rawlinson*[27] the Supreme Court found that a seemingly neutral job qualification relating to height and weight in effect denied equal opportunity to women and was unconstitutional. Despite these rulings that favor women as a group, others, such as *Kahn* v. *Shevin*,[28] perpetuate unequal treatment of women before the law.

Opposition from sophisticated and well-funded religious and new right groups continues unabated. While not always successful, these groups have created a need for diversion of enormous resources and energy in order to prevent legislative proposals from being decimated by crippling amendments, endless delays, and innumerable procedural challenges.

Finally, despite conservative countermovements, the states have become more central arenas for the women's movement.

[20] 404 U.S. 71 (1971).
[21] 411 U.S. 677 (1973).
[22] 419 U.S. 522 (1975).
[23] 420 U.S. 636 (1975).
[24] 97 S. Ct. 1021 (1977).
[25] 414 U.S. 632 (1974).
[26] 400 U.S. 542 (1971).
[27] 97 S. Ct. 2720 (1977).
[28] 416 U.S. 351 (1974).

Of course, the impact of feminists varies from area to area as organization and prevailing political culture differ. To date, state-based legislative and other policy-oriented efforts often have been successful. Sixteen states have enacted equal rights amendments, for example. States have often been leaders in efforts to free marriage and divorce laws from sex-based stereotypes, to use one's own choice of surname, to gain fairer laws dealing with sexual assault, and to aid displaced homemakers. In fact, the tendency to turn attention away from national politics and toward the state and local arenas has accelerated in a Washington climate hostile to increased spending and to such issues as affirmative action and civil rights. During the first half of the 1980s, the states and localities have proven to be especially responsive and receptive to continuing and expanding policy initiatives. They have been willing to allocate funds for domestic violence and maternal and child health-care projects and to provide support for affirmative action and "comparable worth." For this reason, feminist groups and their allies have turned more to state and local governments to achieve their goals. Groups such as NOW, NARAL, and NWPC, as well as other women's groups with local chapters and memberships, are of course best able to play effective roles at these levels of government.

The 1980 elections marked the first time since authoritative election polls were begun in 1952 that a wide gap in voting appeared between the sexes. Women split their vote virtually evenly between Carter and Reagan, while men supported Reagan with 54 percent of their vote (to 37 percent for Carter).[29] An ABC News General Exit Election Poll found a significant difference between men's and women's votes for Carter based on desire to remain out of war and on the Equal Rights Amendment, with more women aged 30-39 citing Reagan's stand on the ERA as their reason for voting against him than any other single issue (32 percent).[30]

[29] *New York Times*, Nov. 9, 1980, 28.

[30] *ABC News General Exit Election Poll*, Tables 6, 8, and 18. Data made available by Jeffrey Alderman, Director, ABC News, Political Unit.

Presuming the continued existence of an electoral gender gap, women's groups were led to unusual levels of activity during the 1984 presidential campaign. They played a major role in promoting and securing the nomination of Representative Geraldine Ferraro as the Democratic vice presidential nominee. Democratic hopefuls for President and Vice President first indicated their belief in the importance of a "women's vote" by speaking before a coalition of women's groups, including the Women's Campaign Fund, NOW, AAUW, and NWPC, to seek backing and endorsement.[31] A survey of Democratic convention delegates was undertaken by the NWPC to demonstrate support for a female vice presidential candidate. Meetings were held with Mondale advisors to pressure successfully for the Ferraro candidacy. NOW and NWPC broke with their nonpartisan tradition to endorse the Democratic ticket, and their PACs, together with those of NARAL and other groups, were extremely involved in election activities as well. In a related move, a 65-member women's vote project in which NOW, NCLW, AAUW, BPW, and GFWC participated, sought to register their own 15 million members and other women as well.[32] While the Ferraro presence on the ticket did not prove to be a magnet for women voters as had been hoped, women were slightly more likely to support Mondale than men,[33] and in some congressional and senate races feminist activity proved to be significant. Women appear to have provided a margin of victory in Iowa, where right-wing Senator Roger Jepson was defeated and in Illinois where Democrat Paul Simon unseated Republican Senator Charles Percy.[34] John Kerry's congressional victory in Massachusetts was aided by the women's vote, as was Madeline Kunin's bid for the governorship of Vermont. Exit polls also indicated that a majority of women supported North Carolina Governor James Hunt in

[31] *National Women's Times*, Aug.-Sept. 1984, 1, 4.
[32] *Washington Post National Weekly Edition*, March 5, 1984, 24.
[33] *Congressional Quarterly Weekly Report*, Jan. 26, 1985, 147.
[34] *National NOW Times*, Nov.-Dec. 1984, 2-3.

his bid for the U.S. Senate, although he was not able to defeat the conservative incumbent Jesse Helms.

A record number of women were elected between 1980 and 1984 to Congress and to state and local legislative positions. Although many of these women are not feminists, it is well to recall a 1977 study done by the Center for American Women and Politics at Rutgers University. The study found that, regardless of ideological identification, women legislators of both parties took more feminist positions on issues such as abortion, the ERA, child care, and social security for homemakers than did their male counterparts.[35] Without asserting that such survey results may necessarily translate into public policy, we can at least say that the potential for building upon the already established "policy network" described throughout this volume obviously exists.

The upheaval caused by the November 1980 elections galvanized feminists and their supporters into greater organizational efforts.[36] Grassroots organization was identified as more essential for influencing policy. It is also possible that the coming decade will see more emphasis on cementing gains already made, while engaging also in new legislative initiatives. In this political climate, the decision to pursue economic rights issues as encompassed in the Economic Equity Act was probably the most effective strategy that could have been devised. Such issues as pension reform, which not only affect women but entire families, are most likely to engender broad-based support as long as they do not create questions of cost, revenue loss, and major role changes for women in society. The focus on incremental policy efforts, framed in the guise of equity, continues to accrue some gains.[37]

The flexibility with which strategies for influencing policy are employed by feminists will continue. The strategy that may have the most profound long-term effect is the expansion of

[35] *New York Times*, Nov. 4, 1980, B8.
[36] *New York Times*, Nov. 7, 1980, A16.
[37] *Congressional Quarterly Weekly Report*, April 23, 1983, 787.

the movement from leadership-based lobbying efforts to constituency-based organizations—though to date the constituency groups such as NOW and NARAL have small memberships compared to the size of their potential constituencies. Grassroots electoral activity, first attempted on a major scale in 1980 and continued in 1982 and 1984, may, in conjunction with expanded membership cadres, also prove to be important and may facilitate expanded influence for women's groups. Effective impact on issues such as employment and child care will need to involve more women workers themselves in feminist politics, a trend only in its incipient stages.

An overriding problem for the entire feminist community is funding. Thus far, financial resources have limited the scope of activity for the organizations considered in this volume. Unless financial opportunities increase, political participation may not be able to expand. Women's organizations have entered politics largely at the policy-making stage. Until 1980 their activity was not, as just noted, focused on electoral activity. Certainly additional funding would facilitate such activity and might foster additional successes. Feminists have made significant gains in the federal policy-making process, but their continued efforts to achieve broad change in established societal roles must contend with the numerous obstacles our political system has erected at every turn.

THE FUTURE OF FEMINIST POLITICS

We have seen that for women activists, there are no easy victories, but considerable success may be achieved by intensive organizational intervention—at all stages of the decision-making process, including the implementation stage. Incremental policy making tends to prevail, although it is our contention that issues perceived as narrow in scope may have a profound impact on the role of women in society. If the women's movement continues to abide by the "political rules of the game" and if parameters are drawn around issues selected for advocacy, so that opposing groups are muted, feminists will continue to be successful political participants in an age of declining parties and pluralist expansion of interest-group politics.

EPILOGUE

The organized women's movement has always focused its attention on several fronts simultaneously. In the last decade of the twentieth century this trend has continued. The issues that excited the imaginations of women activists in earlier years—freedom of choice, equal educational opportunity, and economic equity—remain as focal points of the movement. However, new issues have become important to the movement's agenda. Some of these new issues were of only local interest until national publicity put them on "center stage" for the national women's movement.

The emergence of violence against women as a public policy concern differs from many of the other issues addressed in this volume. It is an issue that emerged locally and later moved onto the national agenda. Changes in abortion laws, which became the focal point of the national women's movement in the 1970s, were initiated at state and local levels as well. The reproductive rights movement in states such as Hawaii, Illinois, and New York helped galvanize the national campaign.[1] Many of the other issues on which women's rights groups have focused their attentions were initiated by national organizations and filtered downward to local groups.

In earlier editions of this volume we contended that narrower equity issues are more likely to produce success than role change issues that often produce intense and irreconcilable political conflict. Abortion rights is a role change issue further complicated by religious and moral beliefs. This is the issue that has faced the most resistance. Violence against women has been portrayed as an equity concern—since it is based on the principle of equal protection of the law—but it is deeply rooted in sex role relationships. Thus, success in curtailing violence against women has been limited despite legislative efforts to counter the problem. Equal educational opportunity is also seen as an equity concern. Women have had some success in breaking down barriers in educational institutions, though complete equality has not been realized, especially in the area of athletics.

The "glass ceiling" and sexual harassment were conceived as equity issues, emanating from Title VII of the 1964 Civil Rights Act's concern with workplace equity for women. Providing for equal opportunity in the work force entails the redistribution of power and resources, issues that always provoke powerful opposition. And sexual harassment, which is related to violence against women, often turns into a role change issue that makes it more difficult to resolve.

ABORTION POLITICS: MORE OF THE SAME?

Freedom of choice has been a highly visible issue for the women's movement since the Supreme Court's 1973 decision in *Roe* v. *Wade*.[2] Women retain the constitutional right to have an abortion, though access to this right has been severely limited for many women. Women's reproductive rights is an issue that continues to be defined in terms of role change, and role change issues are still very difficult for women's rights activists to alter. In the case of abortion rights, religious and moral positions are used by right-to-life activists to justify their antichoice position.

Efforts to maintain access to abortion services have been spearheaded by the National Abortion and Reproductive Rights Action League (NARAL), Planned Parenthood, and the Reproductive Rights Project of the ACLU. Many other organizations have been involved in these efforts, and in some of the more recent abortion rights cases reaching the Supreme Court hundreds of organizations have signed amici briefs.[3]

The first post *Roe* v. *Wade* limitations were imposed when Congress initially adopted the Hyde Amendment in 1976. The Hyde Amendment is still attached to the appropriations for the Department of Health and Human Services. In addition, the State Department appropriation denies abortion services to Peace Corps volunteers, and the Defense Department appropriation denies abortion services to military personnel and their dependents. In the past several years national legislative limitations have been reinforced by state restrictions, some of which have been upheld by the Supreme Court. For example, laws requiring mandatory 24-hour waiting periods, parental notification for minors seeking abortions, informed consent, and preabortion counseling have been upheld by the Court as not providing an "undue burden" on women.

The Supreme Court has remained active in the area of abortion rights. In 1989 in *Webster* v. *Reproductive Health Services,*[4] the court upheld a woman's right to have an abortion but instituted the principle of fetal viability. In this decision the court upheld a Missouri law that permitted abortions to be performed only up to the time of fetal viability. The plurality opinion was written by Chief Justice William Rehnquist. Justice Sandra Day O'Connor wrote a concurring opinion in which she agreed with the fetal viability portion of the Missouri law on the grounds that it did not constitute an "undue burden" on a pregnant woman. The trimester principle developed in *Roe* v. *Wade* was replaced in the Webster decision by this principle of fetal viability, in effect drawing the line between legal and illegal abortions. The principle of "undue burden" was used by the court in its 1992 decision in *Planned Parenthood of Southeastern Pennsylvania et al.* v. *Casey.*[5] The practical outcome of the "undue burden" test is a wide disparity in the availability of abortion from state to state. Many states have enacted restrictive regulations—using the "undue burden test"—requiring waiting periods, parental permission, and information about fetal development, in order to discourage abortion.

During the 1980s, the Reagan and Bush administrations vigorously attacked abortion rights through legislation, support for antichoice lawsuits, and subversion of the intent of the laws they were charged with upholding, as well as through the appointment of countermovement sympathizers to the federal bench and to leadership positions in federal agencies. By the late 1980s, antiabortion judges dominated the lower federal courts,[6] and their influence far outlives that of those who appointed them. The following Clinton administration supported reproductive rights: President Clinton signed into law the Freedom of Access to Clinic Entrances Act, repealed the "gag" rule that prohibited doctors in federally funded clinics from providing abortion counseling, lifted the ban on fetal tissue research, and repealed the policy that denied U.S. funding to countries that provide abortion counseling. Clinton also encouraged research and testing of RU 486, a "morning after" pill that could transform the debate about abortion.

However, despite these positive initiatives, during the late 1980s and 1990s radical right organizations and right-to-life groups supported by the Catholic Church and other religious organizations have intensified their campaign against a woman's right to choose to terminate her pregnancy. There have been congressional and court challenges to the rights guaranteed by *Roe* v. *Wade*. Also, right-to-life groups such as Operation Rescue, which began in 1988, have blocked access to abortion clinics (five hundred blockades from 1987 to 92),[7] harassed medical providers of these services, bombed clinics, and killed providers. The angry rhetoric of the right-to-life movement has helped provoke the violence that has led to death and destruction. These activities have successfully frightened doctors and limited the number of physicians willing to provide abortion services.

One further point must be noted in regard to the availability of abortion services. Most medical school programs do not provide abortion training to their students. Even obstetrical residencies often do not train doctors to perform abortions. In 1975, 93 percent of U.S. medical schools offered training in abortion to obstetrics residents, and 26 percent required it. By 1992, one-third of these schools were not giving any abortion training, even when residents requested it, and only 12 percent included it as a requirement.[8]

The result of this paucity of abortion training is that when abortion-providing physicians retire or are intimidated into cessation of services there are often no trained doctors to replace them. In some regions in the country, especially in the upper Midwest and in the South, there are no abortion providers at all. In 1983, the Alan Guttmacher Institute found that 42 percent of obstetricians performed these services.[9] According to a Kaiser Family Foundation survey published by 1995, one-third of practicing obstetricians performed abortions. In 1982 nearly 3,000 hospitals, clinics, and physician offices provided abortion services. By 1992 the number had declined 18 percent to 2,380.[10] Few hospitals provide abortion services and only 7 percent of rural counties had even one abortion provider.[11]

Despite the extraordinary conflict surrounding the issue, the prochoice movement survives as a relatively strong movement capable of acting simultaneously in several arenas.[12] Abortion rights continued to focus feminist activism in the 1980s and 1990s in response to adverse court rulings and legislative enactments, harassment of clinics, and clinic bombings and deaths. Abortion rights activities drew large numbers of participants, including younger women and men. NOW rejoined NARAL as a national rights organization dedicated to abortion rights. In April 1989 NOW sponsored a demonstration that drew from 300,000 to 600,000 participants; NARAL's membership grew from 200,000 in 1989 to 400,000 in 1990.[13] NOW's membership has also increased, and Planned Parenthood and the ACLU, allies in the struggle for prochoice, also saw significant increases in contributions and memberships.[14] In April 1996 President Clinton vetoed a bill banning late-term abortions on the grounds that it did not make an exception for women's health. Pope John Paul decried the President's decision, highlighting the continuing controversial nature of this issue.[15]

TITLE IX: MORE OF THE SAME, PART 2?

In the second edition of *Women and Public Policies* we noted that women had made substantial progress in their efforts to achieve educational parity with men. The area of college sports provides an example: the National Collegiate Athletic Association (N.C.A.A.) reported that in 1971–72 fewer than 30,000 women participated in collegiate sports. In 1994–95 that number had increased to over 100,000. The visibility of star women athletes as well as the availability of college scholarships has encouraged more women to participate in organized sports. Track and field events are a good example of this phenomenon. In 1972–73 just over 62,000 high school girls participated in track and field events. The comparable figure for 1994–95 was nearly 346,000. However, obstacles to equity remain, as two recent studies make clear. *How Schools Shortchange Girls,* published in 1992 by the American Association of University Women analyzes Title IX and other gender-related educational issues. The study found that during the 1980s, the U.S. Office of Civil Rights, which had been in conservative hands, had not actively pursued Title IX enforcement.[16] Title IX violations continued in athletics and in higher level science and math classes. The study also found that local administrators were often unaware of the need to address unequal educational opportunities between the sexes. A 1996 study by the National Association for Women in Education (NAWE) also found an unwelcome environment in college classrooms. This report followed on the heels of an American Bar Association study that found that women at law schools endured condescension and hostility.[17] The NAWE study reported that women continue to get less attention, fewer opportunities to speak, and are more likely to drop out of school than men.

In the administrative, legislative, and judicial arena, issues related to gender equity in sports continue to play a key role. Congress has threatened to end the Department of Education's Office of Civil Rights' funding if clarification of the meaning of "equitable opportunities to play sports" is not forthcoming.[18] Supporters of football and other traditionally men's sports continue to challenge the equity concept, feeling that Title IX has hurt men's sports and relies too heavily on proportionality as the sole test of compliance. Advocates from such groups as the National Women's Law Center (NWLC) contend that there are continuing efforts to weaken Title IX.[19] Brown University and Louisiana State University are battling allegations in the courts that their sports programs have treated women athletes unfairly.[20] Recent rulings have found that, although universities have treated athletics as a male domain, they have not always intentionally discriminated against women.[21] Thus, equity in sports and in the classroom continues to be a controversial issue in which role equity begins to shade into role change.

DOMESTIC VIOLENCE

Violence against women is not a new problem. The movement to protect women from batterers began in the United States in the mid-1970s. Until quite recently, violence against women was assumed to be a private matter and women were socialized into believing that if men beat them they had in some way aroused, and therefore deserved, their anger.

How serious is the problem of domestic violence? FBI Uniform Crime Statistics indicate that in the United States 4 women die every day at the hands of their husbands or boyfriends. This amounts to about 1,400 deaths a year. The official domestic assault statistics report 572,000 attacks a year. Since most women do not report attacks to the authorities, a conservative estimate of the real number of assaults on women by spouses or boyfriends is between 2 and 4 million each year. It is estimated that 170,000 of these assaults require doctor's care, emergency room attention, or hospitalization. In 1983 the U.S. Department of Justice reported that a woman is beaten every 15 seconds.[22] The FBI Uniform Crime Statistics reported that in 1991 domestic violence was the leading cause of injury to women between the ages of 15 and 44. One in five women who are the victims of spousal violence report that they have been beaten repeatedly by the same person. In 1992 the U.S. Surgeon General reported that battered women are more likely to suffer miscarriages and to have low-birth-weight babies than are other women. When he introduced the Violence Against Women Act, Senator Joseph Biden (D–Del.) reported that 50 percent of all homeless women and children are victims of violence in their homes. As the Senate Judiciary Committee heard at their hearings on the Violence Against Women Act, there are three times as many animal shelters in the United States as there are shelters for battered women and their children.[23]

The emergence of domestic violence on the women's movement issue agenda was locally initiated. The first shelter for battered women opened in 1974 in Minnesota—the St. Paul Women's Advocates, which still exists today. Initial efforts at funding and legal reform came at the state and local level. In addition, some funding initiatives were established by private foundations in the 1980s.[24] The challenge for many shelter providers has been to provide financial security without surrendering feminist attitudes regarding hierarchy and to maintain participatory processes and autonomy as well as the empowerment of battered women. In the late 1970s, national women's groups began to mobilize their energies in response to these concerns. The NOW Task Force on Battered Women/Domestic Violence was founded in 1976, and the National Coalition Against Domestic Violence (NCADV) was founded in 1977.

Domestic violence gained national attention as the result of a White House meeting in July 1977 (after which the NCADV was founded). The U.S. Civil Rights Commission held hearings in 1978, which led to the creation of an Office of Domestic Violence. Other agencies, including the Law Enforcement Assistance Administration (LEAA) and the Department of Housing and Urban Development (HUD) provided limited funding for service provision.[25] Efforts to gain funding for shelters began in 1977, but no legislation was passed due to opposition from right-wing groups that derailed the passage of any bill after the 1980 election.

In 1981 the Family Protection Act was introduced into Congress. This legislation sought to prohibit funding for domestic violence programs. Apparently, the notion of permitting governmental intervention in marriage, even to prevent violence, was "too great a taboo to be challenged" at the time.[26]

However, during the next decade, virtually all fifty states passed legislation protecting battered women, and most provided some funding for shelters and improved intervention by the criminal justice system.[27] Some states have used surcharges on marriage licenses to provide financing for battered women's services. It is likely that lessons learned by women's organizations at the state level proved useful in the national arena: the creation of broad-based coalitions, bipartisan support, and the neutralization of right-wing efforts through the use of nonthreatening symbols such as saving the family and ending violence.[28]

Continuing success at the state level was an indication that concern for battered women had evolved into a legitimate subject for public discussion. Documentation and media attention through such television programs as *The Burning Bed, 60 Minutes,* and the *Phil Donahue Show* kept up the pressure. The adoption of the less threatening (to men) term "domestic violence" helped feminists present the issue of wife battering in a more inclusive way—

girlfriends, divorcees, the elderly, and victims of incest all qualified for protection. This approach deemphasized wives as victims and sought to strengthen the family by reducing violence and providing better protection for women. The lesson from the arena of child abuse—that in order to receive federal attention a social problem has to be widespread and cut across class lines—held true with domestic violence.

Opposition to violence against women is an issue that all women's rights groups endorse. Domestic violence has been framed as an equity issue based on an understanding that the legal system has failed to protect battered women adequately. Given the reluctant welfare state in the United States, generating funds for shelters has proven difficult although not impossible to achieve. A feminist discourse and analysis has had some impact on the legislative process as it developed.[29]

In 1984, following almost six years of congressional pressure and activism, the Family Violence Prevention and Services Act (which had initially been introduced by Senator Barbara Mikulski, D–Md.) was signed into law. Included in an amendment to this legislation were some funds for battered women's shelters. Seed money for shelter provision was provided in appropriations of $8 million over several years. This legislation still continues to fund direct services. Emerson Dobash and Russell Dobash suggest that the passage of this legislation was a "monument to the energy, hard work, increased political sophistication, alliance building and tactics" of women, particularly so because the first Reagan administration was a period of conservative agendas and laissez faire social policies.[30]

In 1994, after several years of prodding Congress to act, the Violence Against Women Act was enacted into law as part of an omnibus crime bill. Senator Joseph Biden (D–Del.), a longtime champion of this legislation, was the chair of the Senate Judiciary Committee. Victoria Nourse, the Judiciary Committee Counsel, was instrumental in focusing attention on domestic violence in the legislative process.[31] Senator Biden and his staff consulted a variety of women's groups as they developed the legislation. The women's rights movement participated through the Violence Against Women Act Task Force, organized by Pat Reuss of the NOW Legal Defense and Education Fund, with the strong participation of such groups as the National Women's Law Center, NOW, the Women's Legal Defense Fund and NCADV, and most recently, a newly formed 501 (c) (4) group established to lobby Congress, the National Network to End Domestic Violence.[32]

The legislation as it finally emerged was a testament to the successful use of a classic "insider/outsider" strategy employed by the women's rights community and its allies. Through the efforts of Senator Biden and other legislative "insiders," a major bipartisan coalition in Congress— including Republican Senators Orren Hatch (R–Utah) and Robert Dole (R–Kans.), and Democratic senators Robert Byrd (D–W.Va.) and George Mitchell (D–Maine) as well as Representatives Connie Morella (R–Md.) and Pat Schroeder (D–Colo.)—was constructed. The "outsider" women's lobbying community, which had originally pressed for increased legislative attention to the issue, joined forces with groups representing a broad constituency, including the civil rights community and health activists. In addition, support was forthcoming from prochoice activists, Catholic Charities, Feminists for Life, the Nurses Task Force on Violence, the Girl Scouts, the General Federation of Women's Clubs (GFWC), and the Junior League.[33] Grassroots efforts were also undertaken by mobilizing local unions and shelter activists. Support also came from moderate Republicans, conservatives who decried violence against women, liberals who wanted more support for shelters and other interventions, and grassroots individuals and community leaders. The support of President Clinton, whose family history includes domestic violence, was significant as well. Opposition to the legislation by forces on the right was directed at public interference in private—that is, family—matters and the extension of the federal government into the domain of the states and localities. Though the battle to pass the legislation was six years in the making, the bill that was passed by Congress and signed by President Clinton did finally provide the framework for protection that women's groups sought.

The 1994 Violence Against Women Act, defined by many women's rights activists as one of the most important pieces of legislation for women passed in this decade, mandates interstate enforcement of protective orders, a National Domestic Violence Hotline, training for state and federal judges, civil rights remedies for victims of gender-related crimes, and some aid for battered immigrant women. In addition, it provides additional federal money for shelters. The law provides that most of the funding be distributed though the Department of Health and Human Services and the Department of Justice. A special task force is responsible for administering the funds, and an advisory committee is to meet quarterly to help set policy. A total of $1.6 billion was authorized for programming, to be allocated through fiscal year 2000. For fiscal year 1995, $26 million was authorized, allotting $500,000 to each state. Grants were provided to local governments, state agencies, nonprofit victim services programs, and Indian tribes to create and strengthen law enforcement and prosecution services. Grants were also given to substate jurisdictions for police and prosecutor training so that they can better identify and respond to violent crimes against women. Additional grants will be provided for hotlines, rape crisis centers, child abuse programs, community domestic intervention programs, counseling, and the like.[34] Despite budgetary cutbacks, federal funding for shelters for fiscal year 1996 increased, with a total of $47.6 million provided through the Violence Against Women Act and the Family Violence Prevention and Services Act. In addition, $175 million was appropriated for law enforcement training and services.[35] In February 1996, as a result of the act's passage, President

Clinton inaugurated a national domestic violence hotline. Funding for prevention of domestic violence covered in the legislation will be secured through the Crime Bill Trust Fund.

In the past ten years, due to continued pressure and several notorious cases involving celebrities, domestic violence has become a pressing public concern. In the mid-1990s the battered women's movement now includes a large number of participants: women's rights organizations, feminist public officials and legislators, volunteers and activists at community shelters, community-based supporters and educators, supportive law enforcement personnel, and lawyers. The battered women's movement has utilized a variety of tactics to pass, implement, and monitor new policy.

SEXUAL HARASSMENT

In the 1970s the problems many women who entered the workforce had to confront—unwelcome sexual advances and conditions that required sexual acquiescence to move up the employment and salary ladder—was given a name by women's rights activists. The situation that so many working women faced and had been hesitant to discuss was called "sexual harassment." But it was not until Anita Hill accused Clarence Thomas of sexual harassment in 1991 and Thomas' subsequent appointment to the Supreme Court that questions relating to sexual harassment became the focus of continued national media and public attention.

Women's awareness of sexual harassment was raised by the hearings. Some women who previously had been hesitant to address the issue began to demand changes in behavior. Of course, many victims still find it easier not to come forward and deal with the problem.[36] The Equal Employment Opportunity Commission (EEOC) has, however, reported a 50 percent increase in reported cases of sexual harassment since the Thomas hearings.

The issue of sexual harassment was raised in the public arena by the Thomas-Hill hearings at the Senate Judiciary Committee, which brought the issue a degree of public awareness that had not existed previously, though there had been some public awareness and response to the problem as early as 1980. In 1980 the EEOC issued regulations that defined sexual harassment as a form of sex discrimination prohibited under Title VII of the Civil Rights Act of 1964.[37] In addition, even prior to these EEOC regulations, Title IX of the Education Amendments of 1972 prohibited sexual harassment and required federally funded institutions to maintain grievance procedures for students and faculty. It is important to remember, however, that the debate surrounding Title IX never focused on sexual harassment.

The Supreme Court entered the sexual harassment debate in 1986, in *Meritor Savings Bank, FSB v. Vinson.*[38] The Court held that the employer is responsible for preventing sexual harassment in the workplace. In other words, employers were seen as responsible for preventing a "hostile environment." Also defined by the Court in their decision was the principle of "quid pro quo." In other words, if sexual favors are required in order to maintain a job or to advance in an organization there is a "quid pro quo," and this violates Title VII of the Civil Rights Act of 1964.

In 1993 the Supreme Court in *Harris* v. *Forklift Services*[39] restated and refined the principle of hostile environment. In a unanimous decision the court described harassment as "an environment that a reasonable person would find hostile or abusive." The decision, written by Justice Sandra Day O'Connor, refined the hostile environment principle by saying that "while psychological harm, like any other relevant factor, may be taken into account, no single factor is required." A hostile environment may be determined by the severity and frequency of the conduct, whether it is physically threatening or humiliating and whether it interferes with an employee's job performance. The decision went on to say that "Title VII comes into play before the harassing behavior leads to a nervous breakdown." [40]

Several additional events that brought the issue of sexual harassment into public view should be mentioned. The Tailhook incident in 1991, in which male naval air force officers harassed their female colleagues, brought the issue onto the front pages of newspapers and onto the evening news and talk shows. Also, in 1995, Senator William Packwood, longtime Republican senator from Oregon, was forced to resign his Senate seat in response to multiple accusations of inappropriate sexual advances. It is perhaps significant that after the initial complaints were made against Senator Packwood he claimed that he did not understand the problem. He did not think that he had behaved inappropriately.

Women activists have helped to redefine the boundaries of acceptable workplace behavior. By defining sexual harassment as a role equity issue, the problem is identified as one that can be rectified. Though the Court and Congress have supported women, the problem has not disappeared. Thus, in a 1995 report issued by the U.S. Merit Systems Protection Board, 44 percent of female federal workers and 19 percent of male workers who responded to a mailed questionnaire replied that they had been sexually harassed. Almost identical percentages were found in the surveys conducted in 1980 and 1987.[41] The Board suggested that it is possible that the numbers remained so high because of heightened awareness of the problem.[42]

ECONOMIC OPPORTUNITY AND THE GLASS CEILING

In 1987 the Department of Labor published *Workforce 2000,* a report that discussed changes taking place in the economy and the workforce. Included in the report was a discussion of the increasing importance of women and minorities in the workforce. This report makes clear that increasing numbers of women and minorities are employed in American organizations, both in the public and the private sectors. However, it is also clear that women and minorities have not been promoted into top management positions. This phenomenon was first described as a "glass ceiling" by the *Wall Street Journal* in 1986.

The term "glass ceiling" refers to the limits women confront in both the public and the private sector as they strive to advance in their careers. More precisely, "glass ceiling" describes "the artificial barriers, based on attitudinal or organizational bias, that prevent qualified individuals from advancing within their organization and reaching their full potential." [43] In 1995, 46 percent of the U.S. workforce was female in contrast to 40.4 in 1983. In 1990 women on average earned 75.9 percent of what men earned. [44] The comparable figure for 1983 was 66.7 percent. Many women have experienced great success in the paid workforce, both in the private and the public sector. Women have become physicians, attorneys, and business administrators. Entering classes in medical schools, law schools, and business schools have often achieved gender parity. However, women have discovered that their professional successes are limited because of an invisible barrier, "glass ceiling," that halts their professional advancement.

According to the U.S. Department of Labor, in the first quarter of 1995 women held only 5 percent of senior-level management positions in the nation's 1,000 largest companies. Only two women were chief executives of these organizations, the same number as 20 years ago. [45] However, more women were members of corporate boards. In 1994 75 percent of Fortune 1,000 companies had at least one woman on their board, up from 69 percent in 1993. [46] Sheila Wellington, president of Catalyst, a nonprofit consulting and research group that conducts an annual survey on women's successes in business, observed that chief executives tend to look to their peers to fill positions on corporate boards and that their peers are rarely women. [47]

Despite increasing opportunities for women in fields

once closed to them, working women continue to be clustered into relatively few occupations. In 1992 the six most prevalent occupations for women were secretary, teacher, cashier, manager and administrator, registered nurse, and bookkeeper and accounting clerk. Over one-third of employed women worked in these fields. With the exception of registered nurses, women in these fields on average earn less then men in the same professions.[48]

In 1991 Congress enacted the Civil Rights Act of 1991. Many groups lobbied Congress and the President to support this legislation, with the Leadership Conference on Civil Rights coordinating their efforts. Women's rights groups as well as black civil rights groups, organizations representing the aged, and groups representing the disabled participated in the coalition. NOW, in its *Statement of Principles,* stated that "we are helping women break through the 'glass ceiling' of the executive suite and break loose of the 'sticky floor.' "[49] This legislation was designed to restore and strengthen laws protecting women and minorities from job discrimination. It also expanded the remedies for women who are victims of intentional discrimination. In addition, it required that a Glass Ceiling Commission be established in the Department of Labor.

The twenty-one-member Glass Ceiling Commission was established after the law was enacted and was chaired by the Secretary of Labor. Members included elected officials and representatives of professions and businesses. The commission grew out of the 1987 report and the economic realities that women confronted in the work place. Elizabeth Dole, then Secretary of Labor, was instrumental in establishing the Commission, and Lynn Martin, who replaced Dole as Secretary of Labor in the Bush administration, chaired the first Glass Ceiling Commission. The first report of the Glass Ceiling Commission did not provide any remedies to the workplace constraints imposed upon women. In fact, establishing the commission and publishing its first two reports in 1991 and 1992 seem to have been symbolic gestures to Republican women who believed that the Republican administration had to do something to respond to equity-based demands. Donna Shavlick, the Director of the Office of Women's Affairs at the American Council on Education, suggested that these early reports provided no remedies for women and thus generated very little response. She submitted that the primary outcome was the use of the "glass ceiling" concept as a buzzword without any meaningful mobilization.[50]

The basic message of the 1992 report was simple and stated the problem well: "While progress has been made in the work place by minorities and women, the commitment and actions that led to this progress must be maintained and enhanced if the goal of full and equal employment opportunity is to be realized."[51] Three years later, in the introduction to the final report of the Glass Ceiling Commission, Secretary of Labor Robert Reich noted that "the glass ceiling is not only an egregious denial of social justice that affects two-thirds of the population, but a serious economic problem that takes a huge financial toll on American business." He went on to say that "equity demands that we destroy the glass ceiling. Smart business demands it as well."[52]

CONCLUSIONS

These are not the only issues that the women's rights community has addressed during the past decade. They have supported child day-care advocates in their campaigns for more public support for day-care services, and they have been involved in successful efforts to enact parental leave legislation. The Family Leave and Medical Leave Act of 1993 was signed into law by President Clinton after two vetoes by his predecessor George Bush. Women's political strength was a factor in the ultimate enactment of this legislation. Lobbying on this issue was coordinated by the Council of Presidents, a coordinating body for heads of Washington-based women's organizations, founded in

1985. As Ferree and Hess note, "passing the law was a long term proactive victory for the movement."[53]

Issues relating to economic equity and equal educational opportunity are still key concerns of the women's rights community. But efforts to prevent the erosion of health and welfare benefits to women and children and the elderly (who are disproportionately female) has not been a central component of the women's rights agenda. In part, this is a function of definition. These issues are defined as welfare and health issues and not as gender issues. In fact, the attack on poor women and children is both punitive and clear. Welfare "reform" proposals often seek to limit benefits to women and girls who are welfare recipients when they give birth to additional children (child exclusion), require that teenage welfare recipients reside with their parents, limit benefits to a five-year lifetime grant, and require that recipients work in dead-end jobs that pay less than the minimum wage.[54]

In addition to attacks on poor women, attacks on all women have been manifest through efforts to eliminate affirmative action at the state and national levels. In 1995 in California, the Board of Regents repealed affirmative action for admissions and hiring in the University of California system. An executive order banning other state affirmative action programs was signed by Governor Pete Wilson. A 1996 California state ballot initiative would dismantle all remaining affirmative action programs in public employment, education, and contracting.[55] A coalition of 150 women's groups and civil rights groups have joined together in the Campaign for Women's Rights and Civil Rights to mount a campaign against the referendum. The groups that spearheaded this coalition represent a wide range of women's groups and civil rights groups, including the YWCA, the NAACP-LDEF, NOW, the Feminist Majority, and several California-based organizations.[56]

At the same time that affirmative action is under assault

in California, a case decided by the Fifth Circuit Court in March 1996, *Hopwood* v. *State of Texas,*[57] found that the University of Texas acted illegally by implementing affirmative action in its admissions process. The effect of this ruling is expected to deter other higher education institutions from continuing to use affirmative action in admissions.

President Clinton has continued to provide moderate support for affirmative action, while backing away from its more controversial aspects. Thus, there is a moratorium on any new federal programs that reserve contracts exclusively for companies owned by women and minorities.[58] The Feminist Expo, held in February 1996 in Washington, D.C., specifically sought to rally young and older feminists in a fight to preserve affirmative action.[59] The Expo highlighted voter registration efforts in support of continued commitment to anti-sex discrimination policies to increase opportunity for women and people of color.

The women's rights community continues to be successful in utilizing the pluralist strategy that won them early success, and their successes are greatest when they define issues in terms of role equity rather than role change, define them narrowly, control the parameters of debate, and build incrementally on earlier efforts. When people suggest that the women's rights movement has passed its peak and is on a downhill slide, they overlook the continuing and even expanded efforts of groups—most of which are not visible to the public—that have improved conditions for women and that continue to strive to correct the inequities that women still confront as a result of their gender.

NOTES

1. Suzanne Staggenborg, *The Pro Choice Movement* (New York: Oxford Univ. Press, 1991), 27.

2. 410 U.S. 413 (1973).

3. Barbara Hinkson Craig and David M. O'Brian, *Abortion and American Politics* (Chatham NJ: Chatham House, 1993), 333.

4. 492 U.S. 490 (1989).

5. 112 S.Ct. 2791 (1992).

6. Staggenborg, *The Pro Choice Movement*, 3.

7. Myra Marx Ferree and Beth Hess, *Controversy and Coalition: The New Feminist Movement across Three Decades of Change* (New York: Twayne, 1994), 162.

8. Amy Goldstein, "Abortions: Still Legal but Less Available," *Washington Post Weekly Edition* (30 Jan.–5 Feb. 1995), 32.

9. Christine Russell, "Abortion Is Falling Out of Favor among Ob-Gyns." *Washington Post Weekly Edition* (23–29 Oct. 1995), 32.

10. Ibid.

11. Ferree and Hess, *Controversy and Coalition*, 164.

12. Staggenborg, *The Pro Choice Movement*, 136.

13. Nancy Whittier, *Feminist Generation: The Persistence of the Radical Women's Movement* (Philadelphia: Temple Univ. Press, 1995), 200.

14. Staggenborg, *The Pro Choice Movement*, 133.

15. Alison Mitchell, "A Veto with Drama," *New York Times* (12 April 1996), A1, A24.

16. Jere Longman, "How the Women Won," *New York Times Magazine*, 23 June 1996, 28. American Association of University Women Educational Foundation, *How Schools Shortchange Girls* (Washington, DC: American Association of University Women, 1992), 8.

17. Ben Gofe, "Classroom Climate Found Still 'Chilly' for Women," *Chronicle of Higher Education* (1 March 1996), A38.

18. *Chronicle of Higher Education* (4 August 1995), A26. Douglas Lederman, "House Bill Targets Enforcement of Federal Sex Bias Law in College Sports," *Chronicle of Higher Education* (29 Sept. 1995), A65.

19. Ibid.

20. AAUW, *How Schools Shortchange Girls*, 8.

21. Gofe, "Classroom Climate."

22. Cindy Hanford, "March to Demand Full Domestic Violence Funding," *National Now Times* (March 1996), 6.

23. *Domestic Violence: The Facts—A Handbook to STOP Violence* (Boston: National Clearinghouse for the Defense of Battered Women, undated). Reprinted on the Safetynet Home Page, World Wide Web, 1995.

24. Claire Reinelt, "Moving into the Terrain of the State: The Battered Woman's Movement and the Politics of Engagement," *Feminist Organizations: Harvest of the New Woman's Movement*, Myra Marx Ferree and Patricia Yancey Martin, eds. (Philadelphia: Temple Univ. Press, 1995), 86.

25. Joyce Gelb, "The Politics of Wife Abuse," *Families, Politics, and*

Public Policy, Irene Diamond, ed. (New York: Longman, 1983), 254–55. Emerson Dobash and Russell Dobash, *Women, Violence and Social Change* (London: Routledge, 1992), 128.

26. Gelb, "The Politics of Wife Abuse," 257.

27. Ibid., 258.

28. Ibid.

29. Dobash and Dobash, *Women, Violence and Social Change,* 142–44.

30. Ibid.

31. Telephone interview with Leslie Wolfe, Executive Director, Center for Women Policy Studies, 20 April 1996.

32. Telephone interview with Beth Clark, Policy Advocate, Nancy Turner, former Policy Advocate, and Sherry Ettleson, Policy Advocate, National Network to End Domestic Violence, 21 April 1996.

33. Telephone interview with Pat Reuss, National Organization for Women—Legal Defense and Education Fund, 20 April 1996.

34. Robin Abb and Margaret Sewell, "Ending Gender-Based Violence a Priority," *National NOW Times* (Jan. 1995). Reprinted on the NOW World Wide Web Site.

35. John Murawski and Grant Williams, "The Budgets Winners and Losers," *The Chronicle of Philanthropy* (16 May 1996), 33.

36. Marian Lief Palley and Howard A. Palley, "The Thomas Appointment: Defeats and Victories for Women," *PS* 25 (September 1992), 475.

37. EEOC, 29 C. F. R. Chapter XIV, Part 1604.11.

38. 477 U.S. 57 (1986).

39. 114 S.Ct. 367 (1993).

40. Ibid.

41. Bill McAllister, "The Problem That Won't Go Away," *Washington Post Weekly Edition,* (20–26 Nov. 1995), 33.

42. Ibid.

43. Robert B. Reich, "Breaking the Glass Ceiling" (Washington, DC: U.S. Department of Labor, Glass Ceiling Commission, 1995). Reprinted on the University of Maryland World Wide Web site.

44. "Comparing Women Around the World," *The Wall Street Journal* (26 July 1995), B1. The data for 1993 is from the U.S. Department of Labor, Women's Bureau, *Facts on Working Women* (Washington, DC: U.S. Department of Labor, December 1993), N. 93–5, 4.

45. Paulette Thomas, "Success at a Huge Personal Cost," *The Wall Street Journal* (26 July 1995), B1.

46. "More Women Are Finding Room at the Top, Business Survey Says," *New Journal* (28 Sept. 1995), B3.

47. Ibid.

48. *Facts on Working Women,* 4–5.

49. "General Information about NOW" (Jan. 1995). Reprinted on the National Organization for Women World Wide Web Site.

50. Telephone interview with Donna Shavlick, Director, Office of Women's Affairs, American Council on Education, 6 May 1996.

51. *Pipelines of Progress—An Update of the Glass Ceiling Initiative* (Washington, DC: U.S. Department of Labor, Glass Ceiling Commission, August 1992). Reprinted on the University of Maryland World Wide Web site.

52. Reich, "Breaking the Glass Ceiling."

53. Ferree and Hess, *Controversy and Coalition,* 190.

54. American Civil Liberties Union Reproductive Freedom Project, *Background Briefing* (April 1995).

55. Campaign for Women's Rights and Civil Rights, "No on CCRI." Reprinted on the CCRI World Wide Web Site, 10 May 1996.

56. Ibid.

57. No. 94–50554, 1996 USApp5th (18 March 1996).

58. Steven Holmes, "Moratorium Called on U.S. Minority Program," *New York Times* (8 March 1996), 1.

59. The Feminist Majority and the Feminist Majority Foundation, "First-Ever National Feminist Exposition Draws Over 3200 Feminists From Across The Nation Despite Winter Storm." Feminist Majority and Feminist Foundation World Wide Web Site, 5 Feb. 1996.

APPENDIX 1: INTERVIEWS

The materials for the case studies were derived in large measure from interviews with leaders of feminist groups, congressional and administrative decision makers, and staff assistants. Many feminist leaders were interviewed at least twice—once for organizational information and once for policy-oriented information. Interviews lasted from one to three hours and were often followed by telephone conversations. They were conducted from 1975 to 1979 and in 1984 and 1985.

A list of persons interviewed (with the affiliations they had at the time of their interviews and locations of the interviews) follows as does a list of questions (in Appendix 2).

Abshire, Pat—Staff, Senate Banking and Currency Committee, Washington, D.C.

Baer, Sheila—Office of Senator Robert Dole (R-Kan.), Washington, D.C.

Bailey, Barbara—Aide to Representative Ed Koch (D-N.Y.), Washington, D.C.

Beck-Rex, Marguerite—Executive Director, SPRINT, Washington, D.C.

Benshoof, Janet—Staff Attorney, ACLU-RFP, New York

Berresford, Susan—Vice President, Ford Foundation, New York

Braun, Eleanor—Executive Director, NWPC, Washington, D.C.

Brown, Cindy—Deputy Director, OCR, HEW, Washington, D.C.

Bryce, Msgr.—Director, Pro-Life Office, National Conference of Catholic Bishops, Washington, D.C.

Bucher, Jeffrey—Federal Reserve Board of Governors, Washington, D.C.

Burris, Carole—Director, Women's Lobby, Washington, D.C.

Campbell, Sharyn—Staff Attorney, Bank Americard and NOW Task Force on Credit, Washington, D.C.

Case, Daniel—Actuary, American Life Insurance Council, Washington, D.C.

Chapman, Jane Roberts—Director, CWPS, Washington, D.C.

Clohesy, Stephanie—Executive Director, NOW-LDEF, New York

Collins, Mary Jane—Vice President, NOW, Washington, D.C.

Cooper, Ranni—Associate Director, Women's Campaign Fund, Washington, D.C.

Cox, William—Director, National Committee for a Human Life Amendment, Washington, D.C.

De Poy, Marilyn—AFSCME, Washington, D.C.

Dickson, Barbara—Aide to Senator Birch Bayh (D-Ind.), Washington, D.C.

Dornan, Robert—Representative (R-Calif.), Washington, D.C.

Doughty, Diane—Lobbyist, NOW, Washington, D.C.

Dubrow, Evelyn—Lobbyist, ILGWU, Washington, D.C.

Dunkle, Margaret—Staff Attorney, HEW, Washington, D.C.

Flemming, Arthur—Director, U.S. Commission on Civil Rights, Washington, D.C.

Florio, James—Representative (D-N.J.), Cherry Hill, N.J.

Forman, Maxine—Director of Policy Analysis, WEAL, Washington, D.C.

Forrest, Winn—Planned Parenthood Federation of America, New York

Gates, Margaret—Co-Director, CWPS, Washington, D.C.

Ginsberg, Ruth Bader—Professor of Law, Columbia University, founder and Advisory Committee member, ACLU-WRP, New York
Glasser, Ira—Director, ACLU, New York
Glickstein, Howard—Professor of Law, Howard University, Washington, D.C.
Gold, Sally—Staff Attorney, Federal Trade Commission, Washington, D.C.
Goldfarb, Lewis—Staff Attorney, Federal Reserve Board Task Force on Credit, Washington, D.C.
Goldsmith, Judy—Vice President, NOW, Washington, D.C.
Gordon, Robin—Director of Public Relations, PEER, Washington, D.C.
Hart, Janette—Deputy Director, Federal Reserve Board, Office of Savings and Consumer Affairs, Washington, D.C.
Hartnett, Cathy—Associate Director, Voters for Choice, Washington, D.C.
Holstein, Charles—Aide to Representative Leonore Sullivan (D-Mo.), Washington, D.C.
Horowitz, Michael—Counsel to the Director, Office of Management and Budget, Washington, D.C.
Howitt, Idell—Staff Attorney, Federal Reserve Board Task Force on Credit, Washington, D.C.
Koch, Edward—Representative (D-N.Y.), New York
Kohn, Margaret—Staff Attorney, NWLC, Washington, D.C.
Kramer, William—Attorney, Squire, Sanders & Dempsey (counsel to NCAA), Washington, D.C.
Law, Sylvia—Professor of Law, New York University, ACLU-RFP Advisory Committee, New York
Leitzer, Ellen—Staff Attorney, ACLU, Washington, D.C.
Lichtman, Judith—Director, WLDF, Washington, D.C.
Lipson, Linda—Director, Congressional Clearinghouse on Women's Rights, Washington, D.C.

Loiello, Elaine—NARAL, Washington, D.C.

Loukas, Helen—Staff, U.S. Commission on Civil Rights, Washington, D.C.

Malcolm, Ellen—Staff, NWPC, Washington, D.C.

Markman, Steven—Director and Chief Counsel, Constitutional Subcommittee of the Senate Judiciary Committee, Washington, D.C.

Middleman, Mike—Deputy Assistant Director, OCR, HEW, Task Force on Athletics, Washington, D.C.

Miller, Kathy—Staff ACLU, Washington, D.C.

Moran, Ann E.—Tax Counsel, U.S. Senate Finance Committee, Washington, D.C.

Moss, Ann—Director, Women's Pension Project of the Pensions Rights Center, Washington, D.C.

Mulhauser, Karen—Executive Director, NARAL, Washington, D.C.

Neas, Ralph—Executive Director, Leadership Conference on Civil Rights, Washington, D.C.

Neier, Aryeh—former Director, ACLU, New York

Northrup, Graham—Staff, House Financial Institutions Subcommittee, Washington, D.C.

Norton, Eleanor Holmes—Chair, EEOC, Washington, D.C.

Novick, Lee—Aide to Representative Bella Abzug (D-N.Y.), Washington, D.C.

O'Donnell, Anne—Director, National Right to Life Committee, Washington, D.C.

Ossonlinick, Carolyn—Assistant, Office of Senator Edward Kennedy (D-Mass.), Washington, D.C.

Parr, Carol—Executive Director, WEAL Fund, Washington, D.C.

Paul, Eve—Legal Director, National Planned Parenthood Federation, New York

Peratis, Kathleen—Executive Director, ACLU-WRP, New York

Picker, Jane—founder, Board member, Women's Law Fund, New York

Pinzler, Isabelle Katz—Director, ACLU-WRP, New York

Polikoff, Nancy—Staff, CWPS, Washington, D.C.

Polivy, Margot—Counsel to AIAW, Washington, D.C.

Quinlan, Alice—OWL, Washington, D.C.

Radigan, Ann—Director, Congressional Caucus for Women's Issues, Washington, D.C.

Rauh, Joseph—Attorney, Rauh, Silard & Lichtman, Washington, D.C.

Reuss, Pat—Legislative Director, WEAL, Washington, D.C.

Rinkers, Martha—Legislative Assistant, Office of Representative Barbara Mikulski (D-Md.), Washington, D.C.

Ross, Susan—Professor, George Washington University Law School, Washington, D.C.

Salinger, Noel—ACLU, New York

Sandler, Bernice "Bunny"—Director, Project on the Status and Education of Women, Association of American Colleges, Washington, D.C.

Schub, Judy—Director of Public Policy, The National Federation of Business and Professional Women, Washington, D.C.

Segal, Phyllis—Legal Director, NOW-LDEF, New York

Shack, Barbara—Attorney, New York Civil Liberties Union, New York

Smith, Delores—Federal Reserve Board, Washington, D.C.

Statial, Sanna—Chief of Staff, Office of Senator Packwood (R-Ore.), Washington, D.C.

Steele, Celia—Staff, NOW-LDEF (PEER), Washington, D.C.

Steenland, Sally—National Caucus for Working Women, Washington, D.C.

Tatel, David—Attorney, Hogan and Hartson; former Director OCR, HEW, Washington, D.C.

Thornton, Maureen—Legal Staff, LWV, Washington, D.C.
Wayne, Claudia—National Commission on Pay Equity, Washington, D.C.
Werner, Carol—Staff, NARAL, Washington, D.C.

Beth Clark, Policy Advocate, National Coalition Against Domestic Violence (NCADV). Telephone interview, 12 April 1996.
Sherry Ettleson, Policy Advocate, National Network to End Domestic Violence. Telephone interview, 21 April 1996.
Pat Reuss, Senior Policy Analyst, NOW Legal Defense and Education Fund (NOW-LDEF). Telephone interview, 21 April 1996.
Donna Shavlick, Director, Office of Women's Affairs, American Council on Education. Telephone interview, 6 May 1996.
Nancy Turner, former Policy Advocate, NCADV. Telephone interview, 21 April 1996.
Leslie Wolff, Executive Director, Center for Women Policy Studies. Telephone interview, 20 April 1996.

APPENDIX 2: QUESTIONNAIRE

For Groups

1. What is your average annual budget?
2. How many people are employed in your office—in professional and other capacities? What is the percentage of attorneys on the staff?
3. How was your group created: a) an issue, b) an individual, c) a crisis, d) split off from another group, e) other?
4. Is your source of funding largely from a) membership dues, b) foundations, c) the U.S. government or other governmental sources, d) other? Which foundations are your major donors?
5. Is your organization dominated by its board or professional staff in terms of policy making? How is the board elected?
6. Please give an example of how one specific policy strategy was determined. How was the decision-making process structured?
7. Does your office allocate most of its resources to: a) lobbying, b) research, c) publicity, d) litigation, e) monitoring the political process, f) testifying before Congress and the executive branch, g) constituency lobbying, h) other? Explain.
8. Are you a membership organization? If yes, how many members do you have? Do you have local chapters? How many and where?
9. Do you participate in coalitions with other groups? With which groups are you most closely associated? Is your relationship with it/them structured or informal?

10. How would you assess your organization's effectiveness?
11. On what issues has your organization had the most impact?
12. What strategy used by your organization has had the most impact: a) lobbying, b) litigation, c) publicity, d) protest, e) monitoring, f) testifying, g) other?
13. What is your tax status: 501(c)(3) or (c)(4)? What is your relationship with groups that have another tax status?
14. Is there one dominant figure within your organization—within the feminist political community?
15. Does one group play a dominant role in feminist politics? Which one?
16. Does your organization specialize in a particular issue area?

For Individuals

1. Why did you seek out a career in feminist politics?
2. What is your background, education, career training? Law degree or other advanced degree?
3. What is your current salary?
4. What is the nature of the job you performed?
5. Do you desire to remain in present job?
6. What is your assessment of your personal effectiveness?
7. What is your assessment of group's effectiveness? Which techniques are most effective: a) lobbying, b) monitoring, etc.?
8. Does your group specialize in one particular issue area?
9. Which other groups are you closest to politically? What is the nature of your relationship?

INDEX

abortion: divisiveness of, 10; erosion of free choice regarding, xi, 5, 154–56; historical background, 130–34; politics of, 133–44; post-1982 developments, xi, xii, 156–60, 220–24; Pregnancy Discrimination Act and, 170–72, 200; pro-life vs. pro-choice, 129–61; as role change issue, 201–202; symbolism in, 10

Abortion Information Exchange, 156

Abzug, Bella (Rep.), 70, 83, 136

access to power: ECOA passage and, 61–63; of feminist groups, 38–39

Ad Hoc Committee in Defense of Life, 149

Adams v. *Califano,* 113

administrative positions for women in education, 98, 164–66, 209–11

administrative process and rights legislation, 77–79, 112–14, 203

advocacy activities of women's groups, 54

Aetna Insurance Co., 187

AFL-CIO, 167–68

Age Discrimination Act, 120

Aid to Families with Dependent Children (AFDC), xviii, 175–76

alimony as financial resource, 66–67

Allstate Insurance Co., 187

"alternative structures," 17

Alyeska Pipeline Service Co. v. *Wilderness Society,* 41

American Association of University Professors (AAUP), 100

American Association of University Women (AAUW), 18, 23, 182; abortion politics, 150; ECOA passage, 74; electoral politics, 214; pension equity, 189; survey of women in educational posts, 98

American Bankers Association, 81

American Citizens Concerned for Life, 148, 159, 169

American Civil Liberties Union (ACLU): abortion politics, 150–53, 155, 223; as force for litigation, 30–31, 51; lobbying on 'women's issues, 31; Pregnancy Discrimination Act, 170. *See also* Reproductive Freedom Project; Reproductive Rights Project; Women's Rights Project

American Council of Life Insurance (ACLI), 180, 184

American Council on Education (ACE), 58, 100

American Express, 187

American Federation of State, County, and Municipal Employees (AFSCME), 183, 196

American Life Lobby, 156, 159

American Medical Association, 150–51

136–37; lobbying efforts against, 54

IBM, 168
Impact of the Hyde Amendment on Federally Funded Abortions, 55
"in kind" services from sponsoring groups, 44
In the Running, 54–55, 112
incentives for group involvement, 15, 37–39
incest and abortion, 137–38
inclusivity of women's groups, 207
income levels: abortion politics and, 157–58; credit discrimination and, 89–90
incremental change, 193, 207; need to focus on, 8; vs. fundamental change, 7
information clearinghouses, feminist groups as, 55–56
"in-process" benefits, 15–16
insurance equity, 175, 178–87
insurance industry, 168
intercollegiate athletics, 95; revenue-producing, 104–105. *See also* NCAA
interest group theory, 1, 6–10, 12, 14
interlocking directorates among feminist groups, 59–60
Internal Revenue Service, 187
International Union of Electrical, Radio, and Machine Workers (IUE), 167–68, 183
International Women's Year (1977), 57, 144, 209
internship programs, 39, 55–56
Interstate Association of Commissions on the Status of Women, 83
interview procedures, 6
issue-oriented politics, 202–203; Title IX passage, 93

Jackson, Jesse, 151
Javits, Jacob (Sen.), 104, 115
Jepsen, Roger (Sen.), 158, 214
Johnson, Lyndon B., 99
Judicial Selection Panel, 58
Justice, Department of, 91

Kahn v. *Shevin,* 212
Kanter, Rosabeth, 20
Kellogg Foundation, 45
Kennedy, Edward (Sen.), 121–22, 190
Kennelly, Barbara (Rep.), 204
Kentucky, abortion laws in, 130
Kerry, John, 214
Kingdon, John, 142
Know, Holly, 39 n.6, 73–75, 116
Kohn, Margaret, 39 n.6, 101
Koop, Everett C., 159
Kunin, Madeline, 214

Labor, U.S. Department of: funding by, 40; Women's Bureau, 66
labor force, women, 16, 65–66, 163–66, 210
labor unions: abortion and, 150; comparable worth, 196; insurance equity, 183; support of pregnancy discrimination, 167
leadership: coalition-building and, 56–59; continuity of, xx; decentralization, 21; executive vs. charismatic, 20; modification of leadership role, 20–21; training, 55–56
Leadership Conference on Civil Rights (LCCR), 58, 120, 150, 182–83, 235
League of Women Voters (LWV): abortion politics, 151; class-action suit on